The
New Oxford Book of
Christian Verse

The New Oxford Book of Christian Verse

Chosen and edited by
Donald Davie

Oxford   New York

OXFORD UNIVERSITY PRESS

Oxford University Press, Walton Street, Oxford OX2 6DP

Oxford New York Toronto
Delhi Bombay Calcutta Madras Karachi
Petaling Jaya Singapore Hong Kong Tokyo
Nairobi Dar es Salaam Cape Town
Melbourne Auckland

and associated companies in
Berlin Ibadan

Oxford is a trade mark of Oxford University Press

First published 1981
Reprinted 1983, 1985, 1986, 1987, 1989

British Library Cataloguing in Publication Data
The new Oxford book of Christian verse.
I. Davie, Donald
821'.05   PR1195.C48   80-49703
ISBN 0-19-213426-4

Printed and bound in Great Britain by
Biddles Ltd, Guildford and King's Lynn

CONTENTS

CONTENTS

CONTENTS

CONTENTS

viii

CONTENTS

CONTENTS

x

CONTENTS

CONTENTS

CONTENTS

CONTENTS

CONTENTS

CONTENTS

INTRODUCTION

'The Oxford Book of Christian Verse' ... but what do we mean, in that expression, by 'Christian'? What do we have to find in a passage of verse before we have the right to call it 'Christian'? It is surely very hard to answer this question even when we consider only the verse written in our own day, or in the present century; and as soon as we begin to think of the verse of previous centuries, the difficulty becomes much greater. For English-speakers may disagree about whether at the present day they live in the latest phase of something called Christendom, or in the aftermath of whatever it was that once went by that name. But all must agree that through most of the centuries when English verse has been written, virtually all the writers of that verse quite properly and earnestly regarded themselves as Christians. Moreover most of those Christians did not suppose that their Christianity stopped when they came out through the church-door, or got up off their knees after praying; for most of them politics, for instance, or even amorous dalliance, were affairs that had to be found a place within the framework of Christian apprehensions and convictions. If they were cruel and faithless in their politics, or lecherous and faithless in their loves, they knew this about themselves, and they thought they knew that the name for such behaviour was not for instance 'maladjustment', but *sin*. They knew this even when they knew that they would go on 'sinning', and even when they declared with a certain bravado that they meant to go on doing so. And so from one point of view most of the political poems of past centuries, and even most of the love-poems (including the most ribald) ought to be regarded as Christian poems. Indeed it is not just from one point of view that they can be thus regarded. That point of view is the only one that measures up to the historically attested facts, and to the claim made by all religions—by Islam no less than by Christianity—to govern and encompass all of human behaviour. Christian and non-Christian alike, we need to recognize that as soon as we automatically exclude from 'Christian verse' poems that deal directly and impartially with what goes on in a corrupt law-court, in a whorehouse, or in the mind of a hired assassin, we are rigging the evidence from the first, and pre-judging the issue. As soon as we set up 'Christian verse' as a category on a par with, say, 'political verse' or 'comic verse', we are making a distinction that the truly devout and thinking Christian is obliged to repudiate. In doing so, we run a great risk, and I'm not sure it is a risk we have a right to. We may as well admit that the very concept, 'Christian verse', is one that won't stand up to close scrutiny.

However Lord David Cecil, when in 1940 he edited the first *Oxford Book of Christian Verse*, plainly decided that the risk, though perilous, was worth taking. He must have decided to *pretend* that there was a category called 'Christian verse' which excluded poems of political partisanship and sexual dalliance. For plainly poems of these kinds were not what readers expected to find when they opened Lord David's *Oxford Book*; and the same must be true of readers of this anthology, which aspires to succeed to Lord David's. For this there is after all some respectable precedent, in that past centuries customarily distinguished between sacred verse and secular verse. And although as we have seen this can only be a rough-and-ready distinction, it is one that previous generations found practicable, and one that we must adhere to: sacred verse is what we are concerned with, and the verse that we think of as 'secular' is to be excluded, even though the borderline between sacred and secular cannot in the last analysis be defined.

What readers did not find in Lord David's anthology, and must not expect to find in this one, is verse which fails to measure up strictly in *artistry* to the best of the secular verse written through the same centuries. This is easy to say, and to agree to; but there is something called 'devotional verse', to which it may seem that this criterion of artistry need not, and probably should not, apply. For it is not hard to think of verses which, though deficient in artistry, could well, because of the purity and sweetness of their spiritual sentiment, minister to the private worshipper in his devotions more effectively than verse which is a great deal better written. Accordingly it seems that 'Christian verse' must be thought of as distinct from 'devotional verse'. And I must confess that this distinction has weighed so much with me, that rightly or wrongly I have in my own mind abandoned the carefully neutral word 'verse' for the more exalted word 'poetry'. I have tried not to include any verse that is not also poetry, in a rather exacting sense. And this partly explains why, though I have taken a wider range than my predecessor both in space and time, I have found myself including considerably fewer poems than he did.

Talk of 'artistry' will mislead us, if it suggests that we ought to look especially for poems that are formally sumptuous and elaborate. On the contrary, the persistent strain of asceticism in Christianity has meant that in every age Christian poets, when they tried to write sacred poems, have fallen in with those theories of poetry which, from the Ancients to the present day, put a specially high value on what is called 'the *plain* style', in which elaboration is avoided. Any anthologist is deceiving both himself and his readers if he pretends that his own preferences and proclivities have played no part in his selection; accordingly I freely admit that I am specially drawn to the plain style myself, and hence that another anthologist could legitimately have chosen more poems written in a more aureate and florid style—this despite the fact that I have taken unusually many pieces from Christopher Smart, whom I take to be a very ornate and florid writer indeed. But looking for the plain style brings with it one great advantage: it enables us to pay due respect to that sort of Christian verse of which the late Robert Lowell wrote, in 'Waking Early Sunday Morning':

> O Bible chopped and crucified
> in hymns we hear but do not read,
> none of the milder subtleties
> of grace or art will sweeten these
> stiff quatrains shovelled out four-square—
> they sing of peace, and preach despair;
> yet they gave darkness some control,
> and left a loophole for the soul.

I hope that none of the congregational hymns printed here do in fact 'preach despair', though it is true that most of them preach doctrines more bleakly challenging than most modern Christians are accustomed to. Our greatest hymn-writers—Isaac Watts and Charles Wesley and William Cowper, all of whom are here represented more fully than is usual—did indeed, as Robert Lowell says, for the most part deny themselves 'the milder subtleties', alike in doctrinal content and in artistic form. But subtlety is not everywhere nor at all times an artistic virtue, and certainly mildness is not—a bleak boldness is just as legitimate a formal effect for a poet to aim at, and indeed it is one of the effects particularly aimed at by the plain style. Watts and Wesley and Cowper, and others among the great hymn-writers, were themselves subtle and sophisticated men who applied themselves to perfect for their hymns a style that should not be subtle but plain—and this for the good reason that they wanted to speak plainly to plain men and women, to the unlettered but devout worshippers in the pews. And these hymns, these poems, have thus spoken to many generations, as they speak still every Sunday morning across the English-speaking world—to plain people who (and this may be the most important point) conceive themselves to have no knowledge of English poetry, and no traffic with it. In this they are wrong: their memories are stocked, though they may not know it, with scraps and tags (if no more) from some very sturdy and admirable poems. To pretend otherwise, by tacitly excluding all but a few such poems from the canon of English poetry, smacks of the worst sort of 'élitism'. And so for offering as reading-matter so many (yet fewer than I would like) of these 'hymns we hear but do not read', I would plead a *democratic* justification. Among the pleas, never long stilled, that poetry be brought 'to the people', we habitually overlook this poetry that *has* been brought to the people, and still abides with them. There is more to be said of this.

If there are pressing reasons for applying rather stringent standards of formal artistry to poems that we want to consider as Christian, this argument applies as well to the *content* of poems, to what they say as well as how they say it. For if professed Christianity must in 1980 think of itself as embattled, and closing ranks against numerous assailants (often enough sincere and candid ones from outside, and muddled ones from inside), then Christian poetry can allow itself even fewer liberties in doctrine than as regards artistic workmanship. For in such a situation nothing can be more tempting, yet none more fatal in the long run, than to settle for the 'religiose', by embracing any poetry that acknowledges and apprehends the numinous or the spiritual. Not all poems that answer to this description are what the worst of them are: the expression of indefinitely oceanic feelings for a something 'beyond', yeasty yearnings towards 'the transcendent'. Yet it must surely be for the exclusion of such poems, good and bad, that this anthology is still called a book of *Christian* verse, rather than (what would be more ingratiating and might seem more liberal) *religious* verse. W. B. Yeats is one example that springs to mind of a poet who is without doubt a greatly religious poet, who is no less clearly a non-Christian poet, the member of a church whose doctrine—though glancingly divulged by fragments in Yeats's poetry and prose—has yet to be formulated. And once one reflects, perhaps with some wistfulness, how good it would be to represent Yeats in this anthology, one soon realizes that there is hardly a poet, however explicitly atheistic or sceptical, who could be excluded as soon as the flood-gates were thus opened. This holds, surely, even for that special class of agnostic and often very moving poems that wish to believe, though they cannot —such poems as Philip Larkin's 'Church Going' or Thomas Hardy's 'The Oxen'. These too, it seems, must be excluded. For Christianity is a religion with a doctrine, a body of dogma. And so it may seem that we can approach a first definition of Christian poetry: it will be poetry that appeals, either explicitly or by plain implication (and in whatever spirit—rebelliously for instance, or sardonically, as often with Emily Dickinson) to some one or more of the distinctive doctrines of the Christian church: to the Incarnation pre-eminently, to Redemption, Judgement, the Holy Trinity, the Fall.

We ought to note that these are quite different from the principles of Christian ethics, such as Hope or Charity; for these can be, and often are, espoused by non-Christians also. They can be called specifically 'Christian' only when they are espoused or practised for specifically Christian reasons and on specifically Christian grounds, reasons and grounds which take us back immediately to matters like Incarnation or Atonement or Redemption. Thus a poem which breathes as pure a spirit of charity as any Christian poem could, is not therefore a Christian poem—unless we are quite wrong about the current need for some stringency in understanding what is Christian and what is not.

On the other hand Christian faith rests not alone, nor even mainly, on a body of doctrine. It rests also, and perhaps pre-eminently, on a narrative, a narrative of historical events: in the first place, events in the lifetime of a particular Being, His lifespan historically recorded. But then, as between narrative and doctrine it seems that we have a distinction without much of a difference. For the narrative of Christ's life gives us doctrines, for instance Incarnation and Atonement, in narrative form; just as the doctrines only give us the narrative in propositional (though paradoxical) form. This means that the most seemingly artless verse-narratives of the Nativity or the Crucifixion, as of related events like the Annunciation or the Transfiguration, certainly belong in Christian poetry. No one is likely to doubt this; in fact the danger is once again that we shall agree too readily. For such narratives are surely *not* Christian poetry so long as they are told just as picturesque or pathetic episodes; they become Christian poetry only when the teller of them reveals in his telling the doctrinal implications of the story he tells. Such poems may be, or may seem to be, artless; but if they are to be worth anything they must not be for instance mawkish or sensational. The distinction is at its clearest, perhaps, in the case of narratives or enactments of those stories from the Old Testament which may be seen as foreshadowing or prophesying the events of the New. Unless that foreshadowing is plainly implied by the poet, his poem is not Christian. For example, Robert Graves's splendid 'Angry Samson' is not a Christian poem, for all that it depends for its fable on a passage of what Christians regard as Holy Scripture. It is not enough to say that a poem, to be a Christian poem, must have at its core something either doctrinal or scriptural; it must treat of scripture to show how scripture embodies doctrine, and of doctrine to show how it has scriptural authority. Moreover, 'doctrinal' in this connection must include the sacramental, as when the Atonement is held to be enacted afresh in every Eucharist or 'Lord's Supper'. And only the poet who tells the story of the Last Supper showing himself aware of its eucharistic implications, can be thought to have satisfied the requirement of *doctrine*. On the other hand, among the sacraments recognized by most Christian churches, notably by the Church of England, there is holy matrimony; and so some epithalamia—for instance Richard Crashaw's (no. 84) and John Keble's (no. 179)—must be acknowledged as sacred poetry which earns a place in an anthology like this one.

In such an anthology no author is more important than 'Anon.', and I hope he figures in these pages as prominently as he should. He does however present the anthologist—that is to say, the critic—with certain peculiar and vexing problems. We see him, the anonymous poet, as the undifferentiated voice of the English-speaking folk in his place and in his time. But even this may be wrong; when we consider texts from the thirteenth or fourteenth centuries, though no specific name is attached to the text, this may be due only to the accidental attrition of historical records. And thus we may be dealing not with the voice of the anonymous folk, but with an independent and highly conscious master whose name for ultimately accidental reasons has not been transmitted to us. (And if it had been transmitted, the mere name, unsupported by biographical information, would not help.) In any case, though we plainly should require artistry of such texts as of any others, 'artistry' takes on a rather different meaning as soon as we envisage the possibility that the text before us is not the product of ordering and contrivance by one intelligence, 'the artist's', but rather the end-product of manipulation and adaptation by many intelligences, all anonymous, through many generations. Our ideas and procedures, as judicious readers, are derived from a notion of the artist as highly individual; and they are ill adapted to dealing with works of art that we have to recognize as, on the contrary, *communal*. The great temptation, in this situation, is to let pass gaucheries that we would not tolerate if the text before us came over a signature that we could recognize, for instance Edmund Spenser's. I cannot be sure that in all cases I have resisted this temptation; cannot be sure for instance that 'The Holy Well' (no. 26) is presented here for its intrinsic merit, and not for its intriguing relationship to a similarly anonymous piece three centuries later, 'The Bitter Withy' (no. 214). But after all, an anthology of Christian Verse would be inadequate if it did not acknowledge the astonishing persistence over many centuries, at a sub-terranean level, of certain Christian topics; and in order to make that point, it seemed justifiable to relax more than a little the requirement of 'artistry'. No such special pleading is called for, to justify including 'The Heavenly Aeroplane' (no. 259); this anonymous poem from the 1930s is offered as a sturdy composition in its own right, in which an initial conceit is sustained with impressive consistency and inventiveness. Any one who reads it as 'amusing' or 'quaint' is condescending to it in a way that was not intended.

The congregational hymn is one sort of Christian poem which, though certainly not anonymous, all the same has never been copyrighted in the author's name in the way that we take for granted with secular poems. For although the hymn that we are called on to sing in church may bear at its foot or at its head the name of Charles Wesley or Isaac Watts, the text that we sing from our hymn-book is likely to differ in important respects from any text that Wesley or Watts authorized. And in any case the order of service will as like as not direct us to 'omit verses 3 and 5'. A unitarian hymn-book will claim for Isaac Watts a hymn that has been tampered with throughout so as to remove any even implicit reference to the Holy Trinity; and not for doctrinal reasons but merely to placate some squeamish Anglican sensibility, Watts's 'When I survey the wondrous cross' (no. 116) is in *Hymns Ancient and Modern* shorn of its vividly emblematic fourth stanza. It may seem that in all such cases the anthologist is in duty bound to recover and present the pristine text, and in many cases I have done so. Not in all, however. For there are many cases where the version sung and treasured through generations is, thanks to the good sense and good taste of choirmasters and congregations through many generations, superior to the original; and even when it is not manifestly superior, it remains true that the amended version is part of the accumulated heritage of Christian people, where the original is not. Bishop Thomas Ken for instance was a saint of the English Church, but as a poet (a poet writing moreover for schoolboys!) he was thin and garrulous. His 'Glory to thee, my God, this night' (no. 109), as originally written for the scholars of Winchester College, comprised twelve stanzas, of which however few editors have ever printed more than six, and none in the last century more than seven. Time, by thus eroding Ken's composition— as it has also eroded though less drastically his companion-piece, 'Awake, my soul, and with the sun'—has shown itself a good critic; and the version given here, profiting by that criticism, runs to six stanzas only. It will be found that I have conceived myself at liberty, when printing congregational hymns, sometimes to restore them to their pristine form, but just as often to give them rather in some form more familiar from the hymn-books. And I am not disposed to apologize for this as something less than scholarly. On the contrary, responsible scholarship must surely recognize the congregational hymn as a form of Christian poetry that lies halfway between the anonymous and the copyrighted; as it were *quasi*-anonymous. However it may be at the present day, in past centuries the hymn-writer could not claim copyright in his compositions as the secular writer did. It was his glory and his triumph that his work was taken over by the body of the worshipping folk, who thereafter claimed the right to modify his wording as confidently as they modified the wording of their folk-poetry. And just as scholars, dealing with a Border Ballad like 'Lord Randall' or 'The Twa Corbies', have learned not to take a late version as a corruption of some perhaps irrecoverable original, so in the case of congregational hymns they must acknowledge that a late version, smoothed and adapted through generations of usage, may have more authority than an original version signed perhaps 'John Keble'. The great hymns of the Christian Church are, or have become, folk-poetry; and we treat them properly, with proper gratitude and respect, when we treat them as we treat other folk-poetry.

I find that the poets I have represented most lavishly are Herbert and Vaughan, Smart and Cowper. There is as it were a different competition altogether for poets like Milton and Spenser and Langland; because they mostly need the elbow-room of long poems, these poets can be represented here only, for the most part, by excerpts. Leaving them aside, and recognizing how an anthology like this cannot help but be weighted towards the relatively brief lyric, I am willing for readers to think that I propose to them Herbert and Vaughan, Smart and Cowper, as the masters of the sacred poem in English. There are those who would press John Donne into Herbert's place, or Traherne into Henry Vaughan's. Yet no one surely will protest that too many pages have been given to Herbert, or too many to Vaughan. There will be general agreement that in any Book of Christian Verse these two seventeenth-century masters must figure very large; and for my own part, when I was debating whether such and such a poem deserved to be included, the question presented itself in the form: 'Does it deserve to appear between the same covers as Herbert's "The Collar" or his "Church-monuments"?' More eyebrows will be raised at finding Smart and Cowper, from the next century, given equal prominence. Christopher Smart may be left to speak for himself. But it is worth making the case for William Cowper because in order to do so we have to clear our minds about the status of the congregational hymn as poetry, and also about what is meant by 'the plain style'.

Our resistance to considering hymns as poems has something to do with our sense that, because the sentiments professed by a church congregation have to be unexceptionable, the verses which express those sentiments cannot have all the honesty that we expect of poets, even of Christian poets like Hopkins, or Donne in his Holy Sonnets, who speak of their Maker only of and for themselves, not for themselves in communion with others. This may be true of Hopkins, but is I suspect a misreading of Donne, who does not inherit any of the romantic individualism that is inherited by the Victorian Father Hopkins; the Holy Sonnets are not cries from a lonely and agonized heart, though we may read them as if they were. However that may be, if on these grounds we tend to think that Cowper's Olney Hymns are not quite poems, the best hymnologists, we find, think that they are not quite hymns—partly because, whereas Watts and Wesley and Cowper's Olney collaborator John Newton are uttering their hymns as it were from the pulpit, Cowper is one of those who sit at their feet, reporting faithfully how it seems to him, there, in the pew. Perhaps the clearest example is 'Sometimes a light surprises' (no. 162). One may have read this poem, or more probably sung it, many and many a time before realizing that the crucial word in it is the first. 'Sometimes'—only sometimes, not always, not even very often! The 'holy contemplation' that is thereafter evoked, the sweet security, the unforced adoration— all this is distinctly *not* what any one, it seems, should expect to experience at all often, in church or out of it. It is *not* presented as the normal condition of the Believer. Above all therefore it is *not* the pay-off, the guaranteed reward for going to church and trying to behave well. On the contrary one earns such fitful and infrequent benefits (though 'earn' is the wrong word anyway, for a Calvinist such as Cowper) only by first suffering through afflictions and desolations —the 'season of clear shining' comes only 'after rain', only 'when comforts are declining'; and there is no guarantee that it will come, even then. Similarly, one sings anyway; the consoling words that one sings strike dully and inertly Sunday after Sunday (one is even, so some might say, 'insincere' in singing them); it is only *sometimes*, on one or two Sundays out of many, that 'a light surprises' and the words take on heartfelt meaning, 'while he sings'. Regular worshippers can decide for themselves if this doesn't accurately state what public worship is, in their experience of it. If it does, then the sentiments expressed are indeed unexceptionable but also disconcertingly honest. An evangelist, or even the earnest incumbent in the pulpit, would surely prefer not to have the insecurity of the whole arrangement announced quite so bleakly. After all, they want those pews filled! In any case, once one has taken the force of 'sometimes', the poem affects a fusion of states of feeling that one would have sworn were incompatible: of grateful security ('But he will bear us through') with wistfulness, even weariness, almost resentment. The opening word of the poem casts a beam of pathos and qualification across everything that comes after. And yet it would be wrong, surely, to call this 'subtle'; it is only our inattentiveness that makes it seem so. The word 'some-times' means just what it says, and it is not slipped over on us, or slyly slipped in when we are not looking. In short, though these are not 'stiff quatrains shovelled out four-square', few indeed of 'the milder subtleties of grace or art' are called on to sweeten these verses. In particular the modern reader will feel the lack of those subtleties that come under the heading of 'imagery'. But to use images sparingly, and seldom to seek them except in commonplaces, is characteristic of the plain style.

At any rate this note is constant, with Cowper. 'Oh! for a closer walk with God' (no. 160) is not a pious ejaculation, but a demand to know when 'a season of clear shining' will be vouchsafed once more, how much longer he must wait for it. There is an almost mutinous suspicion of having been cheated in the bargain:

> Where is the blessedness I knew
>   When first I saw the Lord?
> Where is the soul-refreshing view
>   Of Jesus and his word?
>
> What peaceful hours I once enjoyed!
>   How sweet their memory still!
> But they have left an aching void
>   The world can never fill.

According to Calvinist doctrine, this was not supposed to happen. Once 'saved' (as Cowper was sure that he had been), the elect were supposed never thereafter to lose the blissful assurance of their elec-tion. But Cowper, who suffered from long periods of suicidal depres-sion, knew that it hadn't worked out like that for him; and his struggle with this agonizing puzzle was the chief concern of his religious life. Accordingly, the second half of his hymn consists of something more than formulaic breast-beating:

> Return, O holy Dove, return,
>   Sweet messenger of rest;
> I hate the sins that made thee mourn,
>   And drove thee from my breast.
>
> The dearest idol I have known,
>   Whate'er that idol be;

> Help me to tear it from thy throne,
> And worship only thee.
>
> So shall my walk be close with God,
> Calm and serene my frame;
> So purer light shall mark the road
> That leads me to the Lamb.

'Sin' in a poem like this is less an action, or a course of actions, than it is a state: the state of mind and feeling which ensures that however often the worshipper sings, only *sometimes* will the light surprise; the habitual inattention and worse which makes it certain that on nineteen Sundays out of twenty nothing will happen, and worship won't 'work'. This is the block that is in the worshipper himself; and it's a block that he can't with the best will in the world remove, because this is the sin that is 'original', rooted in human nature and ineradicable therefore except by God's intervention, the gift of His grace. The light 'surprises'; try as one may, it cannot be switched on, simply because, as Cowper says elsewhere, 'No strength of Nature can suffice/To serve the lord aright . . .' And so there can be no recourse but prayer: 'Return . . . return . . . Help me . . .' *So* (and not otherwise) 'shall my walk be close with God'—that's to say, only if God chooses to make it so. The patness of the 'So shall . . .' (as it were, Q.E.D!) comes over as almost sardonic. It all sounds so simple! But 'So shall' means something quite different from 'So all I have to do is . . .' And yet, here once again, Cowper has not been laying a trap for us. If we fall into a trap, it is one we have dug for ourselves; the poem, in sober earnestness, simply enunciates what Cowper takes to be orthodox doctrine, and he has found it vindicated by his own experience. It is the doctrine that is 'subtle', not the poem that meditates upon it.

For some parts or aspects of Calvinist doctrine, the word that the modern reader will find, even the Christian reader, is not 'subtle' but rather 'appalling'. For instance, when Cowper wrote (no. 161) 'God moves in a mysterious way,/His wonders to perform', he seems to have had in mind, as such 'wonders', chiefly those unforeseeable calamities against all the odds which even today our lawyers can define only as 'acts of God'. One such was the subject of one of his secular poems: the freakish foundering of a warship, 'The Royal George', not when she was in action nor on the high seas but by the harbour-wall. Another such, we cannot help but think, was the curious fate visited by God upon his poet, doomed to try to kill himself insanely every few years. The lines that we sing or say as meaning, 'Despite appearances, everything is under control', do in fact mean that, but mean it in a more horrific way than most of us are aware of:

Judge not the Lord by feeble sense,
  But trust him for his grace;
Behind a frowning providence
  He hides a smiling face.

His purposes will ripen fast,
  Unfolding ev'ry hour;
The bud may have a bitter taste,
  But sweet will be the flow'r.

The 'smiling face' that looked down when the Royal George keeled over, and 'Kempenfelt went down/With twice four hundred men', wears a smile inhuman enough to satisfy Sir William Empson, or any one else nowadays who cannot justify God's ways to man. And of course any Christian is at liberty to protest that this isn't the creed that *he* professes. The anthologist however is not a theologian: the Christianity that he is concerned with is the faith that, in all its varieties, has been professed and practised through the centuries, and the variety of the faith that Cowper's poem expounds is to be found long before Cowper's time, and indeed before John Calvin's. Accordingly this way of following through what we mean by God's omnipotence deserves its place in this anthology, as do more consolatory explanations of the same mystery.

The bleakness of the doctrine may seem to go along with the bleakness of Cowper's verses simply as poetry. A reader may protest that he expects more 'consolations' from the poetry, even if he can't demand them of the doctrine. And it is surely true that, if all poetry were like this, we should feel we had been put on iron rations. There are legitimate splendours and audacities which this style must deny itself; and on other pages of this collection other styles than this plain one will be found purveying such splendours. Indeed, one reason why we know William Cowper to be a great poet is that in other poems he himself achieves Miltonic and other splendours such as he denied himself when he was writing his Olney Hymns and his Stanzas for the Bills of Mortality. For these he chose to use the plain style—quite deliberately, as we know from certain passages in his Letters.

These, it may seem, are academic niceties with which a reader of this anthology need not concern himself. And indeed it is true that there is no *need* for him to do so. Yet I venture to think he will miss a great deal if he passes over them impatiently. For when a poet chooses a style, or chooses *between* styles, he is making a choice in which his whole self is involved—including, if he is a Christian poet, that part of himself which is most earnestly and devoutly Christian. The question is, for him: what sort of language is most appropriate when I would speak of, or to, my God? And it is not only the puritans among poets who appear to have decided that the only language proper for such exalted purposes is a language stripped of fripperies and seductive indulgences, the most direct and unswerving English. To speak thus plainly has the additional advantage that it ought to be meaningful to plain men and women, the poet's fellow-Christians; but the main reason for choosing it is that when speaking to God, in poetry as in prayer, any sort of prevarication or ambiguity is unseemly, indeed unthinkable.

DONALD DAVIE

1980

ANONYMOUS
7th–10th century

(translated by Michael Alexander)

The Dream of the Rood

Hwaet!
A dream came to me
    at deep midnight
when humankind
    kept their beds
—the dream of dreams!
    I shall declare it.

It seemed I saw the Tree itself
borne on the air, light wound about it,
—a beam of brightest wood, a beacon clad
in overlapping gold, glancing gems
fair at its foot, and five stones
set in a crux flashed from the crosstree.

Around angels of God
    all gazed upon it,
since first fashioning fair.
    It was not a felon's gallows,
for holy ghosts beheld it there,
and men on mould, and the whole Making shone for it
—*signum* of victory!
               Stained and marred,
stricken with shame, I saw the glory-tree
shine out gaily, sheathed in yellow
decorous gold; and gemstones made
for their Maker's Tree a right mail-coat.

Yet through the masking gold I might perceive
what terrible sufferings were once sustained thereon:
it bled from the right side.
    Ruth in the heart.

Afraid I saw that unstill brightness
change raiment and colour
    —again clad in gold

or again slicked with sweat,
    spangled with spilling blood.

Yet lying there a long while
I beheld, sorrowing, the Healer's Tree
till it seemed that I heard how it broke silence,
best of wood, and began to speak:

'Over that long remove my mind ranges
back to the holt where I was hewn down;
from my own stem I was struck away,
    dragged off by strong enemies,
wrought into a roadside scaffold.
    They made me a hoist for wrongdoers.

The soldiers on their shoulders bore me,
    until on a hill-top they set me up;
many enemies made me fast there.
    Then I saw, marching toward me,
mankind's brave King;
    He came to climb upon me.

I dared not break or bend aside
against God's will, though the ground itself
shook at my feet. Fast I stood,
who falling could have felled them all.

Almighty God ungirded Him,
    eager to mount the gallows,
unafraid in the sight of many:
    He would set free mankind.
I shook when His arms embraced me
    but I durst not bow to ground,
stoop to Earth's surface.
    Stand fast I must.

I was reared up, a rood.
    I raised the great King,
liege lord of the heavens,
    dared not lean from the true.
They drove me through with dark nails:
    on me are the deep wounds manifest,
wide-mouthed hate-dents.

2

I durst not harm any of them.
How they mocked at us both!
I was all moist with blood
sprung from the Man's side
after He sent forth His soul.

Wry wierds a many I underwent
up on that hill-top; saw the Lord of Hosts
stretched out stark. Darkness shrouded
the King's corse. Clouds wrapped
its clear shining. A shade went out
wan under cloud-pall. All creation wept,
keened the King's death. Christ was on the Cross.

But there quickly came from far
earls to the One there. All that I beheld;
had grown weak with grief,
yet with glad will bent then
meek to those men's hands,
yielded Almighty God.

They lifted Him down from the leaden pain,
left me, the commanders,
standing in a sweat of blood.
I was all wounded with shafts.

They straightened out His strained limbs,
stood at His body's head,
looked down on the Lord of Heaven
—for a while He lay there resting—
set to contrive Him a tomb
in the sight of the Tree of Death,
carved it of bright stone,
laid in it the Bringer of victory,
spent from the great struggle.
They began to speak the grief-song,
sad in the sinking light,
then thought to set out homeward;
their hearts were sick to death,
their most high Prince
they left to rest there with scant retinue.

Yet we three, weeping, a good while
stood in that place after the song had gone up
from the captains' throats. Cold grew the corse,
fair soul-house.
                    They felled us all.
We crashed to ground, cruel Wierd,
and they delved for us a deep pit.

The Lord's men learnt of it,
His friends found me . . .
it was they who girt me with gold and silver . . .'

ANONYMOUS

13th century

(translated by Donald Davie)

2   *'Thou who createdst everything'*

Thou who createdst everything,
Sweet Father, heavenly King,
Hear me—I, thy son, implore:
For Man this flesh and bone I bore.

Clear and bright my breast and side,
Blood over whiteness spilling wide,
Holes in my body crucified.

Stiff and stark my long arms rise,
Dimness and darkness cloud my eyes;
Like sculpted marble hang my thighs.

Red my feet with the flowing blood,
Holes in them washed through with that flood.
Mercy on Man's sins, Father on high!
Through all my wounds to thee I cry!

ANONYMOUS

c. 1275–1300

('*Wait a Little*')

3

Loverd, thou clepedest me,
And I nought ne answered thee
But wordès slow and sleepy:
'Tholè yet! Thole a litel!'
But 'yet' and 'yet' was endèless
And 'thole a litel' a long way is.

('*Undo!*')

4

Alas, alas, well evil I sped!
For sin Jesu from me is fled,
    That lively fere.
At my door he stands alone
And calls 'Undo!' with rueful moan
    On this manère:

'Undo, my lief, my dovè dear,
Undo! why stand I steken out here?
    I am thy make.
Lo, my head and minè locks
Are all biweved with bloody drops
    For thinè sake.'

ANONYMOUS

(translated by Brian Stone)

from the Harley Lyrics c. 1260–1320

5

'*Now fade the rose and lily-flower*'

Now fade the rose and lily-flower
That once, in summer's balmy hour,
    Gave sweetly out their scent.

---

3 *clepedest*] called   *thole*] wait, or abide   **4** *fere*] companion
     steken] ?stuck   *make*] mate, or match

ANONYMOUS

All queens of plenitude and power,
All ladies bright in palace bower,
   By gliding death are pent.
If man will cast out fleshly lust,
   On heavenly bliss being bent,
Then think of Jesus Christ he must,
   Whose side by spear was rent.

On pleasure forth adventuring
From Peterborough at morning-spring,
   My secret love I weighed,
And grieving it and murmuring
To her who bore the heavenly King,
   For clemency I prayed:
'Beg your Son to grant us grace,
   (For us he dearly paid)
And save us from the loathsome place,
   That house for devils made!'

My heart was shuddering with dread
For fleshly sins on which I fed
   Of which my life was made.
I know not where I shall be led,
To joy or woe, when on the bed
   In death I shall be laid.
My hope in one sole Lady is,
   A Mother and a Maid;
For we shall come to heavenly bliss
   With her healing aid.

Better is her medicine
Than any mead or any wine;
   Her herbs are sweet of scent.
And sure, from Caithness to Dublin,
No doctor is so skilled and fine
   At curing discontent.
A man of vices manifold
   Who longs to change his bent
Can, without paying wealth or gold,
   Win health and high content.

Her cures of penance smoothly run:
My service to her shall be done
   As long as I have life:
To joy and freedom slaves have come
Through that noble, slender one:
   Praise to her blisses five!
Whenever man in sickness is,
   To reach her he should strive;
And through her grace are brought to bliss
   Maid and married wife.

May he who died upon the tree
Grant us sinners clemency,
   Prince of heavenly bowers!
Women, in your gaiety
Think of God's benignity,
   Which falls on us in showers.
Though bright and fair of face you be,
   Decay shall fade your flowers.
Jesu, honoured in high degree,
   Yet may your grace be ours!

ANONYMOUS

14th century

(translated by Donald Davie)

6   *'Moon-like is all other love'*

Moon-like is all other love:
First crescent, then decreasing, gain;
Flower that buds, and soon goes off;
A day that fleets away in rain.

All other love bravely starts out,
But ends with torture, and in tears;
No love can salve the torment out
But that the King of Heaven bears:

For ever springing, ever new,
For ever the full orb, it is
A thing not thinned, from which accrue
Always new sweets, new centuries.

For this love, I all others fled:
Tell me where you may be found!
'Meek Mary is one fountainhead;
But Christ, Christ rather, is the ground.'

I did not find you, Christ found me.
Hold me, hold me fast, or else,
For all that that love steadfast be,
This love of mine swerves as it swells.

And yet, and yet—I *hurt*, the blood
Floods from my heart. My God, I see,
Leaves me in this. So, well and good . . .
Yet still I pray: 'God be with me.'

Alas, what should I do in Rome?
I take a leaf from carnal love:
No mortal troth dare I trust home
Except He help that sits above.

ANONYMOUS (the *Pearl* poet)

14th century

(translated by Brian Stone)

7   from *Cleanness*

I

He who would acclaim Cleanness in becoming style,
And rehearse all the honours she asks as of right,
May find fair forms to further his art:
To utter the opposite would be hard and troublesome.

For he who made all is angry to a marvel
With votaries who follow him with defiled spirits.
Consider the sacred calling of those who sing and read
And approach his presence, priests as we call them:

Attached to him in truth, to his temple they go;
Properly and piously they pace to his altar

And handle his own body in holy communion.
If Cleanness encompass them, how incomparable their reward!

But if their faith is false and failing in courtesy,
Their outsides all honour, their insides corrupted,
They are sinful themselves and sullied altogether,
Hating God and his good rites, goading him to anger.

So clean in his court is that king who rules all,
So upright a householder, so honourably served
By angels of utter purity without and within,
Beautifully bright, in brilliant mantles.

2

'I made them natural means, which I communicated secretly,
And held most holy in my ordinance for humans,
A manner of mating of marvellous sweetness.
In my brain was born the embrace of lovers:

'The modes of love I made for man's utmost delight,
That when two true ones are attached to each other,
Between the man and his mate is such mutual joy
That the purity of Paradise could prove little better;

'Provided each to each is honourably joined
By a still secret voice, unstirred by sight,
With the love-flame leaping, lashed so hot
That all the evils on earth could not quench it.

'But these have spurned my statutes, in scorn of nature,
And couple in contumely by a custom unclean.
I shall strike them sternly for their stinking filth,
As a warning to the world: let men beware for ever.'

3

Yes, that Master is merciful, though mire and muck
Defile you with filth while you fare through life.
Yet you may shine after shrift, though shame once held you,
And be purified by penance, be a pearl of God.

The pearl is praised as priceless among precious stones,
Though its cost in coin is not accounted the highest.
What quality causes this but its colour of purity,
That wins her honour above all other white stones?

For she shines so shimmering, is shaped so round,
Being faultless and flawless—if she is fine indeed—
That however aged or much-handled she becomes,
The pearl is not impaired while proudly esteemed;

But if by chance things change and she be cherished no more,
Her brightness becoming blurred in the box where she lies,
Then but wash her in wine, worthily, as is due,
And by her quality she will become cleaner than before.

So if people are poisoned by opprobrious deeds,
And their souls are sullied, they may seek shrift
And be polished by the priest, when penance is done,
Brighter than the beryl or braided pearls.

But beware, when you're washed in the water of shrift,
And polished like parchment that's perfectly scraped,
That you stain your soul with sin no more,
For your misdoing will then double the disdain of the Lord,

Raising his wrath more rapidly than ever,
His anger much hotter than if you had not washed.
For when a soul is sealed and sanctified as God's,
He holds it wholly his, and have it he will;

But if it reverts to vice, he violently resents it,
As a wrongful robbery, a raid by a thief.
Be vigilant against his vengeance; very angry is God
With those who gainsay his grace and go back to filth.

Though it be but a basin, a bowl or cup,
A small plate or salver that has served God once,
He forbids it to be flung in defilement to the ground,
So abhorrent of evil is the ever-righteous.

WILLIAM LANGLAND

(?1330–1400)

(the B text, translated by Donald Attwater)

8   from *The Book Concerning Piers the Plowman*

1
[*The Entertainment Industry*]

And some chose trade   they fared the better
As it seemeth to our sight   that such men thrive.
And some to make mirth   as minstrels know how
And get gold with their glees   guiltlessly, I hold.
But jesters and janglers   children of Judas,
Feigning their fancies   and making folk fools,
They have wit at will   to work, if they would;
Paul preacheth of them   I'll not prove it here—
Qui turpiloquium loquitur   is Lucifer's hind.

2
[*The Civil Service*]

These lodge in London in Lent   and at other times too.
Some serve the king   and his silver count
In Chequer and Chancery courts   making claim for his debts
Of wards and of wardmotes   waifs and estrays.
And some serve as servants   to lords and ladies,
And instead of stewards   sit in session to judge.
Their Mass and their matins   their canonical hours,
Are said undevoutly   I fear at the last
Lest Christ in his council   accurse will full many.

3
[*Good Works*]

For though ye be true of your tongue   and honestly earn,
And as chaste as a child   that weepeth in church,
Unless ye love loyally   and give to the poor,
Such goods as God sends you   to them gladly giving,
Ye have no more merit   in Mass or in hours
Than Malkin of her maidenhood   that no man desireth.
For James the gentle   judged in his books
That faith without deed   is right nothing worth
And as dead as a door-post   unless actions follow...

4
[*The Age of Reason*]

'I, Conscience, know this Mother-Wit me it taught,
That Reason shall reign and the realms govern.
As it happened to Agag shall happen to others.
Samuel shall slay him and Saul shall be blamed,
And David shall be diademed and subdue them all;
And one Christian king shall care for them all.
  Meed shall no more be master as she is now,
But Love and Lowliness and Loyalty together,
These shall be masters on earth Truth to save.
  'And who trespasseth against Truth or traverseth his will,
Loyalty shall judge him no living man else.
Shall no serjeant for service wear a silk hood
And no fur on his cloak for pleading at bar.
Meed of many misdoers maketh more lords,
And over the lords' laws ruleth the realms.
  'But man's Love shall come yet and Conscience together,
And make Law a labourer such love shall arise
And such peace among the people and a perfect truth
That Jews shall ween in their wits and wax wondrous glad,
That Moses or Messiah be come into this earth,
And have wonder in their hearts that men be so true.'

5
[*God's Mercy*]

'And all the wickedness in this world that man might work or think
Is no more to the mercy of God than a live coal in the sea.'

6
[*A Saint Called 'Truth'*]

A thousand men then came thronging together,
Who cried upward to Christ and to his clean Mother
To have grace to go with them Truth for to seek.
  But there was no wight so wise that he knew the way thither
But blundered like beasts over banks and on hills
A long time, till 'twas late that they a man met
Apparelled as a Paynim in a pilgrim's wise.
He bare a staff bound with a broad strip
In bindweed wise wound about.

A bowl and a bag he bare by his side;
An hundred ampullas on his hat set,
Signs of Sinai and shells of Galicia,
Many a cross on his cloak keys also of Rome
And the vernicle in front so that men should know
And see by his signs what shrines he had sought.
  This folk asked him first from whence he did come.
  'From Sinai', he said 'and from our Lord's sepulchre;
Bethlehem and Babylon I have been in both;
In Armenia, in Alexandria and many other places.
Ye may see by my signs that sit on my hat
That I've walked full wide in wet and in dry,
And have sought good saints for my soul's health.'
  'Knowest thou aught of a saint that men call Truth?
Could'st thou show us the way where that wight dwelleth?'
  'Nay, so help me God!' said the man then,
'I saw never palmer with pike nor with scrip
Ask after him, till now in this place.'
  'Peter!' quoth a plowman and put forth his head,
'I know him as well as a clerk doth his books.
Conscience and Mother-Wit made known his place
And made me swear surely to serve him for ever
Both in sowing and setting so long as I work.
I have been his follower all these fifty winters,
Both sown his seed and driven his beasts,
And watched over his profit within and without.
I dike and I delve and do what Truth biddeth:
Sometimes I sow and sometimes I thresh;
In tailor's and tinker's craft what Truth can devise;
I weave and I wind and do what Truth biddeth.
For though I say it myself I serve him to his pleasure;
I have good hire of him and oftentimes more.
He is the readiest payer that a poor man knoweth;
He withholds not his hire from his servants at even.
He is lowly as a lamb and lovely of speech,
And if ye are wishful to know where that he dwelleth,
I shall show you surely the way to his place.'

GEOFFREY CHAUCER
?1340–1400

9   from *Troilus and Criseyde*

Swich fyn hath, lo, this Troilus for love!
Swich fyn hath al his gretè worthinesse!
Swich fyn hath his estat rëàl above!
Swich fyn his lust, swich fyn hath his noblesse!
Swich fyn, this falsè worldès brotelnesse!—
And thus bigan his loving of Criseyde
As I have told, and in this wise he deyde.

—O yongè fresshè folkès, he or she,
In whiche ay love up-groweth with your age,
Repeireth hom fro worldly vanité!
And of your herte up-casteth the visàge
To th'ilkè God that after his imàge
You made; and thinketh al n'is but a faire
This world, that passeth sone as flourès faire!

And loveth Him, the whiche that right for love
Upon a cros, our soulès for to beye,
First starf, and roos, and sit in hevene above;
For He n'il falsen no wight, dar I seye,
That wol his herte al hooly on him leye!
And sin He best to love is, and most meke,
What nedeth feynèd lovès for to seke?

Lo here, of payens corsèd oldè rites!
Lo here, where alle hir Goddès may availe!
Lo here, thise wrecched worldès appetites!
Lo here, the fyn and guerdon for travaile
Of Jove, Appollo, of Mars, of swich rascaile!
Lo here, the forme of oldè clerkès speche
In poetrye, if ye hir bokès seche!

—O moral Gower, this book I directe
To thee, and to thee, philosophical Strode,
To vouchen-sauf, ther nede is, to correcte,
Of your benignètès and zelès gode.—

9   *Swich fyn*] such an end   *brotelnesse*] brittleness   *starf*] died

And to that sothfast Crist, that starf on rode,
With al myn herte, of mercy evere I preye,
And to the Lord right thus I speke and seye:

Thou oon, and two, and three, eterne on-live,
That regnest ay in three and two and oon,
Uncircumscript, and al maist circumscrive,
Us from visible and invisible foon
Defende, and to thy mercy, everichoon,
So make us, Jesus, for thy mercy digne,
For love of mayde and moder thyn benigne!

10   from *Prologue* to *The Canterbury Tales*

A good man was ther of religioun,
And was a POURE PERSOUN OF A TOUN;
But riche he was of hooly thoght and werk;
He was also a lernèd man, a clerk,
That Cristès Gospel trewely wolde prechè:
His parisshens devoutly wolde he teche.
Benygne he was, and wonder diligent,
And in adversitee ful pacient;
And swich he was y-prevèd oftè sithes.
Ful looth were hym to cursen for his tithes,
But rather wolde he yeven, out of doute,
Unto his pourè parisshens aboute,
Of his offrýng and eek of his substaunce:
Ne koude in litel thyng have suffisaunce.
Wyd was his parisshe, and houses fer asonder,
But he ne laftè nat, for reyn ne thonder,
In sicknesse nor in meschief to visite
The ferreste in his parisshe, muche and lite,
Upon his feet, and in his hand a staf.
This noble ensample to his sheepe he yaf
That firste he wroghte and afterward he taughte.
Out of the gospel he tho wordès caughte,
And this figure he added eek therto,
That if gold rustè what shal iren doo?
For if a preest be foul, on whom we truste,
No wonder is a lewèd man to ruste;
And shame it is, if a prest takè keepe,
A shiten shepherde and a clenè sheepe.

15

Well oughte a preest ensample for to yive
By his clennesse how that his sheepe sholde lyve.
He settè nat his benefice to hyre
And leet his sheepe encombred in the myre,
And ran to Londoun, unto Seint Poules,
To seken hym a chaunterie for soules,
Or with a bretherhed to been withholde;
But dwelte at hoom and keptè wel his folde,
So that the wolf ne made it nat myscarie,—
He was a shepherde, and noght a mercenarie:
And though he hooly were and vertuous,
He was to synful man nat despitous,
Ne of his spechè daungerous ne digne,
But in his techyng déscreet and benygne,
To drawen folk to hevene by fairnesse,
By good ensample, this was his bisynesse.
But it were any persone obstinat,
What so he were, of heigh or lough estat,
Hym wolde he snybben sharply for the nonys.
A bettrè preest I trowe that nowher noon ys;
He waited after no pompe and reverence,
Ne maked him a spicèd conscience,
But Cristès loore, and his Apostles twelve,
He taughte, but first he folwed it hym selve.

ANONYMOUS

late 14th century

11   ('*Quia Amore Langueo*')

In the vale of restless mind
    I sought in mountain and in mead,
Trusting a true love for to find,
    Upon an hill then took I heed;
    A voice I heard—and near I yede—
    In huge dolòur complaining tho:
'See, dear soul, my sidès bleed,
    Quia amore langueo.'

11   *near I yede*] nearer I went   *tho*] then

16

Under this mount I found a tree;
  Under this tree a man sitting;
From head to foot wounded was he,
  His hertè-blood I saw bleeding;
  A seemly man to be a king
    A gracious face to look unto.
  I asked him how he had paining.
    He said: *Quia amore langueo*.

'I am true love that false was never:
  My sister, man's soul, I loved her thus;
Because I would on no wise dissever,
  I left my kingdom glorious;
  I purveyed her a place full precious;
    She flit, I followed; I loved her so
  That I suffered these painès piteous,
    Quia amore langueo.

'My fair love and my spousè bright,
  I saved her fro beating and she hath me bet;
I clothed her in grace and heavenly light,
  This bloody surcote she hath on me set.
  For longing love I will not let;
    Sweetè strokès by these, lo!
  I have loved her ever as I het,
    Quia amore langueo.

'I crowned her with bliss, and she me with thorn;
  I led her to chamber, and she me to die;
I brought her to worship, and she me to scorn;
  I did her reverence, and she me villainy.
  To love that loveth is no maistrỳ;
    Her hate made never my love her foe;
  Ask then no mo questions why,
    Quia amore langueo.

'Look unto mine handès, man!
  These gloves were given me when I her sought;
They be not white, but red and wan,
  Embroidered with blood, my spouse them bought;
  They will not off, I leave them nought,

bet] beaten   *het*] promised   *villainy*] indignity   *wan*] discoloured

17

I woo her with them wherever she go;
These hands full friendly for her fought,
   Quia amore langueo.

'Marvel not, man, though I sit still;
   My love hath shod me wonder strait;
She buckled my feet, as was her will,
    With sharpè nails—well thou maist wait!
    In my love was never deceit,
      For all my members I have opened her to;
    My body I made her heartès bait,
      Quia amore langueo.

'In my side I have made her a nest;
   Look in me how wide a wound is here!
This is her chamber, here shall she rest,
    That she and I may sleep in fere.
    Here may she wash, if any filth were,
      Here is succour for all her woe;
    Come if she will, she shall have cheer,
      Quia amore langueo.

'I will abide till she be ready,
   I will her sue if she say nay;
If she be reckèless, I will be ready,
    If she be dangerous, I will her pray.
    If she do weep, then bid I nay;
      Mine arms be spread to clip her me to;
    Cry onès: I come. Now, soul, assay!
      Quia amore langueo.

'I sit on an hill for to see far,
   I look to the vale; my spouse I see:
Now runs she awayward, now comes she nearer,
    Yet fro my eye-sight she may not be.
    Some wait their prey to make her flee;
      I run tofore to chastise her foe.
    Recover, my soul, again to me,
      Quia amore langueo.

wait] see   *in fere*] together   *reckèless*] thoughtless
    ready] prudent   *dangerous*] haughty

'My sweetè spouse, will we go play?
   Apples be ripe in my gardène;
I shall clothe thee in new array,
   Thy meat shall be milk, honey, and wine.
   Now, dear soul, let us go dine,
     Thy sustenance is in my scrippè, lo!
   Tarry not now, fair spousè mine,
     Quia amore langueo.

'If thou be foul, I shall make thee clean;
   If thou be sick, I shall thee heal,
If thou aught mourn, I shall bemene.
   Spouse, why wilt thou nought with me deal?
   Thou foundest never love so leal;
     What wilt thou, soul, that I shall do?
   I may of unkindness thee appeal,
     Quia amore langueo.

'What shall I do now with my spouse?
   Abide I will her gentleness.
Would she look onès out of her house
   Of fleshly affections and uncleanness,
   Her bed is made, her bolster is bliss,
     Her chamber is chosen, such are no mo.
   Look out at the windows of kindness,
     Quia amore langueo.

'Long and love thou never so high,
   Yet is my love more than thine may be;
Thou gladdest, thou weepest, I sit thee by;
   Yet might thou, spouse, look onès at me!
   Spouse, should I alway feedè thee
     With childès meat? Nay, love, not so!
   I prove thy love with adversity,
     Quia amore langueo.

'My spouse is in chamber, hold your peace;
   Make no noise, but let her sleep.
My babe shall suffer no disease,
   I may not hear my dear child weep;

scrippè] bag   *bemene*] condole with   *leal*] loyal   *disease*] unease

For with my pap I shall her keep.
　　No wonder though I tend her to:
This hole in my side had never been so deep,
　　But *quia amore langueo*.

'Wax not weary, mine own dear wife:
　　What meed is aye to live in comfort?
For in tribulation I run more rife
Oftentimes than in disport;
In wealth, in woe, ever I support,
　　Then, dear soul, go never me fro!
Thy meed is markèd, when thou art mort,
　　Quia amore langueo.'

ANONYMOUS

15th century

12　　　　'*I sing of a maiden*'

I sing of a maiden
　　That is makèless:
King of all kingès
　　To her son she ches.

He came all so stillè
　　There his mother was,
As dew in Aprillè
　　That falleth on the grass.

He came all so stillè
　　To his mother's bower,
As dew in Aprillè
　　That falleth on the flower.

He came all so stillè
　　There his mother lay,
As dew in Aprillè
　　That falleth on the spray.

---

11 *markèd*] assigned　　*mort*] dead
12　*makèless*] matchless, unmated　　*ches*] chose　　*There*] where

ANONYMOUS

Mother and maiden
    Was never none but she;
Well may such a lady
    Goddès mother be.

ANONYMOUS

c. 1450

13   *'Adam lay y-bounden'*

Adam lay y-bounden
    Bounden in a bond;
Four thousand winter
    Thought he not too long;
And all was for an apple
    An apple that he took,
As clerkes finden written
    In theire book.

Ne had the apple taken been,
    The apple taken been,
Ne hadde never our Lady
    A been heaven's queen.
Blessed be the time
    That apple taken was!
Therefore we may singen
    'Deo Gratias!'

WILLIAM DUNBAR

?1465–1520

14   *On the Resurrection of Christ*

Done is a battell on the dragon blak,
Our campioun Chryst confountet hes his force;
The yettis of hell ar brokin with a crak
The signe triumphall rasit is of the croce,
The divillis trymmillis with hiddous voce,

---

14   *campioun*] champion   *yettis*] gates   *trymmillis*] tremble

The saulis ar borrowit and to the blis can go,
Chryst with his blud our ransonis dois indoce:
Surrexit Dominus de sepulchro.

Dungin is the deidly dragon Lucifer,
The crewall serpent with the mortall stang;
The auld kene tegir with his teith on char,
Quhilk in a wait hes lyne for us so lang,
Thinking to grip us in his clows strang;
The mercifull lord wald nocht that it wer so,
He maid him for to felye of that fang:
Surrexit Dominus de sepulchro.

He for our saik that sufferit to be slane,
And lyk a lamb in sacrifice was dicht,
Is lyk a lyone rissin up agane,
And as gyane raxit him on hicht;
Sprungin is Aurora radius and bricht,
On loft is gone the glorius Appollo,
The blisfull day depairtit fro the nycht:
Surrexit Dominus de sepulchro.

The grit victour agane is rissin on hicht,
That for our qúerrel to the deth was woundit;
The sone that wox all paill now schynis bricht,
And dirknes clerit, our fayth is now refoundit;
The knell of mercy fra the hevin is soundit,
The Cristin ar deliverit of thair wo,
The Jowis and thair errour ar confondit:
Surrexit Dominus de sepulchro.

The fo is chasit, the battel is done ceis,
The presone brokin, the jevellouris fleit and flemit;
The weir is gon, confermit is the peis,
The fetteris lowsit and the dungeoun temit,
The ransoun maid, the presoneris redemit;
The feild is win, ourcumin is the fo,
Dispulit of the tresur that he yemit:
Surrexit Dominus de sepulchro.

borrowit] ransomed   *indoce*] endorse   *Dungin*] struck down
on char] ajar   *felye of that fang*] come short of that booty   *dicht*] made ready
raxit him] raised himself   *On loft*] aloft   *done ceis*] made to cease
jevellouris fleit and flemit] gaolers affrighted and put to flight   *temit*] emptied
yemit] kept

ANONYMOUS
15th century

This Endris Night

This endris night I saw a sight,
    A star as bright as day;
And ever among, a maiden sung,
    'Lullay, by, by, lullay.'

This lovely lady sat and sung,
    And to her child did say:
'My son, my brother, father, dear,
    Why liest thou thus in hay?

My sweetest bird thus 'tis required,
    Though thou be king veray;
But nevertheless I will not cease
    To sing, by, by, lullay.'

The child then spake in his talking,
    And to his mother said:
'Yea, I am known as heaven-king,
    In crib though I be laid;

For angels bright down to me light:
    Thou knowest 'tis no nay:
And for that sight thou may'st delight
    To sing, by, by, lullay.'

'Now sweet son, since thou art a king,
    Why art thou laid in stall?
Why dost not order thy bedding
    In some great kingès hall?

Methinks 'tis right that king or knight
    Should be in good array:
And then among, it were no wrong
    To sing, by, by, lullay.'

This endris night] the other night   *ever among*] every now and then
  veray] true   *light*] alight   *no nay*]   not to be denied

'Mary-mother, I am thy child,
    Though I be laid in stall:
For lords and dukes shall worship me,
    And so shall kingès all.

Ye shall well see that kingès three
    Shall come on this twelfth day;
For this behest, give me thy breast,
    And sing, by, by, lullay.'

'Now tell, sweet son, I thee do pray,
    Thou art my love and dear—
How should I keep thee to thy pay,
    And make thee glad of cheer?

For all thy will I would fulfil—
    Thou knowest well, in fay;
And for all this I will thee kiss,
    And sing, by, by, lullay.'

'My dear mother, when time it be,
    Take thou me up on loft,
And set me then upon thy knee,
    And handle me full soft;

And in thy arm thou hold me warm,
    And keep me night and day,
And if I weep, and may not sleep,
    Thou sing, by, by, lullay.'

'Now sweet son, since it is come so,
    That all is at thy will,
I pray thee grant to me a boon,
    If it be right and skill—

That child or man, who will or can
    Be merry on my day,
To bliss thou bring—and I shall sing,
    Lullay, by, by, lullay.'

to thy pay] to thy satisfaction
fay] faith   *right and skill*] right and reasonable

SIR THOMAS WYATT

1503–1542

16   *Psalm 130. 'Out of the depths have I cried unto thee, O Lord'*

From depth of sin and from a deep despair,
> From depth of death, from depth of heartès sorrow,
> From this deep cave of darkness' deep repair,
Thee have I call'd, O Lord, to be my borow.
> Thou in my voice, O Lord, perceive and hear
> My heart, my hope, my plaint, my overthrow,
My will to rise; and let by grant appear
> That to my voice thine ears do well entend.
> No place so far that to thee it is not near;
No depth so deep that thou ne may'st extend
> Thine ear thereto. Hear then my woeful plaint.
> For, Lord, if thou do observe what men offend
And put thy native mercy in restraint,
> If just exaction demand recompense,
> Who may endure, O Lord? Who shall not faint
At such account? Dread, and not reverence
> Should so reign large. But thou seeks rather love,
> For in thy hand is mercy's residence,
By hope whereof thou dost our heartès move.
> I in thee, Lord, have set my confidence;
> My soul such trust doth evermore approve.
Thy holy word of eterne excellence,
> Thy mercy's promise that is alway just,
> Have been my stay, my pillar and pretence.
My soul in God hath more desirous trust
> Than hath the watchman looking for the day,
> By the relief to quench of sleep the thrust.
Let Israel trust unto the Lord alway,
> For grace and favour are his property;
> Plenteous ransom shall come with him, I say,
And shall redeem all our iniquity.

borow] shelter   *pretence*] pretension, claim

WILLIAM BALDWIN
fl. 1547–1549

17   *Christ to his Spouse*

Lo, thou, my Love, art fair;
Myself have made thee so:
Yea, thou art fair indeed,
Wherefore thou shalt not need
In beauty to despair;
For I accept thee so,
            For fair.

For fair, because thine eyes
Are like the culvers' white,
Whose simpleness in deed
All others do exceed:
Thy judgement wholly lies
In true sense of sprite
            Most wise.

18   *Christ, my Beloved*

Christ, my Beloved which still doth feed
    Among the flowers, having delight
        Among his faithful lilies,
Doth take great care for me indeed,
    And I again with all my might
        Will do what so his will is.

My Love in me and I in him,
    Conjoined by love, will still abide
        Among the faithful lilies
Till day do break, and truth do dim
    All shadows dark and cause them slide,
        According as his will is.

17 *culvers' white*] doves

GEORGE GASCOIGNE

1542–1577

Gascoigne's Good-morrow

You that have spent the silent night
In sleep and quiet rest,
And joy to see the cheerful light
That riseth in the east,
Now clear your voice, now cheer your heart,
Come help me now to sing;
Each willing wight come bear a part
To praise the heavenly King.

And you whom care in prison keeps,
Or sickness doth suppress,
Or secret sorrow breaks your sleeps,
Or dolours do distress—
Yet bear a part in doleful wise,
Yea think it good accord
And acceptable sacrifice,
Each sprite to praise the Lord.

The dreadful night with darksomeness
Had overspread the light,
And sluggish sleep with drowsiness
Had overpressed our might:
A glass wherein you may behold
Each storm that stops our breath—
Our bed the grave, our clothes like mould,
And sleep like dreadful death.

Yet as this deadly night did last
But for a little space,
And heavenly day now night is past
Doth show his pleasant face,
So must we hope to see God's face
At last in Heaven on high,
When we have changed this mortal place
For immortality.

And of such haps and heavenly joys
As then we hope to hold,

GEORGE GASCOIGNE

All earthly sights and worldly toys
Are tokens to behold:
The day is like the day of doom;
The sun, the Son of man;
The skies, the heavens; the earth, the tomb
Wherein we rest till then;

The rainbow bending in the sky,
Bedecked with sundry hues,
Is like the seat of God on high,
And seems to tell these news—
That as thereby he promisèd
To drown the world no more,
So by the blood which Christ hath shed
He will our health restore.

The misty clouds that fall sometime
And overcast the skies
Are like to troubles of our time
Which do but dim our eyes;
But as such dews are dried up quite
When Phoebus shows his face,
So are such fancies put to flight
Where God doth guide by grace.

The carrion crow, that loathsome beast
Which cries against the rain,
Both for her hue and for the rest
The Devil resembleth plain;
And as with guns we kill the crow
For spoiling our relief,
The Devil so must we overthrow
With gunshot of belief.

The little birds which sing so sweet
Are like the angels' voice
Which render God his praises meet,
And teach us to rejoice;
And as they more esteem that mirth
Than dread the night's annoy,
So must we deem our days on earth
But hell to heavenly joy—

Unto which joys for to attain
God grant us all his grace,
And send us after worldly pain
In Heaven to have a place,
Where we may still enjoy that light
Which never shall decay.
Lord, for thy mercy lend us might
To see that joyful day.

20 *Gascoigne's Good-night*

When thou hast spent the lingering day in pleasure and delight
Or, after toil and weary way, dost seek to rest at night,
Unto thy pains or pleasures past, add this one labour yet:
Ere sleep close up thine eye to-fast, do not thy God forget,
But search within thy secret thoughts, what deeds did thee befall,
And if thou find amiss in aught, to God for mercy call.
Yea, though thou find nothing amiss which thou canst call to mind,
Yet ever more remember this, there is the more behind;
And think, how well so ever it be that thou hast spent the day,
It came of God, and not of thee, so to direct thy way.
Thus if thou try thy daily deeds, and pleasure in this pain,
Thy life shall cleanse thy corn from weeds, and thine shall be the
    gain,
But if thy sinful sluggish eye will venture for to wink,
Before thy wading will may try how far thy soul may sink,
Beware and wake, for else thy bed, which soft and smooth is made,
May heap more harm upon thy head than blows of enemy's blade.
Thus if this pain procure thine ease, in bed as thou dost lie,
Perhaps it shall not God displease, to sing thus soberly:
'I see that sleep is lent me here, to ease my weary bones,
As death at last shall eke appear, to ease my grievous groans.
My daily sports, my paunch full fed, have caused my drowsy eye,
As careless life, in quiet led, might cause my soul to die;
The stretching arms, the yawning breath, which I to bedward use,
Are patterns of the pangs of death, when life will me refuse;
And of my bed each sundry part in shadows doth resemble
The sundry shapes of death, whose dart shall make my flesh to
    tremble;
My bed itself is like the grave; my sheets, the winding sheet;
My clothes the mould which I must have, to cover me most meet;

The hungry fleas which frisk so fresh, to worms I can compare,
Which greedily shall gnaw my flesh, and leave the bones full bare;
The waking cock that early crows to wear the night away
Puts in my mind the trump that blows before the latter day;
And as I rise up lustily, when sluggish sleep is past,
So hope I to rise joyfully, to Judgement at the last.
Thus will I wake, thus will I sleep, thus will I hope to rise,
Thus will I neither wail nor weep, but sing in godly wise.
My bones shall in this bed remain, my soul in God shall trust,
By whom I hope to rise again from death and earthly dust.'

WILLIAM KETHE

c. 1560

21   *Psalm 100.* '*O be joyful in the Lord, all ye lands*'

> All people that on earth do dwell,
>   Sing to the Lord with cheerful voice;
> Him serve with mirth, his praise forth tell,
>   Come ye before him, and rejoice.
>
> The Lord, ye know, is God indeed;
>   Without our aid he did us make;
> We are his folk, he doth us feed,
>   And for his sheep he doth us take.
>
> Oh enter then his gates with praise,
>   Approach with joy his courts unto;
> Praise, laud, and bless his name always.
>   For it is seemly so to do.
>
> For why, the Lord our God is good;
>   His mercy is for ever sure;
> His truth at all times firmly stood,
>   And shall from age to age endure.

ANONYMOUS
16th century

Hierusalem

Hierusalem, my happy home,
   When shall I come to thee?
When shall my sorrows have an end,
   Thy joys when shall I see?

O happy harbour of the saints,
   O sweet and pleasant soil,
In thee no sorrow may be found,
   No grief, no care, no toil.

There lust and lucre cannot dwell,
   There envy bears no sway;
There is no hunger, heat, nor cold,
   But pleasure every way.

Thy walls are made of precious stones,
   Thy bulwarks diamonds square;
Thy gates are of right orient pearl,
   Exceeding rich and rare.

Thy turrets and thy pinnacles
   With carbuncles do shine;
Thy very streets are paved with gold,
   Surpassing clear and fine.

Ah, my sweet home, Hierusalem,
   Would God I were in thee!
Would God my woes were at an end,
   Thy joys that I might see!

Thy gardens and thy gallant walks
   Continually are green;
There grows such sweet and pleasant flowers
   As nowhere else are seen.

Quite through the streets, with silver sound,
   The flood of life doth flow;
Upon whose banks on every side
   The wood of life doth grow.

There trees for evermore bear fruit,
    And evermore do spring;
There evermore the angels sit,
    And evermore do sing.

Our Lady sings *Magnificat*
    With tune surpassing sweet;
And all the virgins bear their part,
    Sitting about her feet.

Hierusalem, my happy home,
    Would God I were in thee!
Would God my woes were at an end,
    Thy joys that I might see!

ALEXANDER MONTGOMERIE
?1545–?1610

23   *Away Vane World*

Away vane world, bewitcher of my hairt!
My sorowis shawis, my sins maks me to smart!
    Yit will I not dispair
    Bot to my God repair—
        He has mercy ay,
        Thairfor will I pray.
He has mercy ay and lovis me
Thoght by his humbling hand he provis me.

Away, away, too long thou hes me snaird!
I will not tyne more tyme, I am prepaird
    Thy subtill slychts to flie,
    Whilks hes allured me.
        Tho they sweitly smyle,
        Smoothly they begyle:
Tho they sweitly smyle, I feir thame.
I find thame fals, I will forbeir thame.

23   *shawis*] shows   *provis*] tests   *tyne*] lose   *slychts*] wiles

Once more away, shawis loth the world to leave,
Bids oft adieu with it that holds me slave.
    Loth am I to forgo
    This sweet alluring fo.
      Sen thy wayis ar vane,
      Sall I the retane?
Sen thy wayis ar vane, I quyt thee.
Thy pleasuris sall no more delyt me.

A thousand tymis away! Oh, stay no more!
Sweit Chryst conduct, leist subtile sin devore!
    Without thy helping hand
    No man hes strenth to stand.
      Tho I oft intend
      All my wayis to mend,
Tho I oft intend, strength fails ay.
The sair assaults of sin prevailis ay.

Quhat sal I say? Ar all my plesurs past?
Sall worldly lustis now tak thair leiv at last?
    Yea, Chryst, these earthly toyes
    Sall turne in hevinly joyes.
      Let the world be gone,
      I'l love Chryst allone!
Let the world be gone—I cair not.
Chryst is my love alone—I feir not.

EDMUND SPENSER
?1552–1599

24 from *The Faerie Queene, II,* Canto VIII, 1 and 2

And is there care in heaven? and is there love
    In heavenly spirits to these creatures base,
That may compassion of their evils move?
    There is: else much more wretched were the case
    Of men, than beasts. But, O! th' exceeding grace
Of highest God, that loves his creatures so,
    And all his works with mercy doth embrace,
That blessed angels he sends to and fro,
To serve to wicked man, to serve his wicked foe.

EDMUND SPENSER

How oft do they their silver bowers leave,
  To come to succour us, that succour want?
How oft do they with golden pinions cleave
  The flitting skies, like flying pursuivant,
  Against foul fiends to aid us militant?
They for us fight, they watch and duly ward,
  And their bright squadrons round about us plant,
And all for love, and nothing for reward:
O! why should heavenly God to men have such regard?

25   from *Amoretti*

Most glorious Lord of life! that, on this day,
Didst make thy triumph over death and sin;
And, having harrowed hell, didst bring away
Captivity thence captive, us to win:
This joyous day, dear Lord, with joy begin;
And grant that we, for whom thou didest die,
Being with thy dear blood clean washed from sin,
May live for ever in felicity!
And that thy love we weighing worthily,
May likewise love thee for the same again;
And for thy sake, that all like dear didst buy,
With love may one another entertain:
    So let us love, dear Love, like as we ought;
    Love is the lesson which the Lord us taught.

ANONYMOUS
16th century

26   *The Holy Well*

As it fell out one May morning,
  And upon a bright holiday,
Sweet Jesus asked of his dear mother
  If he might go to play.
'To play, to play, sweet Jesus shall go,
  And to play now get you gone;
And let me hear of no complaint
  At night when you come home.'

34

Sweet Jesus went down to yonder town,
  As far as the Holy Well,
And there did see as fine children
  As any tongue can tell.
He said, 'God bless you every one,
  And your bodies Christ save and see!
And now, little children, I'll play with you,
  And you shall play with me.'

But they made answer to him, 'No!
  Thou art meaner than us all;
Thou art but a simple fair maid's child,
  Born in an ox's stall.'
Sweet Jesus turned him round about,
  Neither laughed, nor smiled, nor spoke;
But the tears came trickling from his eyes
  Like waters from the rock.

Sweet Jesus turned him round about,
  To his mother's dear home went he,
And said, 'I have been in yonder town,
  As after you may see:
I have been down in yonder town,
  As far as the Holy Well;
There did I meet with as fine children
  As any tongue can tell.

'I said, "God bless you every one,
  And your bodies Christ save and see!
And now, little children, I'll play with you,
  And you shall play with me."
But they made answer to me "No";
  They were lords' and ladies' sons,
And I the meanest of them all,
  Born in an ox's stall.'

'Though you are but a maiden's child,
  Born in an ox's stall,
Thou art the Christ, the King of Heaven,
  And the Saviour of them all!
Sweet Jesus, go down to yonder town,
  As far as the Holy Well,
And take away those sinful souls,
  And dip them deep in hell.'

'Nay, nay,' sweet Jesus smiled and said;
  'Nay, nay, that may not be,
For there are too many sinful souls
  Crying out for the help of me.'
Then up spoke the angel Gabriel,
  Upon a good set steven,
'Although you are but a maiden's child,
  You are the King of Heaven!'

FULKE GREVILLE, LORD BROOKE
1554–1628

from *Caelica*
Sonnet 89

The *Manicheans* did no idols make
Without themselves, nor worship gods of wood,
Yet idols did in their *Ideas* take,
And figured Christ as on the cross he stood.
    Thus did they when they earnestly did pray,
    Till clearer Faith this idol took away.

We seem more inwardly to know the Son,
And see our own salvation in his blood.
When this is said, we think the work is done,
And with the Father hold our portion good,
    As if true life within these words were laid
    For him that in life never words obeyed.

If this be safe, it is a pleasant way,
The Cross of Christ is very easily borne;
But *six days' labour makes the sabbath day,*
The flesh is dead before grace can be born,
    The heart must first bear witness with the book,
    The earth must burn, ere we for Christ can look.

Sonnet 96

In those years when our Sense, Desire and Wit
Combine, that Reason shall not rule the heart,
Pleasure is chosen as a Goddess fit

26 *Upon a good set steven*] ? resoundingly

The wealth of Nature freely to impart;
Who like an Idol doth apparel'd sit
In all the glories of Opinion's art:
    The further off, the greater beauty showing,
    Lost only, or made less, by perfect knowing.

Which fair Usurper runs a Rebel's way,
For though elect of Sense, Wit and Desire,
Yet rules she none but such as will obey,
And to that end becomes what they aspire;
Making that torment, which before was play,
Those dews to kindle, which did quench the fire;
    Now Honour's image, now again like lust,
    But earthly still, and end repenting must.

While man who, Satyr-like, then knows the flame
When kissing of her fair-appearing light,
He feels a scorching power hid in the same,
Which cannot be revealèd to the sight,
Yet doth by over-heat so shrink this frame
Of fiery apparitions in delight,
    That as in Orbs where many passions reign,
    What one Affection joys, the rest complain.

In which confusèd sphere Man being plac'd
With equal prospect over good or ill,
The one unknown, the other in distaste,
Flesh, with her many moulds of Change and Will,
So his affections carries on, and casts
In declination to the error still,
    As by the truth he gets no other light
    But to see *Vice, a restless infinite.*

By which true map of his Mortality
Man's many Idols are at once defaced,
And all hypocrisies of frail humanity
Either exilèd, waivèd, or disgraced;
Fall'n nature by the streams of vanity
Forc'd up to call for grace above her placed:
    Whence from the depth of fatal desolation
    Springs up the height of his Regeneration.

Which light of life doth all those shadows war
Of woe and lust, that dazzle and enthrall,

Whereby man's joys with goodness bounded are,
And to remorse his fears transformèd all;
His six days' labour past, and that clear star,
Figure of Sabbath's rest, rais'd by this fall.
    For God comes not till man be overthrown;
    Peace is the seed of grace, in dead flesh sown.

Flesh but the *Top*, which only *Whips* make go,
The *Steel* whose rust is by afflictions worn,
The *Dust* which good men from their feet must throw,
A *living-dead thing*, till it be newborn,
A *Phoenix-life*, that from self-ruin grows,
Or *Viper* rather through her parents torn,
    A *boat*, to which the world itself is Sea,
    Wherein the mind sails on her fatal way.

29
Sonnet 105

Three things there be in Man's opinion dear:
Fame, many *Friends*, and *Fortune*'s dignities;
False visions all, which in our sense appear
To sanctify desire's Idolatries.

For what is *Fortune*, but a wat'ry glass?
Whose crystal forehead wants a steely back,
Where rain and storms bear all away that was,
Whose shape alike both depths and shallows wrack.

Fame again, which from blinding power takes light,
Both *Caesar*'s shadow is, and *Cato*'s friend,
The child of humour, not allied to right,
Living by oft exchange of wingèd end.

And many *Friends*, false strength of feeble mind,
Betraying equals, as true slaves to might,
Like *Echoes* still send voices down the wind,
But never in adversity find right.

Then, Man (though virtue of extremities
The middle be, and so hath two to one,
By Place and Nature constant enemies,
And against both these no strength but her own)
    Yet quit thou for her Friends, Fame, Fortune's throne;
    Devils, there many be, and Gods but one.

SIR PHILIP SIDNEY

1554–1586

30 *(Splendidis Longum Valedico Nugis)*

Leave me, O Love, which reaches but to dust;
  And thou, my mind, aspire to higher things;
Grow rich in that which never taketh rust;
  Whatever fades but fading pleasure brings.
Draw in thy beams, and humble all thy might
  To that sweet yoke where lasting freedoms be;
Which breaks the clouds and opens forth the light,
  That doth both shine and give us sight to see.
O take fast hold; let that light be thy guide
  In this small course which birth draws out to death,
And think how evil becometh him to slide,
  Who seeketh heaven, and comes of heavenly breath.
    Then farewell, world; thy uttermost I see;
    Eternal Love, maintain thy life in me.

ALEXANDER HUME

?1557–1609

31 *Of the Day Estivall*

O perfite light, quhilk schaid away
The darkenes from the light,
And set a ruler ou'r the day,
Ane uther ou'r the night;

Thy glorie when the day foorth flies,
Mair vively dois appeare,
Nor at midday unto our eyes
The shining sun is cleare.

The shaddow of the earth anon
Remooves and drawes by,
Sine in the East, when it is gon,
Appeares a clearer sky.

31   *Day Estivall*] Summer's Day   *schaid away*] separated   *sine*] then

39

ALEXANDER HUME

Quhilk sunne perceaves the little larks,
The lapwing and the snyp,
And tunes their sangs like natures clarks,
Ou'r midow, mure and stryp.

Bot everie bais'd nocturnall beast
Na langer may abide,
They hy away baith maist and least,
Them selves in house to hide.

They dread the day fra thay it see,
And from the sight of men
To saits and covars fast they flee,
As lyons to their den.

Our Hemisphere is poleist clein,
And lightened more and more,
While everie thing be clearely sein
Quhilk seemèd dim before.

Except the glistering astres bright,
Which all the night were cleere,
Offuskèd with a greater light,
Na langer dois appeare.

The golden globe incontinent
Sets up his shining head,
And ou'r the earth and firmament
Displayes his beims abroad.

For joy the birds with boulden throts,
Agains his visage shein,
Takes up their kindelie musicke nots
In woods and gardens grein.

Up braids the carefull husbandman
His cornes and vines to see,
And everie tymous artisan
In buith worke busilie.

snyp] snipe   *stryp*] rill   *bais'd*] dismayed   *saits and covers*] homes
          and hiding-places   *astres*] stars   *offusked*] obscure
                incontinent] at once   *boulden*] swollen
          braids] springs   *tymous*] early   *buith*] covered stall

40

The pastor quits the slouthfull sleepe
And passis forth with speede,
His little camow-nosèd sheepe
And rowtting kie to feede.

The passenger from perrels sure
Gangs gladly foorth the way:
Briefe, everie living creature
Takes comfort of the day.

The subtile mottie rayons light,
At rifts thay are in wonne,
The glansing phains and vitre bright
Resplends against the sunne.

The dew upon the tender crops,
Lyke pearlès white and round,
Or like to melted silver drops,
Refreshes all the ground.

The mystie rocke, the clouds of raine,
From tops of mountains skails,
Cleare are the highest hils and plaine,
The vapors takes the vails.

Begaried is the saphire pend,
With spraings of skarlet hew,
And preciously from end till end
Damasked white and blew.

The ample heaven of fabrik sure
In cleannes dois surpas
The chrystal and the silver pure
Or clearest poleist glas.

The time sa tranquill is and still
That na where sall ye find,
Saif on ane high and barren hill,
Ane aire of peeping wind.

---

camow-nosed] flat-nosed   *rowtting*] lowing   *mottie*] containing motes
rifts] cracks   *in wonne*] got in   *phains*] vanes   *vitre*] window pane
skails] clears   *begaried*] ornamented   *pend*] vault   *spraings*] streaks
saif] except

All trees and simples great and small
That balmie leife do beir,
Nor thay were painted on a wall,
Na mair they move or steir.

Calme is the deepe and purpour se,
Yee smuther nor the sand,
The wals that woltring wont to be
Are stable like the land.

Sa silent is the cessile air
That every cry and call,
The hils, and dails, and forrest fair,
Againe repeates them all.

The rivers fresh, the callor streames,
Ou'r rockes can softlie rin,
The water cleare like chrystall seames
And makes a pleasant din.

The fields and earthly superfice
With verdure greene is spread,
And naturallie but artifice,
In partie coulors cled.

The flurishes and fragrant flowres,
Throw Phoebus fostring heit,
Refresht with dew and silver showres
Casts up ane odor sweit.

The cloggèd busie humming beis,
That never thinks to drowne,
On flowers and flourishes of treis
Collects their liquor browne.

The sunne maist like a speedie post
With ardent course ascends,
The beautie of the heavenly host
Up to our zenith tends,

simples] medicinal herbs   smuther] smoother   wals] waves
woltring] rolling   cessile] yielding   callor] cool   superfice] surface
partie] motley   flurishes] blossoms   clogged] burdened

42

ALEXANDER HUME

Nocht guided be na Phaeton
Nor trainèd in a chyre,
But be the high and haly On,
Quhilk dois all where impire.

The burning beims downe from his face
Sa fervently can beat
That man and beast now seekes a place
To save them fra the heat.

The brethles flocks drawes to the shade
And frechure of their fald,
The startling nolt as they were made
Runnes to the rivers cald.

The heards beneath some leaffie trie,
Amids the flowers they lie,
The stabill ships upon the sey
Tends up their sails to drie.

The hart, the hynd and fallow deare
Are tapisht at their rest,
The foules and birdes that made the beare
Prepares their prettie nest.

The rayons dures descending downe
All kindlis in a gleid,
In cittie nor in borroughstowne
May nane set foorth their heid.

Back from the blew paymented whun
And from ilk plaister wall
The hote reflexing of the sun
Inflams the aire and all.

The labourers, that timelie raise,
All wearie faint and weake
For heate downe to their houses gaise,
Noone-meate and sleepe to take.

chyre] chariot   nolt] cattle   made] mad
tapisht] crouching   beare] noise   gleid] flame
paymented whun] whinstone made into pavement

43

The callour wine in cave is sought,
Mens brothing breists to cule;
The water cald and cleare is brought,
And sallets steipt in ule.

Sume plucks the honie plowm and peare,
The cherrie and the pesche,
Sume likes the reamand London beare
The bodie to refresh.

Forth of their skepps some raging bees
Lyes out and will not cast,
Some uther swarmes hyves on the trees,
In knots togidder fast.

The corbeis and the kekling kais
May scarce the heate abide,
Halks prunyeis on the sunnie brais,
And wedders back and side.

With gilted eyes and open wings
The cock his courage shawes,
With claps of joy his breast he dings,
And twentie times he crawes.

The dow with whisling wings sa blew
The winds can fast collect,
His pourpour pennes turnes mony hew
Against the sunne direct.

Now noone is went, gaine is mid-day,
The heat dois slake at last,
The sunne descends downe west away,
Fra three of clock be past.

A little cule of braithing wind
Now softly can arise,
The warks, throw heate that lay behind,
Now men may enterprise.

brothing] sweating
sallets] salads   *ule*] oil   *reamand*] foaming   *beare*] beer
skepps] hives   *corbeis*] crows   *kekling kais*] chattering jackdaws
halks prunyeis] hawks preen   *wedders*] ruffles   *dow*] pigeon   *warks*] works

ALEXANDER HUME

Furth fairis the flocks to seeke their fude,
On everie hill and plaine,
Ilk labourer as he thinks gude
Steppes to his turne againe.

The rayons of the sunne we see
Diminish in their strength,
The schad of everie towre and tree
Extended is in length.

Great is the calme, for everie quhair
The wind is sitten downe,
The reik thrawes right up in the air
From everie towre and towne.

Their firdoning the bony birds,
In banks they do begin,
With pipes of reides the jolie hirds
Halds up the mirrie din.

The maveis and the philomeen,
The stirling, whissilles loud;
The cuschetts on the branches green
Full quietly they crowd.

The gloming comes, the day is spent,
The sun goes out of sight,
And painted is the occident
With pourpour sanguine bright.

The skarlet nor the golden threid,
Who would their beautie trie,
Are nathing like the colour reid
And beutie of the sky.

Our west horizon circuler,
Fra time the sunne be set,
Is all with rubies (as it wer)
Or rosis reid ou'rfret.

schad] shadow   *reik*] smoke
firdoning] piping   *maveis*] song-thrush   *philomeen*] nightingale
stirling] starling   *cuschetts*] wood-pigeons   *crowd*] coo
gloming] twilight   *ou'rfret*] embroidered

45

ALEXANDER HUME

What pleasour were to walk and see,
Endlang a river cleare,
The perfite forme of everie tree
Within the deepe appeare?

The salmon out of cruifs and creils
Up hailed into skowts,
The bels and circles on the weills
Throw lowpping of the trouts.

O! then it were a seemely thing,
While all is still and calme,
The praise of God to play and sing
With cornet and with shalme.

Bot now the hirds with mony schout
Cals uther be their name:
'Ga, Billie, turne our gude about,
Now time is to go hame.'

With bellie fow the beastes belive
Are turnèd fra the corne,
Quhilk soberly they hameward drive
With pipe and lilting horne.

Throw all the land great is the gild
Of rustik folks that crie,
Of bleiting sheepe fra they be fild,
Of calves and routing ky.

All labourers drawes hame at even,
And can till uther say:
'Thanks to the gracious God of heaven,
Quhilk send this summer day.'

---

cruifs] fishing cruives (i.e. wattled hedges built on tidal flats for catching fish)
skowts] cobles (flat-bottomed boats)   *weills*] wells
shalme] shawn (medieval instrument like an oboe)   *gude*] livestock
fow] full   *gild*] clamour

Of Gods Omnipotencie

O everie living warldly wight,
Awake and dres your selfe with speede
To serve and praise the God of might,
From whome all bountie dois proceede:
For gif ye drift, and still refuse,
The heavens and earth will you accuse.

The brutall beasts but ony stryfe,
They willinglie his voice obay;
The creàtures that hes na life
Sets forth his glorie day by day;
The earth, the aire, the sea, and fire
Are subject all to his impire.

The heaven it is his dwelling place,
The earth his littil fute-stule law,
His warks are all before his face;
Of hearts the secreits he dois knaw,
And everie thing as in a glas
He seis before it cum to pas.

The swift and active fierie spreits,
The Cherubins of substance pure,
They walk amang the holie streits
And makes him daylie service sure:
Yea, at all times they readie stand,
To gang and cum at his command.

When Jonah in the sea was cast,
By lot, for safetie of the leave,
A mightie Quhaill did follow fast,
Prepard the prophet to receave;
Quhilk at command did him devore,
Sine brought him safely to the shore.

And as Elijah lurking lay,
Lang solitar by Cherith side,
The ravens left their common pray
His sustenance for to provide;
As they were chargèd him to feede,
They brought him daylie flesh and bread.

but] without   *law*] low   *the leave*] the rest   *sine*] thereafter

Quha learned Balaams brutall asse
The angell of the Lord to knaw?
A foote she forward wald not pas,
That way where she him standing saw,
Bot spake that marvell was to see
Against hir maisters crueltie.

The roaring lions fiers and fell,
Brought up and baited ay with bloud,
They spard the godly Daniell,
Exposed to them in place of fude:
Sa fishes, fouls, and ravenous beists,
Of God maist high they hald the heists.

The verie devils dare nocht rebell
Against his Majestie and might,
The spreits uncleane he did expell
Forth of the pure possessèd wight,
Quha but his priviledge divine
Durst na way enter in the swine.

Into the prophets mouthes the spreit
Of lies could never enter in,
Quhile he did licence first intreate
Of God the Lord, for Ahabs sin;
Quhilk be that meanes did him entyse
His awin defait till enterprise.

His halie statute to fulfill,
And potent power to declaire,
The massive earth reposis still,
Suspended in the cessil eire;
And at hir dew appointed houres
Brings forth maist pleasant fruits and floures.

Quhat thing is fiercer nor the sea?
Mair raging nor the awfull deepe?
Quhilk back retird at his decrie,
And dois her bounds and marchis keepe;
Syne at his charge apart stude by,
To make his hoste a passage dry.

hold the heists] observe the behests   *but*] except for   *cessil*] yielding
nor] than

Without the subtile air but dout
Na plaint nor living thing may lest;
Therefore it cleaves the earth about,
And is in everie place possest,
Then as his godlie wisedome wald,
Decernes the seasons hett and cald.

The brimstane and the burning fire
Maist sudenely from heaven fell downe
For to consume into this yre
Baith Sodome, and Gomorrah towne;
But in the firie furnace he
Preservèd safe the children three.

The mightie winds blaws to and fra,
From everie airth be day and night,
We heare them thudding by us ga,
Yet not conceaves them with our sight;
Bot in a clap the Lord to please,
Their blasts they quietly appease.

Like flocks of fowls the clouds above
Furth flies and covers all the sky;
Againe they suddenly remoove,
We wat not where nor reason why;
Bot till obey his holy law
They poure out rain, sharpe haile, and snaw.

Behald the fearefull thunder crack,
And fierie flauchts sa violent,
Appeares nocht in the cloudis black,
Quhile be the highest they be sent;
The harts of men are dasht with feare
Sik lights to see, and claps to heare.

The heaven sa high, sa cleare of hew,
Declares his power passing weill:
Sua swift of course ay recent new,
Revolving like a turning wheill,
Nane knowes whereof the globe is made,
Quhais beautie at na time dois fade.

but dout] without doubt   *airth*] direction   *flauchts*] flakes

49

ALEXANDER HUME

He made the Sun a lampe of light,
A woll of heate to shine by day,
He made the Moone to guide the night
And set the starnis in gud array,
Orion, Pleiads, and the Urse,
Observes their dew prescrivèd course.

O Poets, paganes impudent,
Quhy worship ye the planets seaven?
The glore of God be you is spent
On Idols and the hoste of heaven,
Ye pride your pens mens eares to pleis,
With fables and fictitious leis.

Your knowledge is bot ignorance,
Your cunning curiositie;
I find your facund eloquence
Repleete with fekles fantasie;
Ye never knew the lively rod
Nor gospell of the sun of God.

He is above Mercurius
Above Neptunus on the sea,
The winds they knaw not Eolus,
Their is na Jupiter but he,
And all your Gods baith great and small
Are of na force for he is all.

Bot sonnes of light ye knaw the trueth,
Extoll the Lord with heart and minde,
Remove all stayes and sluggish sleuth,
Obey his voice for he is kinde;
That heaven and earth may witnes beare,
Ye love that God which bought you deare.

---

woll] well   *starnis*] stars   *the Urse*] the Great Bear (constellation)
                    leis] lies   *sleuth*] sloth

ROBERT SOUTHWELL
1561–1595

33 *Look Home*

Retirèd thoughts enjoy their own delights,
As beauty doth, in self-beholding eye;
Man's mind a mirror is, of heavenly sights,
A brief, wherein all marvels summèd lie;
Of fairest forms and sweetest shapes the store,
Most graceful all, yet thought may grace them more.

The mind a creature is, yet can create,
To nature's patterns adding higher skill;
Of finest works, wit better could the state
If force of wit had equal power of will;
Devise of man in working hath no end;
What thought can think, another thought can mend.

Man's soul, of endless beauties image is,
Drawn by the work of endless skill and might;
This skilful might gave many sparks of bliss,
And to discern this bliss a native light.
To frame God's image as his worths required,
His might, his skill, his word, and will conspired.

All that he had, his image should present;
All that it should present, he could afford;
To that he could afford, his will was bent,
His will was followed with performing word.
Let this suffice, by this conceive the rest:
He should, he could, he would, he did the best.

34 *New Prince, New Pomp*

Behold a silly tender babe
  In freezing winter night
In homely manger trembling lies:
  Alas! a piteous sight.

33 *brief*] abridgement, summary

51

The inns are full; no man will yield
    This little pilgrim bed;
But forced he is with silly beasts
    In crib to shroud his head.

Despise not him for lying there;
    First what he is inquire:
An orient pearl is often found
    In depth of dirty mire.

Weigh not his crib, his wooden dish,
    Nor beasts that by him feed;
Weigh not his mother's poor attire,
    Nor Joseph's simple weed.

This stable is a Prince's court,
    This crib his chair of state,
The beasts are parcel of his pomp,
    The wooden dish his plate.

The persons in that poor attire
    His royal liveries wear;
The Prince himself is come from heaven.
    This pomp is prizèd there.

With joy approach, O Christian wight,
    Do homage to thy King;
And highly praise this humble pomp
    Which he from heaven doth bring.

35 *The Burning Babe*

As I in hoary winter's night
    Stood shivering in the snow,
Surpris'd I was with sudden heat,
    Which made my heart to glow;

And, lifting up a fearful eye
    To view what fire was near,
A pretty Babe all burning bright
    Did in the air appear;

Who, scorchèd with excessive heat,
    Such floods of tears did shed
As though his floods should quench his flan
    Which with his tears were fed.

'Alas' (quoth he) 'but newly born,
    In fiery heats I fry,
Yet none approach to warm their hearts,
    Or feel my fire, but I.

My faultless breast the furnace is;
    The fuel, wounding thorns;
Love is the fire, and sighs the smoke,
    The ashes, shame and scorns.

The fuel Justice layeth on,
    And Mercy blows the coals,
The metal in this furnace wrought
    Are men's defilèd souls;

For which, as now on fire I am
    To work them to their good,
So will I melt into a bath
    To wash them in my blood.'

With this he vanished out of sight,
    And swiftly shrunk away,
And straight I callèd unto mind
    That it was Christmas Day.

MARY HERBERT, COUNTESS OF PEMBROKE
1561–1621

from *The Sidney Psalter*

36   *Psalm 58. 'Do ye indeed speak righteousness, O*
                congregation?'

    And call ye this to utter what is just,
        You that of justice hold the sov'reign throne?
    And call ye this to yield, O sons of dust,
        To wrongèd brethren ev'ry man his own?

O no: it is your long malicious will
    Now to the world to make by practice known
With whose oppression you the balance fill,
    Just to yourselves, indiff'rent else to none.

But what could they, who ev'n in birth declin'd
    From truth and right to lies and injuries?
To show the venom of their cankered mind
    The adder's image scarcely can suffice;
Nay, scarce the aspic may with them contend,
    On whom the charmer all in vain applies
His skilfullest spells, aye missing of his end
    While she self-deaf and unaffected lies.

Lord, crack their teeth! Lord, crush these lions' jaws!
    So let them sink as water in the sand;
When deadly bow their aiming fury draws,
    Shiver the shaft ere past the shooter's hand.
So make them melt as the dishousèd snail
    Or as the embryo, whose vital band
Breaks ere it holds, and formless eyes do fail
    To see the sun, though brought to lightful land.

O let their brood, a brood of springing thorns,
    Be by untimely rooting overthrown;
Ere bushes waxed, they push with pricking horns,
    As fruits yet green are oft by tempest blown.
The good with gladness this revenge shall see,
    And bathe his feet in blood of wicked one,
While all shall say: 'The just rewarded be,
    There is a God that carves to each his own.'

37   *Psalm 74. 'O God, why hast thou cast us off*
for ever?'

        O God, why hast thou thus
        Repuls'd, and scatter'd us?
    Shall now thy wrath no limits hold,
        But ever smoke and burn
        Till it to ashes turn
    The chosen folk of thy dear fold?

Ah! think with milder thought
On them whom thou hast bought
And purchasèd from endless days!
Think of thy birthright lot
Of Sion, on whose plot
Thy sacred house supported stays.

Come, Lord, O come with speed!
This sacrilegious seed
Root quickly out, and headlong cast;
All that thy holy place
Did late adorn and grace,
Their hateful hands have quite defac'd.

Their beastly trumpets roar
Where heavenly notes before
In praises of thy might did flow;
Within thy temple they
Their ensigns oft display,
The ensigns, which their conquest show.

As men with axe on arm
To some thick forest swarm
To lop the trees which stately stand,
They to thy temple flock
And, spoiling, cut and knock
The curious works of carving hand.

Thy most, most holy seat
The greedy flames do eat
And have such ruthless ruin wrought
That all thy house is rased,
So rased and so defac'd
That of that all remaineth nought.

Nay, they resolvèd are
We all alike shall fare,
All of one cruel cup shall taste.
For not one house doth stand
Of God in all the land
But they by fire have laid it waste.

MARY HERBERT

We see the signs no more
We wont to see before;
Nor any now with spirit divine
Amongst us more is found,
Who can to us expound
What term these dolours shall define.

How long, O God, how long
Wilt thou wink at the wrong
Of thy reviling, railing foe?
Shall he that hates thy name,
And hatred paints with shame,
So do, and do for ever so?

Woe us! what is the cause
Thy hand its help withdraws,
That thy right hand far from us keeps?
Ah let it once arise
To plague thine enemies
Which now, embosomed, idly sleeps!

Thou art my God, I know,
My King, who long ago
Didst undertake the charge of me;
And in my hard distress
Didst work me such release
That all the earth did wond'ring see.

Thou by thy might didst make
The seas in sunder break,
And dreadful dragons which before
In deep or swam or crawl'd,
Such mortal strokes appall'd
They floated dead to ev'ry shore.

Thou crush'd that monster's head
Whom other monsters dread,
And so his fishy flesh didst frame
To serve as pleasing food
To all the ravening brood
Who had the desert for their dame.

Thou wondrously didst cause,
Repealing nature's laws,

From thirsty flint a fountain flow,
  And of the rivers clear
  The sandy beds appear,
So dry thou mad'st their channels grow.

  The day array'd in light,
  The shadow-clothèd night,
Were made, and are maintain'd, by thee.
  The sun, and sun-like rays,
  The bounds of nights and days,
Thy workmanship no less they be.

  To thee the earth doth owe
  That earth in sea doth grow,
And sea doth earth from drowning spare;
  The summer's corny crown,
  The winter's frosty gown,
Nought but thy badge, thy livery are.

  Thou, then, still one, the same,
  Think how thy glorious name
These brain-sick men's despite has borne,
  How abject enemies
  The Lord of highest skies
With cursèd, taunting tongues have torn.

  Ah! give no hawk the power
  Thy turtle to devour
Which sighs to thee with mourning moans;
  Nor utterly out-rase
  From tables of thy grace
The flock of thy afflicted ones.

  But call thy league to mind,
  For horror all doth blind,
No light doth in the land remain;
  Rape, murder, violence,
  Each outrage, each offence,
Each where doth range, and rage and reign.

  Enough, enough we mourn!
  Let us no more return
Repuls'd with blame and shame from thee;

But succour us oppress'd
And give the troubled rest
That of thy praise their songs may be.

Rise, God, plead thine own case;
Forget not what disgrace
These fools on thee each day bestow;
Forget not with what cries
Thy foes against thee rise,
Which more and more to heav'n do grow.

38   *Psalm 115. 'Not unto us, O Lord, not unto us'*

Not us, I say, not us,
But thine own name respect, eternal Lord,
And make it glorious
To show thy mercy and confirm thy word.
Why, Lord, why should these nations say:
'Where doth your God now make his stay?'

You ask where our God is?
In heav'n enthron'd, no mark of mortal eye;
Nor hath, nor will he, miss
What likes his will, to will effectually.
What are your idols? we demand:
Gold, silver, works of workmens' hand.

They mouths, but speechless, have;
Eyes, sightless; ears, no news of noise can tell;
Who them their noses gave
Gave not their noses any sense of smell;
Nor hands can feel, nor feet can go,
Nor sign of sound their throats can show.

And wherein differ you
Who, having made them, make of them your trust?
But Israel, pursue
Thy trust in God, the target of the just.
O Aaron's house, the like do ye:
He is their aid, their target he.

All that Jehovah fear
Trust in Jehovah, he our aid and shield.
   He us in mind doth bear,
He will to us abundant blessings yield;
Will evermore with grace and good
Bless Jacob's house, bless Aaron's brood.

   Bless all that bear him awe,
Both great and small. The conduits of his store
   He never dry shall draw,
But you and yours enrich still more and more.
Blest, O thrice blest, whom he hath chose,
Who first with heav'ns did earth enclose.

   Where height of highest skies
Removèd most from floor of lowly ground
   With vaulted roof doth rise,
Himself took up his dwelling there to found.
To mortal men he gracious gave
The lowly ground to hold and have.

   And why? His praise to show;
Which how can dead men, Lord, in any wise?
   Who down descending go
Into the place where silence lodgèd lies?
But save us. We thy praise record
Will now, and still: O praise the Lord!

39   *Psalm 139. 'O Lord, thou hast searched me, and
known me'*

   O Lord in me there lieth nought
     But to thy search revealèd lies:
       For when I sit
       Thou markest it;
     No less thou notest when I rise.
   Yea, closest closet of my thought
     Hath open windows to thine eyes.

   Thou walkest with me when I walk;
     When to my bed for rest I go,
       I find thee there,
       And ev'rywhere;

Not youngest thought in me doth grow,
No, not one word I cast to talk,
   But yet unuttered thou dost know.

If forth I march, thou goest before,
   If back I turn, thou com'st behind;
      So forth nor back
      Thy guard I lack,
   Nay on me too thy hand I find.
Well I thy wisdom may adore,
   But never reach with earthy mind.

To shun thy notice, leave thine eye,
   O whither might I take my way?
      To starry sphere?
      Thy throne is there.
   To dead men's undelightsome stay?
There is thy walk, and there to lie
   Unknown in vain I should assay.

O Sun, whom light nor flight can match,
   Suppose thy lightful, flightful wings
      Thou lend to me,
      And I could flee
   As far as thee the ev'ning brings,
Ev'n led to West he would me catch
   Nor should I lurk with western things.

Do thou thy best, O secret night,
   In sable veil to cover me,
      Thy sable veil
      Shall vainly fail;
   With day unmask'd my night shall be,
For night is day, and darkness light,
   O father of all lights, to thee.

Each inmost piece in me is thine:
   While yet I in my mother dwelt,
      All that me clad
      From thee I had.
   Thou in my frame hast strangely dealt;
Needs in my praise thy works must shine,
   So inly them my thoughts have felt.

Thou, how my back was beam-wise laid
   And raft'ring of my ribs, dost know;
       Know'st ev'ry point
       Of bone and joint,
   How to this whole these parts did grow,
In brave embroid'ry fair array'd
   Though wrought in shop both dark and low

Nay, fashionless, ere form I took,
   Thy all-and-more-beholding eye
       My shapeless shape
       Could not escape;
   All these, time-framed successively
Ere one had being, in the book
   Of thy foresight enroll'd did lie.

My God, how I these studies prize
   That do thy hidden workings show!
       Whose sum is such
       No sum so much,
   Nay, summ'd as sand, they sumless grow.
I lie to sleep, from sleep I rise,
   Yet still in thought with thee I go.

My God, if thou but one wouldst kill,
   Then straight would leave my further chas
       This cursèd brood
       Inur'd to blood
   Whose graceless taunts at thy disgrace
Have aimèd oft, and, hating still,
   Would with proud lies thy truth outface.

Hate not I them, who thee do hate?
   Thine, Lord, I will the censure be.
       Detest I not
       The cankered knot
   Whom I against thee banded see?
O Lord, thou know'st in highest rate
   I hate them all as foes to me.

Search me, my God, and prove my heart,
   Examine me, and try my thought;
       And mark in me

If aught there be
That hath with cause their anger wrought.
If not (as not) my life's each part,
    Lord, safely guide from danger brought.

40   *Psalm 147. 'Praise ye the Lord'*

Sing to the Lord, for what can better be
    Than of our God that we the honour sing?
With seemly pleasure what can more agree
    Than praiseful voice, and touch of tunèd string?
    For lo, the Lord again to form doth bring
        Jerusalem's long ruinated walls;
And Jacob's house, which all the earth did see
        Dispersèd erst, to union now recalls;
    And now by him their broken hearts made sound,
    And now by him their bleeding wounds are bound.

For what could not, who can the number tell
    Of stars, the torches of his heav'nly hall;
And tell so readily, he knoweth well
    How ev'ry star by proper name to call?
    What great to him, whose greatness doth not fall
        Within precincts? whose power no limits stay?
Whose knowledges all number so excel,
        Not numb'ring number can their number lay?
    Easy to him, to lift the lowly just;
    Easy, to down proud wicked to the dust.

O then Jehovah's causeful honour sing,
    His, whom our God we by his goodness find!
O make harmonious mix of voice and string
    To him by whom the skies with clouds are lin'd;
    By whom the rain, from clouds to drop assign'd,
        Supples the clods of summer-scorchèd fields,
Fresheth the mountains with such needful spring,
        Fuel of life to mountain cattle yields,
    From whom young ravens careless old forsake,
    Croaking to him of alms, their diet take.

The stately shape, the force of bravest steed,
  Is far too weak to work in him delight;
No more in him can any pleasure breed
  In flying footman, foot of nimblest flight.
  Nay, which is more, his fearers in his sight
      Can well of nothing but his bounty brave;
Which, never failing, never lets them need
      Who fix'd their hopes upon his mercies have.
  O then, Jerusalem, Jehovah praise,
  With honour due thy God, O Sion, raise.

His strength it is thy gates doth surely bar;
  His grace in thee thy children multiplies;
By him thy borders lie secure from wars,
  And finest flour thy hunger satisfies.
  Nor means he needs; for fast his pleasure flies,
      Borne by his word, when aught him list to bid.
Snow's woolly locks by him wide scatter'd are,
      And hoary plains with frost, as ashes, hid;
  Gross icy gobbets from his hand he flings,
  And blows a cold too strong for strongest things.

He bids again, and ice in water flows,
  As water erst in ice congealèd lay;
Abroad the southern wind, his melter, goes;
  The streams relenting take their wonted way.
  O much is this, but more I come to say:
      The words of life he hath to Jacob told;
Taught Israel, who by his teaching knows
      What laws in life, what rules he wills to hold.
  No nation else hath found him half so kind,
  For to his light, what other is not blind?

WILLIAM SHAKESPEARE
1564–1616

41   *Sonnet 146*

Poor soul, the centre of my sinful earth,
Fooled by these rebel powers that thee array,
Why dost thou pine within and suffer dearth,
Painting thy outward walls so costly gay?

Why so large cost, having so short a lease,
Dost thou upon thy fading mansion spend?
Shall worms, inheritors of this excess,
Eat up thy charge? Is this thy body's end?
Then, soul, live thou upon thy servant's loss,
And let that pine to aggravate thy store;
Buy terms divine in selling hours of dross;
Within be fed, without be rich no more:
   So shalt thou feed on Death, that feeds on men,
   And Death once dead, there's no more dying then.

ANONYMOUS

42   *'If I could shut the gate'*

If I could shut the gate against my thoughts
  And keep out sorrow from this room within,
Or memory could cancel all the notes
  Of my misdeeds, and I unthink my sin:
How free, how clear, how clean my soul should lie,
Discharged of such a loathsome company!

Or were there other rooms without my heart
  That did not to my conscience join so near,
Where I might lodge the thoughts of sin apart
  That I might not their clam'rous crying hear;
What peace, what joy, what ease should I possess,
Freed from their horrors that my soul oppress!

But, O my Saviour, who my refuge art,
  Let thy dear mercies stand 'twixt them and me,
And be the wall to separate my heart
  So that I may at length repose me free;
That peace, and joy, and rest may be within,
And I remain divided from my sin.

ANONYMOUS

c. 1615

Miserere, My Maker

Miserere, my Maker,
O have mercy on me, wretch, strangely distressèd,
Cast down with sin oppressèd;
Mightily vexed to the soul's bitter anguish,
E'en to the death I languish.
Yet let it please Thee
To hear my ceaseless crying:
Miserere, miserere, I am dying.

Miserere, my Saviour,
I, alas, am for my sins fearfully grievèd,
And cannot be relievèd
But by Thy death, which Thou didst suffer for me,
Wherefore I adore Thee.
And do beseech Thee
To hear my ceaseless crying:
Miserere, miserere, I am dying.

Holy Spirit, miserere,
Comfort my distressèd soul, grieved for youth's folly,
Purge, cleanse and make it holy;
With Thy sweet due of grace and peace inspire me,
How I desire Thee.
And strengthen me now
In this, my ceaseless crying:
Miserere, miserere, I am dying.

Sweet was the Song

Sweet was the song the Virgin sung,
When she to Bethelem was come,
And was delivered of her Son,
That blessed JESUS hath to name:
    'Lullaby,
Lullaby, sweet Babe,' quoth she,
'My Son, and eke a Saviour born,
Who hath vouchsafèd from on high

To visit us that were forlorn.
    Lulla, Lulla,
Lullaby, sweet Babe,' sang she;
And sweetly rocked him, rocked him, rocked him,
And sweetly rocked him on her knee.

THOMAS CAMPION
1567–1620

45   *'To Music bent is my retirèd Mind'*

To Music bent is my retirèd mind.
    And fain would I some song of pleasure sing,
But in vain joys no comfort now I find;
    From heavenly thoughts all true delight doth spring.
Thy power, O God, thy mercies, to record,
Will sweeten every note and every word.

All earthly pomp or beauty to express
    Is but to carve in snow, on waves to write.
Celestial things, though men conceive them less,
    Yet fullest are they in themselves of light;
Such beams they yield as know no means to die,
Such heat they cast as lifts the Spirit high.

BARNABE BARNES
c. 1569–1609

46   *God's Virtue*

The world's bright comforter, whose beamsome light
    Poor creatures cheereth, mounting from the deep,
    His course doth in prefixed compass keep;
And, as courageous giant, takes delight
To run his race and exercise his might,
    Till him, down galloping the mountain's steep,
    Clear Hesperus, smooth messenger of sleep,
Views; and the silver ornament of night

Forth brings, with stars past number in her train,
  All which with sun's long borrowed splendour shine.
The seas, with full tide swelling, ebb again;
  All years to their old quarters new resign;
    The winds forsake their mountain-chambers wild,
    And all in all things with God's virtue filled.

BEN JONSON
?1572–1637

47 *To Heaven*

Good and great God, can I not think of thee
  But it must, straight, my melancholy be?
Is it interpreted in me disease
  That, laden with my sins, I seek for ease?
O be thou witness, that the reins dost know
  And hearts of all, if I be sad for show,
And judge me after, if I dare pretend
  To aught but grace, or aim at other end.
As thou art all, so be thou all to me,
  First, midst, and last, converted, one and three;
My faith, my hope, my love; and in this state
  My judge, my witness, and my advocate.
Where have I been this while exil'd from thee,
  And whither rap'd, now thou but stoop'st to me?
Dwell, dwell here still. O, being everywhere,
  How can I doubt to find thee ever, here?
I know my state, both full of shame and scorn,
  Conceiv'd in sin, and unto labour born,
Standing with fear, and must with horror fall,
  And destin'd unto judgement, after all.
I feel my griefs too, and there scarce is ground
  Upon my flesh t'inflict another wound.
Yet dare I not complain, or wish for death
  With holy PAUL, lest it be thought the breath
Of discontent; or that these prayers be
  For weariness of life, not love of thee.

JOHN DONNE
1572–1631

48   *Good Friday, 1613. Riding Westward*

Let man's Soul be a Sphere, and then, in this,
The intelligence that moves, devotion is;
And as the other Spheres, by being grown
Subject to foreign motions, lose their own,
And being by others hurried every day,
Scarce in a year their natural form obey;
Pleasure or business, so, our Souls admit
For their first mover, and are whirl'd by it.
Hence is't, that I am carried towards the West
This day, when my Soul's form bends toward the East.
There I should see a Sun, by rising set,
And by that setting endless day beget;
But that Christ on this Cross did rise and fall,
Sin had eternally benighted all.
Yet dare I almost be glad, I do not see
That spectacle of too much weight for me.
Who sees God's face, that is self life, must die;
What a death were it then to see God die?
It made his own Lieutenant Nature shrink,
It made his footstool crack, and the Sun wink.
Could I behold those hands which span the Poles,
And tune all spheres at once, pierc'd with those holes?
Could I behold that endless height which is
Zenith to us, and our Antipodes,
Humbled below us? or that blood which is
The seat of all our Souls, if not of his,
Made dirt of dust, or that flesh which was worn
By God, for his apparel, ragg'd, and torn?
If on these things I durst not look, durst I
Upon his miserable mother cast mine eye,
Who was God's partner here, and furnish'd thus
Half of that Sacrifice, which ransom'd us?
Though these things, as I ride, be from mine eye,
They are present yet unto my memory,
For that looks towards them; and thou look'st towards me,
O Saviour, as thou hang'st upon the tree;
I turn my back to thee, but to receive
Corrections, till thy mercies bid thee leave.

O think me worth thine anger, punish me,
Burn off my rusts and my deformity,
Restore thine Image so much, by thy grace,
That thou may'st know me, and I'll turn my face.

from *Holy Sonnets*
49   *'Thou hast made me, and shall thy work decay?'*

Thou hast made me, and shall thy work decay?
Repair me now, for now mine end doth haste,
I run to death, and death meets me as fast,
And all my pleasures are like yesterday;
I dare not move my dim eyes any way,
Despair behind, and death before doth cast
Such terror, and my feebled flesh doth waste
By sin in it, which it t'wards hell doth weigh;
Only thou'rt above, and when towards thee
By thy leave I can look, I rise again;
But our old subtle foe so tempteth me
That not one hour my self I can sustain;
Thy Grace may wing me to prevent his art,
And thou like Adamant draw mine iron heart.

50   *'Why are we by all creatures waited on?'*

Why are we by all creatures waited on?
Why do the prodigal elements supply
Life and food to me, being more pure than I,
Simple, and further from corruption?
Why brook'st thou, ignorant horse, subjection?
Why dost thou, bull and boar, so seelily
Dissemble weakness, and by one man's stroke die
Whose whole kind you might swallow and feed upon?
Weaker I am, woe's me, and worse than you,
You have not sinn'd, nor need be timorous.
But wonder at a greater wonder, for to us
Created nature doth these things subdue,
But their Creator, whom sin nor nature tied,
For us, his Creatures and his foes, hath died.

51 *'What if this present were the world's last night?'*

What if this present were the world's last night?
Mark in my heart, O Soul, where thou dost dwell,
The picture of Christ crucified, and tell
Whether that countenance can thee affright.
Tears in his eyes quench the amazing light,
Blood fills his frowns, which from his pierc'd head fell.
And can that tongue adjudge thee unto hell
Which pray'd forgiveness for his foes' fierce spite?
No, no; but as in my idolatry
I said to all my profane mistresses,
'Beauty, of pity, foulness only is
A sign of rigour', so I say to thee:
To wicked spirits are horrid shapes assign'd,
This beauteous form assures a piteous mind.

52 ## from *A Litanie*

The Father

Father of Heaven, and Him, by whom
It, and us for it, and all else for us
        Thou mad'st, and govern'st ever, come
And re-create me, now grown ruinous:
        My heart is by dejection, clay,
        And by self-murder, red.
From this red earth, O Father, purge away
All vicious tinctures, that new fashionèd
I may rise up from death, before I'm dead.

The Son

O Son of God, who seeing two things,
Sin and death, crept in, which were never made,
        By bearing one, tried'st with what stings
The other could Thine heritage invade;
        O be Thou nail'd unto my heart,
        And crucified again.

Part not from it, though it from Thee would part,
But let it be, by applying so Thy pain,
Drown'd in Thy blood, and in Thy passion slain.

The Holy Ghost

O Holy Ghost, whose temple I
Am, but of mud walls, and condensèd dust,
   And being sacrilegiously
Half wasted with youth's fires, of pride and lust,
     Must with new storms be weather-beat;
     Double in my heart Thy flame,
Which let devout sad tears intend; and let
(Though this glass lanthorn, flesh, do suffer maim)
Fire, Sacrifice, Priest, Altar be the same.

GILES FLETCHER
?1588–1623

53   (*Easter Morn*)

Say, earth, why hast thou got thee new attire,
And stick'st thy habit full of daisies red?
Seems that thou dost to some high thought aspire,
And some new-found-out bridegroom mean'st to wed:
Tell me, ye trees, so fresh apparellèd,—
    So never let the spiteful canker waste you,
    So never let the heavens with lightning blast you,—
Why go you now so trimly dressed, or whither haste you?

Answer me, Jordan, why thy crooked tide
So often wanders from his nearest way,
As though some other way thy stream would slide,
And fain salute the place where something lay.
And you, sweet birds that, shaded from the ray,
    Sit carolling and piping grief away,
    The while the lambs to hear you, dance and play,
Tell me, sweet birds, what is it you so fain would say?

And thou, fair spouse of earth, that every year
Gett'st such a numerous issue of thy bride,
How chance thou hotter shin'st, and draw'st more near?
Sure thou somewhere some worthy sight hast spied,
That in one place for joy thou canst not bide:
    And you, dead swallows, that so lively now
    Through the flit air your wingèd passage row,
How could new life into your frozen ashes flow?

Ye primroses and purple violets,
Tell me, why blaze ye from your leavy bed,
And woo men's hands to rent you from your sets,
As though you would somewhere be carrièd,
With fresh perfumes, and velvets garnishèd?
    But ah! I need not ask, 'tis surely so,
    You all would to your Saviour's triumphs go,
There would ye all await, and humble homage do.

ROBERT HERRICK
1591–1674

54   *His Saviour's Words, Going to the Cross*

Have, have ye no regard, all ye
Who pass this way, to pity me
Who am a man of misery?

A man both bruis'd, and broke, and one
Who suffers not here for mine own
But for my friends' transgression?

Ah! Sion's Daughters, do not fear
The Cross, the Cords, the Nails, the Spear,
The Myrrh, the Gall, the Vinegar,

For Christ, your loving Saviour, hath
Drunk up the wine of God's fierce wrath;
Only, there's left a little froth,

Less for to taste, than for to shew
What bitter cups had been your due,
Had He not drank them up for you.

FRANCIS QUARLES

1592–1644

55   *Like to the Arctic Needle*

Like to the arctic needle, that doth guide
  The wand'ring shade by his magnetic pow'r,
And leaves his silken gnomon to decide
  The question of the controverted hour,
First frantics up and down from side to side,
      And restless beats his crystal'd iv'ry case,
      With vain impatience jets from place to place,
And seeks the bosom of his frozen bride;
      At length he slacks his motion, and doth rest
His trembling point at his bright pole's beloved breast.

E'en so my soul, being hurried here and there,
  By ev'ry object that presents delight,
Fain would be settled, but she knows not where;
  She likes at morning what she loathes at night:
She bows to honour; then she lends an ear
      To that sweet swan-like voice of dying pleasure,
      Then tumbles in the scatter'd heaps of treasure;
Now flatter'd with false hope, now foil'd with fear.
      Thus finding all the world's delight to be
But empty toys, good God, she points alone to thee.

But hath the virtued steel a power to move?
  Or can the untouch'd needle point aright?
Or can my wand'ring thoughts forbear to rove,
  Unguided by the virtue of thy sprite?
O hath my leaden soul the art t'improve
      Her wasted talent, and, unrais'd, aspire
      In this sad moulting-time of her desire?
Not first belov'd, have I the power to love?
      I cannot stir, but as thou please to move me,
Nor can my heart return thee love, until thou love me.

The still commandress of the silent night
  Borrows her beams from her bright brother's eye;
His fair aspect fills her sharp horns with light;
  If he withdraw, her flames are quench'd and die.

E'en so the beams of thy enlight'ning sprite,
   Infus'd and shot into my dark desire,
    Inflame my thoughts, and fill my soul with fire,
That I am ravish'd with a new delight;
   But if thou shroud thy face, my glory fades,
And I remain a *Nothing*, all compos'd of shades.

Eternal God! O thou that only art
  The sacred fountain of eternal light,
And blessed loadstone of my better part,
  O thou, my heart's desire, my soul's delight!
Reflect upon my soul, and touch my heart,
    And then my heart shall prize no good above thee;
    And then my soul shall know thee; knowing, love thee;
And then my trembling thoughts shall never start
    From thy commands, or swerve the least degree,
Or once presume to move, but as they move in thee.

56   *On Those that Deserve It*

O, when our clergy at the dreadful Day
Shall make their audit, when the Judge shall say
'Give your accounts. What, have my lambs been fed?
Say, do they all stand sound? Is there none dead
By you defaults? Come shepherds, bring them forth
That I may crown your labours in their worth',
O, what an answer will be given by some!
'We have been silenced; Canons struck us dumb;
The great ones would not let us feed thy flock,
Unless we played the fools and wore a frock;
We were forbid unless we'd yield to sign
And cross their brows—they say, a mark of thine.
To say the truth, great Judge, they were not fed.
Lord, here they be; but Lord, they be all dead.'
Ah, cruel shepherds! Could your conscience serve
Not to be fools, and yet to let them starve?
What if your fiery spirits had been bound
To antic habits, or your heads been crowned
With peacock's plumes, had ye been forced to feed
Your Saviour's dear-brought flock in a fool's weed,
He that was scorned, reviled, endured the curse
Of a base death in your behalf—nay worse,

Swallowed the cup of wrath charged up to the brim—
Durst ye not stoop to play the fools for him?

GEORGE HERBERT
1593–1633

57 *Redemption*

Having been tenant long to a rich Lord,
   Not thriving, I resolvèd to be bold,
   And make a suit unto him, to afford
A new small-rented lease, and cancel th'old.

In heaven at his manor I him sought;
   They told me there, that he was lately gone
   About some land, which he had dearly bought
Long since on earth, to take possession.

I straight return'd and, knowing his great birth,
   Sought him accordingly in great resorts;
   In cities, theatres, gardens, parks, and courts;
At length I heard a ragged noise and mirth

   Of thieves and murderers—there I him espied,
   Who straight, 'Your suit is granted', said, and died.

58 *Jordan*

Who says that fictions only and false hair
Become a verse? Is there in truth no beauty?
Is all good structure in a winding stair?
May no lines pass except they do their duty
   Not to a true, but painted chair?

Is it no verse, except enchanted groves
And sudden arbours shadow coarse-spun lines?
Must purling streams refresh a lover's loves?
Must all be veil'd, while he that reads, divines,
   Catching the sense at two removes?

Shepherds are honest people; let them sing.
Riddle who list, for me, and pull for Prime.
I envy no man's nightingale or spring;
Nor let them punish me with loss of rhyme,
    Who plainly say, 'My God, My King.'

59

Church-monuments

While that my soul repairs to her devotion,
Here I entomb my flesh, that it betimes
May take acquaintance of this heap of dust;
To which the blast of death's incessant motion,
Fed with the exhalation of our crimes,
Drives all at last. Therefore I gladly trust

My body to this school, that it may learn
To spell its elements, and find its birth
Written in dusty heraldry and lines;
Which dissolution sure doth best discern,
Comparing dust with dust, and earth with earth.
These laugh at Jet and Marble put for signs

To sever the good fellowship of dust,
And spoil the meeting. What shall point out them,
When they shall bow, and kneel, and fall down flat
To kiss those heaps which now they have in trust?
Dear flesh, while I do pray, learn here thy stem
And true descent; that when thou shalt grow fat

And wanton in thy cravings, thou mayst know
That flesh is but the glass which holds the dust
That measures all our time; which also shall
Be crumbled into dust. Mark here below
How tame these ashes are, how free from lust,
That thou mayst fit thyself against thy fall.

60

The Windows

Lord, how can man preach thy eternal word?
    He is a brittle, crazy glass;
Yet in thy temple thou dost him afford
    This glorious and transcendent place,
    To be a window, through thy grace.

But when thou dost anneal in glass thy story,
    Making thy life to shine within
The holy Preacher's, then the light and glory
    More rev'rend grows, and more doth win;
    Which else shows waterish, bleak, and thin.

Doctrine and life, colours and light, in one
    When they combine and mingle, bring
A strong regard and awe; but speech alone
    Doth vanish like a flaring thing,
    And in the ear, not conscience, ring.

61   *Virtue*

Sweet day, so cool, so calm, so bright,
The bridal of the earth and sky,
The dew shall weep thy fall tonight;
    For thou must die.

Sweet rose, whose hue angry and brave
Bids the rash gazer wipe his eye,
Thy root is ever in its grave,
    And thou must die.

Sweet spring, full of sweet days and roses,
A box where sweets compacted lie,
My music shows ye have your closes,
    And all must die.

Only a sweet and virtuous soul,
Like season'd timber, never gives;
But though the whole world turn to coal,
    Then chiefly lives.

62   *The Collar*

I struck the board, and cried: 'No more.
    I will abroad.
What? shall I ever sigh and pine?
My lines and life are free; free as the road,
    Loose as the wind, as large as store.

Shall I be still in suit?
Have I no harvest but a thorn
To let me blood, and not restore
What I have lost with cordial fruit?
Sure there was wine
Before my sighs did dry it; there was corn
Before my tears did drown it.
Is the year only lost to me?
Have I no bays to crown it?
No flowers, no garlands gay? all blasted?
All wasted?
Not so, my heart; but there is fruit
And thou hast hands.
Recover all thy sigh-blown age
On double pleasures; leave thy cold dispute
Of what is fit, and not. Forsake thy cage,
Thy rope of sands,
Which petty thoughts have made, and made to thee
Good cable, to enforce and draw,
And be thy law,
While thou didst wink and wouldst not see.
Away! Take heed:
I will abroad.
Call in thy death's head there; tie up thy fears.
He that forbears
To suit and serve his need,
Deserves his load.'
But as I rav'd and grew more fierce and wild
At every word,
Me thought I heard one calling 'Child!'
And I replied, 'My Lord.'

63   *The Pulley*

When God at first made man,
Having a glass of blessings standing by,
'Let us' (said he) 'pour on him all we can;
Let the world's riches, which dispersèd lie,
Contract into a span.'

So strength first made a way;
Then beauty flow'd, then wisdom, honour, pleasure.
When almost all was out, God made a stay,
Perceiving that alone of all his treasure
    Rest in the bottom lay.

'For if I should' (said he)
'Bestow this jewel also on my creature,
He would adore my gifts instead of me,
And rest in Nature, not the God of Nature:
    So both should losers be.

'Yet let him keep the rest,
But keep them with repining restlessness;
Let him be rich and weary, that at least,
If goodness lead him not, yet weariness
    May toss him to my breast.'

64   *Discipline*

Throw away thy rod,
Throw away thy wrath;
      O my God,
Take the gentle path.

For my heart's desire
Unto thine is bent;
      I aspire
To a full consent.

Not a word or look
I affect to own,
      But by book,
And thy book alone.

Though I fail, I weep;
Though I halt in pace,
      Yet I creep
To the throne of grace.

Then let wrath remove;
Love will do the deed;
      For with love
Stony hearts will bleed.

Love is swift of foot;
Love's a man of war,
   And can shoot,
And can hit from far.

Who can scape his bow?
That which wrought on thee,
   Brought thee low,
Needs must work on me.

Throw away thy rod;
Though man frailties hath,
   Thou art God.
Throw away thy wrath.

65
The Pearl
(*Matthew 13:45*)

I know the ways of learning; both the head
And pipes that feed the press, and make it run;
What reason hath from nature borrowèd,
Or of itself, like a good housewife, spun
In laws and policy; what the stars conspire,
What willing nature speaks, what forced by fire;
Both the old discoveries and the new-found seas,
The stock and surplus, cause and history,—
All these stand open, or I have the keys:
      Yet I love Thee.

I know the ways of honour, what maintains
The quick returns of courtesy and wit;
In vies of favours whether party gains;
When glory swells the heart, and mouldeth it
To all expressions both of hand and eye;
Which on the world a true-love-knot may tie,
And bear the bundle, wheresoe'er it goes;
How many drams of spirit there must be
To sell my life unto my friends or foes:
      Yet I love Thee.

I know the ways of Pleasure, the sweet strains,
The lullings and the relishes of it;
The propositions of hot blood and brains;
What mirth and music mean; what love and wit

Have done these twenty hundred years and more.
I know the projects of unbridled store:
My stuff is flesh, not brass; my senses live,
And grumble oft that they have more in me
Than he that curbs them, being but one to five:
                    Yet I love Thee.

I know all these, and have them in my hand:
Therefore not sealèd, but with open eyes
I fly to Thee, and fully understand
Both the main sale and the commodities;
And at what rate and price I have Thy love,
With all the circumstances that may move.
Yet through the labyrinths, not my grovelling wit
But Thy silk-twist let down from heaven to me,
Did both conduct and teach me how by it
                    To climb to Thee.

66   *Love*

Love bade me welcome; yet my soul drew back,
          Guilty of dust and sin.
But quick-ey'd Love, observing me grow slack
          From my first entrance in,
Drew nearer to me, sweetly questioning
          If I lack'd any thing.

'A guest', I answer'd, 'worthy to be here.'
          Love said, 'You shall be he.'
'I the unkind, ungrateful? Ah my dear,
          I cannot look on thee.'
Love took my hand, and smiling did reply,
          'Who made the eyes but I?'

'Truth Lord, but I have marr'd them; let my shame
          Go where it doth deserve.'
'And know you not', says Love, 'who bore the blame?'
          'My dear, then I will serve.'
'You must sit down', says Love,' and taste my meat.'
          So I did sit and eat.

67 *A True Hymn*

My Joy, my Life, my Crown!
My heart was meaning all the day.
Somewhat it fain would say,
And still it runneth muttering up and down
With only this: My Joy, my Life, my Crown!

Yet slight not these few words.
If truly said, they may take part
Among the best in art:
The fineness which a hymn or psalm affords
Is when the soul unto the lines accords.

He who craves all the mind,
And all the soul, and strength, and time,
If the words only rhyme,
Justly complains that somewhat is behind
To make his verse, or write a hymn in kind.

Whereas, if the heart be moved,
Although the verse be somewhat scant,
God doth supply the want;
As when the heart says, sighing to be approved,
'O could I love!' and stops, God writeth, 'Loved.'

68 *The Temper*

How should I praise Thee, Lord! how should my rhymes
Gladly engrave Thy love in steel
If, what my soul doth feel sometimes,
My soul might ever feel!

Although there were some forty heavens or more,
Sometimes I peer above them all;
Sometimes I hardly reach a score,
Sometimes to Hell I fall.

O, rack me not to such a vast extent,
Those distances belong to Thee;
The world's too little for Thy tent,
A grave too big for me.

Wilt Thou meet arms with man, that Thou dost stretch
  A crumb of dust from heaven to hell?
  Will great God measure with a wretch?
    Shall he Thy stature spell?

O let me, when Thy roof my soul hath hid,
  O, let me roost and nestle there;
  Then of a sinner Thou art rid,
    And I of hope and fear.

Yet take Thy way; for sure Thy way is best:
  Stretch or contract me, Thy poor debtor;
  This is but tuning of my breast,
    To make the music better.

Whether I fly with angels, fall with dust,
  Thy hands made both, and I am there;
  Thy power and love, my love and trust,
    Make one place everywhere.

69   *Frailty*

Lord, in my silence how do I despise
    What upon trust
Is stylèd honour, riches, or fair eyes,
    But is fair dust!
  I surname them gilded clay,
    Dear earth, fine grass or hay;
In all, I think my foot doth ever tread
    Upon their head.

But when I view abroad both regiments,
    The world's and Thine,—
Thine clad with simpleness and sad events;
    The other fine,
  Full of glory and gay weeds,
    Brave language, braver deeds,—
That which was dust before doth quickly rise,
    And prick mine eyes.

O, brook not this, lest if what even now
    My foot did tread

Affront those joys wherewith Thou didst endow
                And long since wed
My poor soul, even sick of love,—
                It may a Babel prove,
Commodious to conquer heaven and Thee
                Planted in me.

70   *Peace*

Sweet Peace, where dost thou dwell? I humbly crave,
                Let me once know.
    I sought thee in a secret cave,
                And asked if Peace were there.
A hollow wind did seem to answer, 'No;
                Go seek elsewhere.'

I did; and going did a rainbow note;
                Surely, thought I,
    This is the lace of Peace's coat,
                I will search out the matter.
But while I looked, the clouds immediately
                Did break and scatter.

Then went I to a garden, and did spy
                A gallant flower,
    The Crown Imperial. Sure, said I,
                Peace at the root must dwell.
But when I digged, I saw a worm devour
                What showed so well.

At length I met a reverend good old man,
                Whom when for Peace
    I did demand, he thus began:
                'There was a Prince of old
At Salem dwelt, Who lived with good increase
                Of flock and fold.

'He sweetly lived; yet sweetness did not save
                His life from foes.
    But after death out of His grave
                There sprang twelve stalks of wheat;
Which many wondering at, got some of those
                To plant and set.

'It prospered strangely, and did soon disperse
       Through all the earth;
  For they that taste it do rehearse
    That virtue lies therein;
A secret virtue, bringing peace and mirth
       By flight of sin.

'Take of this grain, which in my garden grows,
       And grows for you;
  Make bread of it; and that repose
    And peace, which everywhere
With so much earnestness you do pursue,
       Is only there.'

71   *The Flower*

How fresh, O Lord, how sweet and clean
Are thy returns! even as the flowers in spring,
  To which, besides their own demean,
The late-past frosts tributes of pleasure bring;
       Grief melts away
       Like snow in May,
As if there were no such cold thing.

Who would have thought my shrivelled heart
Could have recovered greenness? It was gone
  Quite underground; as flowers depart
To see their mother-root, when they have blown;
       Where they together
       All the hard weather,
Dead to the world, keep house unknown.

These are thy wonders, Lord of power,
Killing and quickening, bringing down to hell
  And up to heaven in an hour;
Making a chiming of a passing-bell.
       We say amiss
       This or that is;
Thy word is all, if we could spell.

O that I once past changing were,
Fast in thy Paradise, where no flower can wither!
Many a spring I shoot up fair,
Offering at heaven, growing and groaning thither;
Nor doth my flower
Want a spring shower,
My sins and I joining together.

But while I grow in a straight line,
Still upwards bent, as if heaven were mine own,
Thy anger comes, and I decline;
What frost to that? what pole is not the zone
Where all things burn,
When thou dost turn,
And the least frown of thine is shown?

And now in age I bud again,
After so many deaths I live and write;
I once more smell the dew and rain,
And relish versing. O, my only light,
It cannot be
That I am he
On whom thy tempests fell all night.

These are thy wonders, Lord of love,
To make us see we are but flowers that glide;
Which when we once can find and prove,
Thou hast a garden for us, where to bide.
Who would be more,
Swelling through store,
Forfeit their Paradise by their pride.

THOMAS WASHBOURNE
1606–1687

72   *Upon a Great Shower of Snow that fell on*
May-day, 1654

You that are weather-wise and pretend to know
Long time before, when it will rain or snow,
When 'twill be fair or foul, when hot or cold—
Here stand or gaze a while, I dare be bold

To say you never saw the like; nay more,
You never heard the like of this before.
Since snow in May, you may hereafter make
A famous epoch in your almanac.
Prodigious 'tis, and I begin to fear
We have mistook the season of the year;
'Tis Winter yet, and this is Christmas day,
Which we indeed miscall the first of May.
Summer and Winter now confounded be,
And we no difference betwixt them see,
Only the trees are blossomèd, and so
The Glastonbury hawthorn used to do,
Upon the day of Christ's nativity,
As Camden tells in his Chorography.
The youths for cold creep in the chimney's end,
Who formerly the day did spritely spend
In merry May-games; now they hang the head
And droop, as if they and their sports were dead.
Perhaps some superstitious Cavalier,
That loved to keep his Christmas, will go near
To make an ill interpretation
Of this, and call it a judgement on the Nation
For our despising of that time and season
Against the ancient custom and right reason,
As he conceives, and since we'll not allow
One in December, we have a Christmas now.
But we a better use may make of it;
Though not to our minds the weather fit,
Yet to our soul convert the same, and thence
Extract this wholesome holy inference:
From this unseasonable change of weather
Without us, what's within us we may gather;
When in our hearts the Summer should begin
And graces grow, 'tis Winter by one sin,
All frost and snow, nothing comes up that's good,
And fruits o' th' Spirit nipped are in the bud.
Our May's turned to December, and our sun
Declines before he half his course hath run.
O Thou the Sun of Righteousness! display
Thy beams of mercy, make it once more May
Within our souls; let it shine warm and clear,
Producing in us yet a fruitful year.

Let it dissolve our snow into a shower
Of hot and penitent tears, which may procure
A blessing on the Nation, and at last
A general pardon for all faults are past.

73

The Circulation

Our famous *Harvey* hath made good
The circulation of the blood,
And what was paradox we know
To be a demonstration now.
The like in bodies doth befall
Civil as well as natural,
Such revolutions in them found
That they are always turning round.
We know a kingdom which of late
Converted was into a State;
And from the hands of many men
That State devolved to one again.
We know that wealth, which now doth flow
I' th' City veins, did lately grow
I' th' Country furrows, and the same
Soon runs to the place from whence it came.
We know our body's frame of dust
At first created was, and must
Crumble to dust ere long; we see
Not one from dissolution free.
We know, or (what's equivalent)
Believe our souls, which God first sent
To make our bodies move and live,
Shall go to Him who did them give;
When once their Maker them commands,
They straight return into His hands.
Thus we see almost every thing
Circling about as in a ring.
The Winter-season of the year
Is now turned Summer everywhere;
This Summer will to Winter turn,
And that freeze, which before did burn;
Rivers which borrow from the main
Their streams, do pay them back again.
Since nothing under heaven hath rest
But floating up and down, 'tis best

To look above, and fix mine eyes
Where not a shadow of change lies:
No variation there, but all
Stand still in state pacifical.
Go then, my dust, to dust, but thou my soul
Return unto thy rest above the pole.

EDMUND WALLER
1606–1687

74   from *Last Verses*

The seas are quiet when the winds give o'er;
So calm are we when passions are no more.
For then we know how vain it was to boast
Of fleeting things, so certain to be lost.
Clouds of affection from our younger eyes
Conceal that emptiness which age descries.
The soul's dark cottage, batter'd and decay'd,
Lets in new light through chinks that Time has made;
Stronger by weakness, wiser, men become
As they draw near to their eternal home.
Leaving the old, both worlds at once they view
That stand upon the threshold of the new.

JOHN MILTON
1608–1674

75   *On the Morning of Christ's Nativity*

I

This is the month, and this the happy morn,
Wherein the Son of Heav'n's eternal King,
Of wedded Maid and Virgin Mother born,
Our great redemption from above did bring;
For so the holy sages once did sing,
    That he our deadly forfeit should release,
And with his Father work us a perpetual peace.

2

That glorious form, that light unsufferable,
And that far-beaming blaze of majesty,
Wherewith he wont at Heav'n's high council-table
To sit the midst of Trinal Unity,
He laid aside; and here with us to be,
   Forsook the courts of everlasting day,
And chose with us a darksome house of mortal clay.

3

Say Heav'nly Muse, shall not thy sacred vein
Afford a present to the Infant God?
Hast thou no verse, no hymn, or solemn strain,
To welcome him to this his new abode;
Now while the Heav'n by the sun's team untrod
   Hath took no print of the approaching light,
And all the spangled host keep watch in squadrons bright?

4

See how from far upon the eastern road
The star-led wizards haste with odours sweet:
O run, prevent them with thy humble ode,
And lay it lowly at his blessed feet;
Have thou the honour first thy Lord to greet,
   And join thy voice unto the Angel Quire,
From out his secret altar touch'd with hallow'd fire.

The Hymn

I

It was the winter wild
While the Heav'n-born child,
   All meanly wrapp'd in the rude manger lies;
Nature in awe to him
Had doff'd her gaudy trim,
   With her great Master so to sympathize;
It was no season then for her
To wanton with the sun her lusty paramour.

2

Only with speeches fair
She woos the gentle air
   To hide her guilty front with innocent snow,

And on her naked shame,
Pollute with sinful blame,
    The saintly veil of maiden white to throw;
Confounded, that her Maker's eyes
Should look so near upon her foul deformities.

3

But he, her fears to cease,
Sent down the meek-ey'd Peace;
    She, crown'd with olive green, came softly sliding
Down through the turning sphere
His ready harbinger,
    With turtle wing the amorous clouds dividing,
And waving wide her myrtle wand,
She strikes a universal peace through sea and land.

4

No war, or battle's sound
Was heard the world around:
    The idle spear and shield were high up hung;
The hooked chariot stood
Unstain'd with hostile blood,
    The trumpet spake not to the armed throng;
And kings sat still with awful eye,
As if they surely knew their sovran Lord was by.

5

But peaceful was the night
Wherein the Prince of Light
    His reign of peace upon the earth began:
The winds with wonder whist
Smoothly the waters kissed,
    Whispering new joys to the mild ocean,
Who now hath quite forgot to rave,
While birds of calm sit brooding on the charmed wave.

6

The stars with deep amaze
Stand fix'd in steadfast gaze,
    Bending one way their precious influence;
And will not take their flight,
For all the morning light,
    Or Lucifer that often warn'd them thence;

But in their glimmering orbs did glow,
Until their Lord himself bespake, and bid them go.

7

And though the shady gloom
Had given day her room,
   The sun himself withheld his wonted speed;
And hid his head for shame,
As his inferior flame
   The new-enlightened world no more should need;
He saw a greater Sun appear
Than his bright throne or burning axletree could bear.

8

The shepherds on the lawn,
Or ere the point of dawn,
   Sat simply chatting in a rustic row;
Full little thought they then
That the mighty Pan
   Was kindly come to live with them below;
Perhaps their loves, or else their sheep,
Was all that did their silly thoughts so busy keep.

9

When such music sweet
Their hearts and ears did greet
   As never was by mortal finger strook;
Divinely warbled voice
Answering the stringed noise,
   As all their souls in blissful rapture took;
The air such pleasure loth to lose
With thousand echoes still prolongs each heav'nly close.

10

Nature that heard such sound
Beneath the hollow round
   Of Cynthia's seat, the airy region thrilling,
Now was almost won
To think her part was done,
   And that her reign had here its last fulfilling;
She knew such harmony alone
Could hold all Heav'n and Earth in happier union.

JOHN MILTON

11

At last surrounds their sight
A globe of circular light
    That with long beams the shame-fac'd Night array'd;
The helmed Cherubim
And sworded Seraphim
    Are seen in glittering ranks with wings displayed,
Harping in loud and solemn quire
With unexpressive notes to Heav'n's new-born Heir.

12

Such music (as 'tis said)
Before was never made,
    But when of old the sons of morning sung;
While the Creator great
His constellations set,
    And the well-balanc'd world on hinges hung,
And cast the dark foundations deep,
And bid the welt'ring waves their oozy channel keep.

13

Ring out ye crystal spheres,
Once bless our human ears
    (If ye have power to touch our senses so),
And let your silver chime
Move in melodious time;
    And let the bass of Heav'n's deep organ blow;
And with your ninefold harmony
Make up full consort to th'angelic symphony.

14

For if such holy song
Enwrap our fancy long,
    Time will run back, and fetch the age of gold;
And speckled Vanity
Will sicken soon and die,
    And leprous Sin will melt from earthly mould;
And Hell itself will pass away,
And leave her dolorous mansions to the peering day.

15

Yea, Truth and Justice then
Will down return to men,
  Orb'd in a rainbow; and like glories wearing
Mercy will sit between,
Thron'd in celestial sheen,
  With radiant feet the tissu'd clouds down steering;
And Heav'n as at some festival
Will open wide the gates of her high palace hall.

16

But wisest Fate says no,
This must not yet be so,
  The Babe lies yet in smiling infancy
That on the bitter cross
Must redeem our loss
  So both himself and us to glorify;
Yet first to those ychain'd in sleep
The wakeful trump of doom must thunder through the deep,

17

With such a horrid clang
As on Mount Sinai rang
  While the red fire and smouldering clouds outbrake;
The aged Earth, aghast
With terror of that blast,
  Shall from the surface to the centre shake,
When at the world's last session
The dreadful Judge in middle air shall spread his throne.

18

And then at last our bliss
Full and perfect is,
  But now begins; for from this happy day
Th'old Dragon underground,
In straiter limits bound,
  Not half so far casts his usurpèd sway;
And wroth to see his kingdom fail,
Swinges the scaly horror of his folded tail.

19

The oracles are dumb,
No voice or hideous hum
   Runs through the archèd roof in words deceiving.
Apollo from his shrine
Can no more divine,
   With hollow shriek the steep of Delphos leaving.
No nightly trance or breathèd spell
Inspires the pale-eyed priest from the prophetic cell.

20

The lonely mountains o'er,
And the resounding shore,
   A voice of weeping heard, and loud lament;
From haunted spring and dale
Edg'd with poplar pale
   The parting Genius is with sighing sent;
With flower-inwoven tresses torn
The nymphs in twilight shade of tangled thickets mourn.

21

In consecrated earth,
And on the holy hearth,
   The Lars and Lemures moan with midnight plaint;
In urns and altars round,
A drear and dying sound
   Affrights the flamens at their service quaint;
And the chill marble seems to sweat,
While each peculiar power forgoes his wonted seat.

22

Peor and Baalim
Forsake their temples dim,
   With that twice-battered god of Palestine;
And moonèd Ashtaroth,
Heav'n's queen and mother both,
   Now sits not girt with tapers' holy shine;
The Lybic Hammon shrinks his horn,
In vain the Tyrian maids their wounded Thamuz mourn.

23

And sullen Moloch, fled,
Hath left in shadows dread
   His burning idol all of blackest hue;
In vain with cymbals' ring
They call the grisly king,
   In dismal dance about the furnace blue;
The brutish gods of Nile as fast,
Isis and Orus, and the dog Anubis haste.

24

Nor is Osiris seen
In Memphian grove or green,
   Trampling the unshower'd grass with lowings loud;
Nor can he be at rest
Within his sacred chest,
   Naught but profoundest hell can be his shroud;
In vain with timbrell'd anthems dark
The sable-stoled sorcerers bear his worshipped ark.

25

He feels from Judah's land
The dreaded Infant's hand,
   The rays of Bethlehem blind his dusky eyn;
Nor all the gods beside
Longer dare abide,
   Not Typhon huge ending in snaky twine:
Our Babe, to show his Godhead true,
Can in his swaddling bands control the damnèd crew.

26

So when the sun in bed,
Curtain'd with cloudy red,
   Pillows his chin upon an orient wave,
The flocking shadows pale
Troop to the infernal jail;
   Each fettered ghost slips to his several grave;
And the yellow-skirted fays
Fly after the night-steeds, leaving their moon-loved maze.

27

But see the Virgin blest
Hath laid her Babe to rest.
   Time is our tedious song should here have ending;
Heaven's youngest-teemèd star
Hath fixed her polished car,
   Her sleeping Lord with handmaid lamp attending;
And all about the courtly stable
Bright-harnessed angels sit in order serviceable.

76
          Sonnet
On the late Massacre in Piedmont

Avenge, O Lord, thy slaughter'd Saints, whose bones
  Lie scatter'd on the Alpine mountains cold,
  Ev'n them who kept thy truth so pure of old
  When all our fathers worshipp'd stocks and stones,
Forget not; in thy book record their groans
  Who were thy sheep, and in their ancient fold
  Slain by the bloody Piedmontese that roll'd
  Mother with infant down the rocks. Their moans
The vales redoubled to the hills, and they
  To Heav'n. Their martyr'd blood and ashes sow
  O'er all th'Italian fields where still doth sway
The triple Tyrant; that from these may grow
  A hundredfold who, having learned thy way
  Early may fly the Babylonian woe.

77
          Sonnet
(*On his Blindness*)

When I consider how my light is spent
  Ere half my days, in this dark world and wide,
  And that one talent which is death to hide
  Lodged with me useless, though my soul more bent
To serve therewith my Maker, and present
  My true account, lest he returning chide:
  'Doth God exact day-labour, light denied?'
  I fondly ask. But patience, to prevent

That murmur, soon replies: 'God doth not need
  Either man's work or his own gifts, who best
  Bear his mild yoke, they serve him best, his State
Is Kingly. Thousands at his bidding speed
  And post o'er land and ocean without rest;
  They also serve, who only stand and wait.'

78   from *Paradise Lost*
from Book V (Adam Unfallen)

'O favourable spirit, propitious guest,
Well hast thou taught the way that might direct
Our knowledge, and the scale of nature set
From centre to circumference, whereon,
In contemplation of created things,
By steps we may ascend to God. But say,
What meant that caution joined, "if ye be found
Obedient"? Can we want obedience then
To him, or possibly his love desert,
Who formed us from the dust, and placed us here,
Full to the utmost measure of what bliss
Human desires can seek or apprehend?'
  To whom the angel: 'Son of Heaven and earth,
Attend: that thou art happy, owe to God;
That thou continuest such, owe to thyself,
That is, to thy obedience; therein stand.
This was that caution given thee; be advised
God made thee perfect, not immutable;
And good he made thee, but to persevere
He left it in thy power; ordained thy will,
By nature free, not over-ruled by fate
Inextricable, or strict necessity;
Our voluntary service he requires,
Not our necessitated; such with him
Finds no acceptance, nor can find; for how
Can hearts, not free, be tried whether they serve
Willing or no, who will but what they must
By destiny, and can no other choose?
Myself, and all the angelic host, that stand
In sight of God enthroned, our happy state
Hold, as you yours, while our obedience holds;
On other surety none: freely we serve,
Because we freely love, as in our will

To love or not; in this we stand or fall:
And some are fallen, to disobedience fallen,
And so from Heaven to deepest Hell; O fall
From what high state of bliss, into what woe!'

79   from *Paradise Lost*
from *Book XII* (*Adam Fallen*)

Descended, Adam to the bower where Eve
Lay sleeping ran before, but found her waked;
And thus with words not sad she him received:
   'Whence thou return'st, and whither wentst, I know;
For God is also in sleep; and dreams advise,
Which he hath sent propitious, some great good
Presaging, since, with sorrow and heart's distress,
Wearied I fell asleep: but now lead on;
In me is no delay; without thee here to stay,
Is to go hence unwilling; thou to me
Art all things under Heaven, all places thou,
Who for my wilful crime art banished hence.
This further consolation, yet secure,
I carry hence; though all by me is lost,
Such favour I unworthy am vouchsafed,
By me the promised Seed shall all restore!'
   So spake our mother Eve, and Adam heard,
Well pleased, but answered not; for now too nigh
The archangel stood, and from the other hill
To their fixed station, all in bright array,
The cherubim descended; on the ground,
Gliding metèorous, as evening mist,
Risen from a river, o'er the marish glides,
And gathers ground fast at the labourer's heel,
Homeward returning. High in front advanced,
The brandished sword of God before them blazed,
Fierce as a comet which with torrid heat
And vapour as the Libyan air adust
Began to parch that temperate clime; whereat
In either hand the hastening angel caught
Our lingering parents, and to the eastern gate
Led them direct, and down the cliff as fast
To the subjected plain; then disappeared.
They, looking back, all the eastern side beheld

Of Paradise, so late their happy seat,
Waved over by that flaming brand; the gate
With dreadful faces thronged, and fiery arms:
Some natural tears they dropped, but wiped them soon;
The world was all before them, where to choose
Their place of rest, and Providence their guide;
They, hand in hand, with wandering steps and slow
Through Eden took their solitary way.

80   from *Samson Agonistes*

O how comely it is and how reviving
To the spirits of just men long oppressed,
When God into the hands of their deliverer
Puts invincible might
To quell the mighty of the earth, the oppressor,
The brute and boisterous force of violent men,
Hardy and industrious to support
Tyrannic power, but raging to pursue
The righteous and all such as honour truth!
He all their ammunition
And feats of war defeats
With plain heroic magnitude of mind
And celestial vigour armed;
Their armouries and magazines contemns,
Renders them useless, while
With winged expedition
Swift as the lightning glance he executes
His errand on the wicked, who surprised,
Lose their defence, distracted and amazed.
   But patience is more oft the exercise
Of saints, the trial of their fortitude,
Making them each his own deliverer,
And victor over all
That tyranny or fortune can inflict;
Either of these is in thy lot,
Samson, with might endued
Above the sons of men; but sight bereaved
May chance to number thee with those
Whom patience finally must crown.

SIDNEY GODOLPHIN
1610–1643

81   *'Lord, when the wise men came from far'*

Lord, when the wise men came from far,
Led to thy cradle by a star,
Then did the shepherds too rejoice,
Instructed by thy angels' voice;
Blest were the wise men in their skill,
And shepherds in their harmless will.

Wise men in tracing nature's laws
Ascend unto the highest cause;
Shepherds with humble fearfulness
Walk safely, though their light be less;
Though wise men better know the way,
It seems no honest heart can stray.

There is no merit in the wise
But love (the shepherds' sacrifice).
Wise men, all ways of knowledge past,
To th' shepherds' wonder come at last;
To know, can only wonder breed,
And not to know, is wonder's seed.

A wise man at the altar bows
And offers up his studied vows
And is received; may not the tears
Which spring too from a shepherd's fears,
And sighs upon his frailty spent,
Though not distinct, be eloquent?

'Tis true, the object sanctifies
All passions which within us rise;
But since no creature comprehends
The cause of causes, end of ends,
He who himself vouchsafes to know
Best pleases his creator so.

When then our sorrows we apply
To our own wants and poverty,

When we look up in all distress
And our own misery confess,
Sending both thanks and prayers above,
Then though we do not know, we love.

ANNE BRADSTREET
?1612–1672

82   *To my Dear and Loving Husband*

If ever two were one, then surely we.
If ever man were lov'd by wife, then thee;
If ever wife was happy in a man,
Compare with me ye women if you can.
I prize thy love more than whole mines of gold,
Or all the riches that the East doth hold.
My love is such that rivers cannot quench,
Nor aught but love from thee, give recompense.
Thy love is such I can no way repay,
The heavens reward thee manifold, I pray.
Then while we live, in love lets so persever
That, when we live no more, we may live ever.

83   *In Memory of my dear grandchild Elizabeth
Bradstreet, who deceased August, 1665, being a year
and a half old.*

Farewell dear babe, my heart's too much content,
Farewell sweet babe, the pleasure of mine eye,
Farewell fair flower that for a space was lent,
Then ta'en away unto Eternity.
Blest babe, why should I once bewail thy fate,
Or sigh thy days so soon were terminate,
Sith thou art settled in an Everlasting state?

By nature trees do rot when they are grown,
And plums and apples thoroughly ripe do fall,
And corn and grass are in their season mown,
And time brings down what is both strong and tall.
But plants new set to be eradicate,
And buds new blown to have so short a date,
Is by His hand alone that guides nature and fate.

RICHARD CRASHAW
?1613–1649

84   *Epithalamium*

Come, virgin tapers of pure wax,
   Made in the hive of Love, all white
As snow, and yet as cold, where lacks
   Hymen's holy heat and light;
     Where blooming kisses
       Their beds yet keep
     And steep their blisses
       In rosy sleep;
Where sister buds yet wanting brothers
Kiss their own lips in lieu of others;
Help me to mourn a matchless maidenhead
        That now is dead.

A fine, thin negative thing it was,
   A nothing with a dainty name
Which pruned her plumes in Self-Love's glass
   Made up of fancy and fond fame;
     Within the shade
       Of its own wing
     It sat and played
       A self-crowned king;
A froward flower whose peevish pride
Within itself itself did hide,
Flying all fingers, and even thinking much
        Of its own touch.

This bird indeed the phoenix was
   Late chased by Love's revengeful arrows,
Whose wars now left the wonted pass
   And spared the little lives of sparrows
     To hunt this fool
       Whose froward pride
     Love's noble school
       And courts denied,
And froze the fruit of fair desire
Which flourisheth in mutual fire
'Gainst Nature, who 'mong all the webs she spun
        Ne'er wove a nun.

She, of Cupid's shafts afraid
   Left her own balm-breathing East,
And in a western bosom made
   A softer and a sweeter nest;
     There did she rest
       In the sweet shade
     Of a soft breast
       Whose beauties made
Thames oft stand still and lend a glass
While in her own she saw Heaven's face
And sent him full of her fair name's report
        To Thetis' court.

And now poor Love was at a stand:
   The crystal castle which she kept
Was proof against the proudest hand;
   There in safest hold she slept;
     His shafts' expense
       Left there no smart,
     But bounding thence
       Broached his own heart:
At length a fort he did devise
Built in noble Brampston's eyes,
And aiming thence, this matchless maidenhead
        Was soon found dead.

Yet Love in death did wait upon her
   Granting leave she should expire
In her fumes and have the honour
   T'exhale in flames of his own fire,
     Her funeral pile
       The marriage bed;
     In a sighed smile
       She vanishèd.
So rich a dress of death ne'er famed
The cradles where her kindred flamed;
So sweet her mother-phoenixes of the East
       Ne'er spiced their nest.

With many pretty, peevish trials
   Of angry yielding, faint denyings,
Melting Noes and mild denials,
   Dying lives and short-lived dyings,

With doubtful eyes,
   Half smiles, half tears;
With trembling joys
   And jocund fears,
Twixt the pretty twilight strife
Of dying maid and dawning wife,
Twixt rain and sunshine, this sweet maidenhead
            Alas is dead.

Happy he whose wakeful joys
   Kept the prize of this rich loss;
Happy she whose watery eyes
   Kiss no worse a weeping cross;
         Thrice happy he
            Partakes her store
         Thrice happy she
            Hath still the more.
Think not sweet bride, that faint shower slakes
The fires he from thy fair eyes takes;
Thy drops are salt, and while they think to tame
            Sharpen his flame.

Blest bridegroom, ere the rain be laid,
   Use good weather while it proves;
Those drops that wash away the maid
   Shall water your warm-planted loves;
         Fair youth, make haste
            Ere it be dry:
         The sweet brine taste
            From her moist eye;
Thy lips will find such dew as this is
Best season for a lover's kisses;
And those thy morning stars will better please
            Bathed in those seas.

Nor may thy vine, fair oak, embrace thee
   With ivy arms and empty wishes,
But with full bosom interlace thee
   And reach her clusters to thy kisses;
         Safe may she rest
            Her laden boughs
         On thy firm breast
            And fill thy vows

Up to the brim, till she make even
Their full tops with the fair-eyed heaven,
And heaven to gild those glorious heroes' birth
      Stoop and kiss earth.

Long may this happy heaven-tied band
   Exercise its most holy art,
Keeping her heart within his hand,
   Keeping his hand upon her heart;
     But from her eyes
      Feel he no charms;
     Find she no joy
      But in his arms;
May each maintain a well-fledged nest
Of wingèd loves in either's breast;
Be each of them a mutual sacrifice
      Of either's eyes.

May their whole life a sweet song prove
   Set to two well-composèd parts
By music's noblest master, Love,
   Played on the strings of both their hearts;
     Whose mutual sound
      May ever meet
     In a just round,
      Not short though sweet;
Long may heaven listen to the song
And think it short though it be long;
Oh, prove't a well-set song indeed, which shows
      Sweet'st in the close!

85   *Charitas Nimia: or the Dear Bargain*

Lord, what is man? why should he cost thee
   So dear? what had his ruin lost thee?
Lord, what is man, that thou hast over-bought
   So much a thing of naught?

    Love is too kind, I see, and can
Make but a simple merchantman;
'Twas for such sorry merchandise
Bold painters have put out his eyes.

Alas, sweet Lord, what were't to thee,
If there were no such worms as we?
Heaven ne'ertheless still heaven would be,
    Should mankind dwell
    In the deep hell,
What have his woes to do with thee?

    Let him go weep
    O'er his own wounds;
    Seraphims will not sleep
Nor spheres let fall their faithful rounds.

  Still would the youthful spirits sing,
And still thy spacious palace ring:
Still would those beauteous ministers of light
    Burn all as bright,

  And bow their flaming heads before thee;
Still Thrones and Dominations would adore thee;
Still would those ever-wakeful sons of fire
    Keep warm thy praise
    Both nights and days,
And teach thy loved name to their noble lyre.

  Let froward dust then do its kind,
And give itself for sport to the proud wind.
Why should a piece of peevish care plead shares
In the Eternity of thy old cares?
Why should'st thou bow thy awful breast to see
What mine own madnesses have done with me?

  Should not the King still keep his throne
Because some desperate fool's undone?
Or will the world's illustrious eyes
Weep for every worm that dies?

    Will the gallant sun
    E'er the less glorious run?
Will he hang down his golden head
Or e'er the sooner seek his western bed,
    Because some foolish fly
    Grows wanton and will die?

If I were lost in misery,
What was it to thy heaven and thee?
What was it to thy precious blood
If my foul heart called for a flood?

What if my faithless soul and I
    Would needs fall in
    With guilt and sin?
What did the Lamb that he should die?
What did the Lamb that he should need,
When the Wolf sins, himself to bleed?

    If my base lust
Bargained with death and well-beseeming dust,
    Why should the white
    Lamb's bosom write
    The purple name
    Of my sin's shame?

Why should his unstained breast make good
My blushes with his own heart-blood?

O, my Saviour, make me see
How dearly thou hast paid for me,

That lost again my life may prove
As then in death, so now in love.

RICHARD BAXTER

1615–1691

86   from *A Psalm of Praise*
        (To the Tune of the 148th Psalm)

Ye holy Angels bright,
    Which stand before God's throne,
And dwell in glorious light,
    Praise ye the Lord each one.
        You there so nigh
            Are much more meet
            Than we the feet,
        For things so high.

RICHARD BAXTER

You blessed souls at rest
   That see your Saviour's face,
Whose glory, even the least,
   Is far above our grace;
       God's praises sound,
        As in his sight
        With sweet delight
      You do abound.

All nations of the earth,
   Extol the world's great King;
With melody and mirth
   His glorious praises sing.
        For he still reigns;
         And will bring low
         The proudest foe
      That him disdains.

Sing forth Jehovah's praise,
   Ye saints that on him call;
Magnify him always,
   His holy churches all.
        In him rejoice;
         And there proclaim
         His Holy Name
      With sounding voice.

My soul, bear thou thy part!
   Triumph in God above!
With a well-tuned heart
   Sing thou the songs of love.
        Thou art his own
         Whose precious blood,
         Shed for thy good,
      His love made known.

       *   *

Though human help depart
   And flesh draw near to dust,
Let Faith keep up my heart
   To love God true and just;
        And all my days
         Let no disease
         Cause me to cease
      His joyful praise.

RICHARD BAXTER

Though sin would make me doubt,
  And fill my soul with fears,
Though God seem to shut out
  My daily cries and tears,
      By no such frost
        Of sad delays
         Let thy sweet praise
      Be nipped and lost.

Away, distrustful care!
  I have thy promise, Lord.
To banish all despair,
  I have thy oath and word.
      And therefore I
        Shall see thy face,
        And there thy grace
      Shall magnify.

Though sin and death conspire
  To rob thee of thy praise,
Still towards thee I'll aspire,
  And thou dull hearts canst raise.
      Open thy door;
        And when grim death
        Shall stop this breath
      I'll praise thee more.

With thy triumphant flock
  Then I shall numbered be;
Built on the eternal rock
  His glory we shall see.
      The heavens so high
        With praise shall ring.
        And all shall sing
      In harmony.

The sun is but a spark
  From the eternal light;
Its brightest beams are dark
  To that most glorious sight.
      There the whole Chore
        With one accord
        Shall praise the Lord
      For evermore.

ANDREW MARVELL
1621–1678

87   *Bermudas*

Where the remote *Bermudas* ride
In th'Ocean's bosom unespy'd,
From a small Boat, that row'd along,
The listning Winds receiv'd this Song.
  What should we do but sing his Praise
That led us through the watry Maze,
Unto an Isle so long unknown,
And yet far kinder than our own?
Where he the huge Sea-Monsters wracks,
That lift the Deep upon their Backs.
He lands us on a grassy Stage;
Safe from the Storms, and Prelate's rage.
He gave us this eternal Spring,
Which here enamels every thing;
And sends the Fowls to us in care,
On daily Visits through the Air.
He hangs in shades the Orange bright,
Like golden Lamps in a green Night,
And does in the Pomgranates close
Jewels more rich than *Ormus* shows.
He makes the Figs our mouths to meet,
And throws the Melons at our feet;
But Apples plants of such a price,
No tree could ever bear them twice.
With Cedars, chosen by his hand
From *Lebanon*, he stores the Land;
And makes the hollow Seas, that roar,
Proclaim the Ambergris on shore.
He cast (of which we rather boast)
The Gospel's Pearl upon our Coast,
And in these Rocks for us did frame
A Temple, where to sound his Name.
Oh let our Voice his Praise exalt,
Till it arrive at Heaven's Vault;
Which thence (perhaps) rebounding, may
Echo beyond the *Mexique Bay*.
Thus sung they, in the *English* boat,
An holy and a cheerful note,

And all the way, to guide their Chime,
With falling Oars they kept the time.

88   *The Coronet*

When for the Thorns with which I long, too long,
   With many a piercing wound
   My Saviour's head have crown'd,
I seek with Garlands to redress that Wrong,
   Through every Garden, every Mead
I gather flow'rs (my fruits are only flow'rs)
   Dismantling all the fragrant Towers
That once adorn'd my Shepherdess's head.
And now when I have summ'd up all my store,
   Thinking (so I my self deceive)
   So rich a Chaplet thence to weave
As never yet the king of Glory wore,
   Alas I find the Serpent old
   That, twining in his speckled breast,
   About the flow'rs disguis'd does fold,
   With wreaths of Fame and Interest.
Ah, foolish Man, that would'st debase with them
And mortal Glory, Heaven's Diadem!
But thou who only could'st the Serpent tame,
Either his slipp'ry knots at once untie,
And disintangle all his winding Snare;
Or shatter too with him my curious frame
And let these wither, so that he may die,
Though set with Skill and chosen out with Care;
That they, while Thou on both their Spoils dost tread,
May crown thy Feet, that could not crown thy Head.

HENRY VAUGHAN
1622–1695

89   *Quickness*

False life! a foil and no more, when
     Wilt thou be gone?
Thou foul deception of all men
That would not have the true come on.

Thou art a Moon-like toil; a blind
   Self-posing state;
A dark contest of waves and wind;
A mere tempestuous debate.

Life is a fix'd, discerning light,
   A knowing Joy;
No chance, or fit: but ever bright,
And calm and full, yet doth not cloy.

'Tis such a blissful thing, that still
   Doth vivify,
And shine and smile, and hath the skill
To please without Eternity.

Thou art a toilsome Mole, or less,
   A moving mist;
But life is, what none can express,
A quickness, which my God hath kiss'd.

The Retreat

90

Happy those early days, when I
Shin'd in my angel-infancy!
Before I understood this place
Appointed for my second race,
Or taught my soul to fancy aught
But a white, celestial thought;
When yet I had not walked above
A mile, or two, from my first love,
And looking back (at that short space)
Could see a glimpse of his bright face;
When on some gilded cloud or flower
My gazing soul would dwell an hour,
And in those weaker glories spy
Some shadows of eternity;
Before I taught my tongue to wound
My conscience with a sinful sound,
Or had the black art to dispense
A several sin to every sense,
But felt through all this fleshly dress
Bright *shoots* of everlastingness.

113

O how I long to travel back
And tread again that ancient track!
That I might once more reach that plain
Where first I left my glorious train,
From whence th'Enlightened spirit sees
That shady city of palm-trees;
But (ah!) my soul with too much stay
Is drunk, and staggers in the way.
Some men a forward motion love,
But I by backward steps would move,
And when this dust falls to the urn,
In that state I came, return.

91   *Peace*

My soul, there is a country
  Far beyond the stars,
Where stands a wingèd sentry
  All skilful in the wars.
There, above noise and danger,
  Sweet peace sits crown'd with smiles,
And one born in a manger
  Commands the beauteous files.
He is thy gracious friend
  And (O my soul, awake!)
Did in pure love descend
  To die here for thy sake.
If thou canst get but thither,
  There grows the flower of peace,
The rose that cannot wither,
  Thy fortress, and thy ease.
Leave then thy foolish ranges;
  For none can thee secure
But one, who never changes,
  Thy God, thy life, thy cure.

92   *Ascension Hymn*

They are all gone into the world of light!
   And I alone sit lingering here.
Their very memory is fair and bright,
   And my sad thoughts doth clear.

It glows and glitters in my cloudy breast
   Like stars upon some gloomy grove,
Or those faint beams in which this hill is drest
   After the sun's remove.

I see them walking in an air of glory
   Whose light doth trample on my days;
My days, which are at best but dull and hoary,
   Mere glimmering and decays.

O holy hope! and high humility,
   High as the Heavens above!
These are your walks, and you have shew'd them me
   To kindle my cold love,

Dear, beauteous death! the jewel of the just,
   Shining nowhere but in the dark,
What mysteries do lie beyond thy dust,
   Could man outlook that mark!

He that hath found some fledged bird's nest, may know
   At first sight if the bird be flown;
But what fair well or grove he sings in now,
   That is to him unknown.

And yet, as angels in some brighter dreams
   Call to the soul, when man doth sleep,
So some strange thoughts transcend our wonted themes,
   And into glory peep.

If a star were confin'd into a tomb
   Her captive flames must needs burn there;
But when the hand that locked her up, gives room,
   She'll shine through all the sphere.

O Father of eternal life, and all
   Created glories under thee!
Resume thy spirit from this world of thrall
   Into true liberty.

Either disperse these mists, which blot and fill
   My perspective (still) as they pass,
Or else remove me hence unto that hill
   Where I shall need no glass.

93   *The World*

I saw Eternity the other night
Like a great *Ring* of pure and endless light,
   All calm, as it was bright,
And round beneath it, Time in hours, days, years
     Driv'n by the spheres
Like a vast shadow mov'd, in which the world
   And all her train were hurl'd;
The doting lover in his quaintest strain
     Did there complain,
Near him his lute, his fancy, and his flights,
     Wit's sour delights,
With gloves and knots, the silly snares of pleasure;
     Yet his dear treasure
All scattered lay, while he his eyes did pore
   Upon a flower.

The darksome statesman, hung with weights and woe,
Like a thick midnight-fog moved there so slow
   He did not stay, nor go;
Condemning thoughts (like sad eclipses) scowl
     Upon his soul,
And clouds of crying witnesses without
   Pursued him with one shout.
Yet digged the mole, and lest his ways be found
     Worked underground,
Where he did clutch his prey, but one did see
     That policy;
Churches and altars fed him, perjuries
     Were gnats and flies,
It rained about him blood and tears, but he
   Drank them as free.

The fearful miser on a heap of rust
Sat pining all his life there, did scarce trust
   His own hands with the dust,
Yet would not place one piece above, but lives
     In fear of thieves.
Thousand there were as frantic as himself
   And hugged each one his pelf,
The downright Epicure placed heaven in sense
     And scorned pretence
While others, slipped into a wide excess,
     Said little less;
The weaker sort slight, trivial wares enslave
   Who think them brave,
And poor, despisèd Truth sat counting by
     Their victory.

Yet some, who all this while did weep and sing,
And sing, and weep, soared up into the *Ring*,
   But most would use no wing.
'O fools' (said I) 'thus to prefer dark night
     Before true light,
To live in grots, and caves, and hate the day
   Because it shows the way,
The way which from this dead and dark abode
     Leads up to God,
A way where you might tread the sun, and be
     More bright than he.'
But as I did their madness so discuss
     One whispered thus:
'*This Ring the Bridegroom did for none provide
     But for his bride.*'

94   *Man*

   Weighing the steadfastness and state
Of some mean things which here below reside,
Where birds like watchful clocks the noiseless date
   And intercourse of times divide,
Where bees at night get home and hive, and flowers
     Early, as well as late,
Rise with the sun, and set in the same bowers,

I would (said I) my God would give
The staidness of these things to man! for these
To his divine appointments ever cleave,
   And no new business breaks their peace;
The birds nor sow nor reap, yet sup and dine,
    The flowers without clothes live,
Yet Solomon was never dressed so fine.

   Man hath still either toys, or care,
He hath no root, nor to one place is tied,
But ever restless and irregular
   About this earth doth run and ride;
He knows he hath a home, but scarce knows where,
    He says it is so far
That he hath quite forgot how to go there.

   He knocks at all doors, strays and roams,
Nay, hath not so much wit as some stones have,
Which in the darkest nights point to their homes
   By some hid sense their Maker gave;
Man is the shuttle, to whose winding quest
    And passage through these looms
God ordered motion, but ordained no rest.

95   *The Waterfall*

With what deep murmurs through time's silent stealth
Doth thy transparent, cool, and watery wealth
       Here flowing fall,
       And chide, and call,
As if his liquid loose retinue stayed
Lingering, and were of this steep place afraid,
       The common pass
       Where, clear as glass,
       All must descend
       Not to an end;
But quickened by this deep and rocky grave,
Rise to a longer course more bright and brave.

    Dear stream, dear bank, where often I
    Have sat, and pleased my pensive eye,

Why, since each drop of thy quick store
Runs thither, whence it flowed before,
Should poor souls fear a shade or night,
Who came, sure, from a sea of light?
Or since those drops are all sent back
So sure to thee, that none doth lack,
Why should frail flesh doubt any more
That what God takes, he'll not restore?
O useful Element and clear!
My sacred wash and cleanser here,
My first consigner unto those
Fountains of life, where the Lamb goes,
What sublime truths, and wholesome themes
Lodge in thy mystical, deep streams!
Such as dull man can never find,
Unless that Spirit lead his mind
Which first upon thy face did move,
And hatched all with his quickening love.
As this loud brook's incessant fall
In streaming rings restagnates all,
Which reach by course the bank, and then
Are no more seen, just so pass men.
O my invisible estate,
My glorious liberty, still late!
Thou art the channel my soul seeks,
Not this with cataracts and creeks.

96 *The Dawning*

Ah! what time wilt thou come? when shall that cry,
　'The Bridegroom's coming!' fill the sky?
　Shall it in the evening run
　When our words and works are done?
　Or will thy all-surprising light
　　Break at midnight,
　When either sleep or some dark pleasure
　Possesseth mad man without measure?
　Or shall these early fragrant hours
　　Unlock thy bowers,
　And with their blush of light descry
　Thy locks crowned with eternity?
　Indeed it is the only time
　That with thy glory doth best chime:

All now are stirring, every field
  Full hymns doth yield,
The whole creation shakes off night,
And for thy shadow looks the light;
Stars now vanish without number,
Sleepy planets set, and slumber,
The pursy clouds disband, and scatter;
All expect some sudden matter,
Not one beam triumphs, but from far
  That morning-star.

O at what time soever thou,
Unknown to us, the heavens wilt bow,
And with thy angels in the van
Descend to judge poor careless man,
Grant, I may not like puddle lie
In a corrupt security
Where, if a traveller water crave,
He finds it dead, and in a grave.
But as this restless vocal spring
All day and night doth run, and sing,
And though here born, yet is acquainted
Elsewhere, and flowing keeps untainted;
So let me all my busy age
In thy free services engage,
And though, while here, of force I must
Have commerce sometimes with poor dust,
And in my flesh, though vile, and low,
As this doth in her channel flow,
Yet let my course, my aim, my love
And chief acquaintance be above;
So when that day and hour shall come
In which thyself will be the sun,
Thou'lt find me dressed and on my way
Watching the break of thy great day.

97   *The Revival*

Unfold, unfold! Take in his light,
Who makes thy cares more short than night.
The joys, which with his day-star rise,
He deals to all but drowsy eyes;

And, what the men of this world miss,
Some drops and dews of future bliss.
   Hark! how his winds have changed their note,
And with warm whispers call thee out.
The frosts are past, the storms are gone,
And backward life at last comes on.
The lofty groves in express joys
Reply unto the turtle's voice,
And here in dust and dirt, O here
The lilies of his love appear!

98   *Corruption*

Sure, it was so. Man in those early days
    Was not all stone, and earth,
He shined a little, and by those weak rays
    Had some glimpse of his birth.
He saw heaven o'er his head, and knew from whence
    He came, condemnèd, hither,
And, as first love draws strongest, so from hence
    His mind sure progressed thither.
Things here were strange unto him: sweat, and till,
    All was a thorn, or weed,
Nor did those last but, like himself, died still
    As soon as they did seed.
They seemed to quarrel with him; for that act
    That felled him, foiled them all.
He drew the curse upon the world, and cracked
    The whole frame with his fall.
This made him long for home, as loath to stay
    With murmurers, and foes;
He sighed for Eden, and would often say,
    'Ah, what bright days were those!'
Nor was Heaven cold unto him; for each day
    The valley, or the mountain
Afforded visits, and still paradise lay
    In some green shade, or fountain.
Angels lay leiger here; each bush, and cell,
    Each oak and highway knew them.
Walk but the fields, or sit down at some well,
    And he was sure to view them.
Almighty love! where art thou now? Mad man
    Sits down, and freezeth on.

He raves, and swears to stir nor fire nor fan,
    But bids the thread be spun.
I see, thy curtains are close-drawn; thy bow
    Looks dim too in the cloud.
Sin triumphs still, and man is sunk below
    The centre, and his shroud;
All's in deep sleep, and night; thick darkness lies
    And hatcheth o'er thy people.
But hark! what trumpet's that? What angel cries
    'Arise! Thrust in thy sickle'?

99   *Religion*

My God, when I walk in those groves
And leaves thy spirit still doth fan,
I see in each shade that there grows
An angel talking with a man.

Under a juniper some house,
Or the cool myrtle's canopy,
Others beneath an oak's green boughs,
Or at some fountain's bubbling eye;

Here Jacob dreams and wrestles; there
Elias by a raven is fed,
Another time by the angel, where
He brings him water with his bread;

In Abraham's tent the wingèd guests
(O how familiar then was heaven!)
Eat, drink, discourse, sit down, and rest
Until the cool and shady even;

Nay, thou thyself, my God, in fire,
Whirlwinds, and clouds, and the soft voice
Speak'st there so much, that I admire
We have no conference in these days.

Is the truce broke? or 'cause we have
A mediator now with thee,
Dost thou therefore old treaties waive
And by appeals from him decree?

Or is't so, as some green heads say,
That now all miracles must cease,
Though thou hast promised they should stay
The tokens of the Church, and peace?

No, no; religion is a spring
That from some secret, golden mine
Derives her birth, and thence doth bring
Cordials in every drop, and wine;

But in her long and hidden course
Passing through the earth's dark veins,
Grows still from better unto worse,
And both her taste and colour stains,

Then drilling on, learns to increase
False echoes, and confusèd sounds,
And unawares doth often seize
On veins of sulphur underground;

So poisoned, breaks forth in some clime,
And at first sight doth many please,
But drunk, is puddle, or mere slime
And 'stead of physic, a disease.

Just such a tainted sink we have
Like that Samaritan's dead well,
Nor must we for the kernel crave
Because most voices like the shell.

Heal then these waters, Lord; or bring thy flock,
Since these are troubled, to the springing rock.
Look down, great Master of the Feast! O shine,
And turn once more our water into wine!

100 *The Night*
(*John 2:3*)

Through that pure Virgin-shrine,
That sacred veil drawn o'er thy glorious noon
That men might look and live as glow-worms shine,
    And face the moon,

123

Wise Nicodemus saw such light
As made him know his God by night.

Most blest believer he!
Who in that land of darkness and blind eyes
Thy long expected healing wings could see
When thou didst rise
And, what can never more be done,
Did at midnight speak with the sun!

O who will tell me, where
He found thee at that dead and silent hour!
What hallowed solitary ground did bear
So rare a flower,
Within whose sacred leaves did lie
The fullness of the deity?

No mercy-seat of gold,
No dead and dusty Cherub, nor carved stone,
But his own living works did my Lord hold
And lodge alone;
Where trees and herbs did watch and peep
And wonder, while the Jews did sleep.

Dear night! this world's defeat;
The stop to busy fools; care's check and curb;
The day of Spirits; my soul's calm retreat
Which none disturb!
Christ's progress, and his prayer time;
The hours to which high heaven doth chime.

God's silent, searching flight;
When my Lord's head is filled with dew, and all
His locks are wet with the clear drops of night;
His still, soft call;
His knocking time; the soul's dumb watch,
When Spirits their fair kindred catch.

Were all my loud, evil days
Calm and unhaunted as is thy dark tent,
Whose peace but by some Angel's wing or voice
Is seldom rent;
Then I in Heaven all the long year
Would keep, and never wander here.

But living where the sun
Doth all things wake, and where all mix and tire
Themselves and others, I consent and run
      To every mire,
  And by this world's ill-guiding light
  Err more than I can do by night.

  There is in God, some say,
A deep, but dazzling darkness; as men here
Say it is late and dusky, because they
      See not all clear.
  O for that night! where I in him
  Might live invisible and dim.

JOHN BUNYAN
1626–1688

101   (*The Pilgrim Song*)

Who would true Valour see,
Let him come hither;
One here will Constant be,
Come Wind, come Weather.
There's no Discouragement
Shall make him once Relent
His first avow'd Intent
To be a Pilgrim.

Whoso beset him round
With dismal Stories,
Do but themselves Confound;
His strength the more is.
No Lyon can him fright,
He'll with a Giant fight,
But he will have a right
To be a Pilgrim.

Hobgoblin, nor foul Fiend,
Can daunt his Spirit:

He knows, he at the end
Shall Life Inherit.
Then Fancies fly away,
He'll fear not what men say,
He'll labour Night and Day
To be a Pilgrim.

URIAN OAKES

1631–1681

102 from *An Elegie upon the Death of the Reverend
Mr Thomas Shepard*

I

Away loose-reined careers of Poetry!
The celebrated Sisters may be gone;
We need no mourning women's elegy,
No forced, affected, artificial tone.
    Great and good *Shepard*'s dead! Ah, this alone
    Will set our eyes abroach, dissolve a stone.

Poetic raptures are of no esteem,
Daring hyperboles have here no place,
Luxuriant wits on such a copious theme
Would shame themselves, and blush to shew their face.
    Here's worth enough to overmatch the skill
    Of the most stately poet-laureate's quill.

Exuberant fancies useless here I deem,
Transcendent virtue scorns feigned elegies;
He that gives *Shepard* half his due may seem,
If strangers hear it, to hyperbolize.
    Let him that can, tell what his virtues were,
    And say: This star moved in no common sphere.

Here need no spices, odours, curious arts,
No skill of Egypt, to embalm the name
Of such a worthy. Let men speak their hearts,
They'll say: He merits an immortal fame.
    When *Shepard* is forgot, all must conclude
    This is prodigious ingratitude.

But live he shall in many a grateful breast,
Where he hath reared himself a monument,
A monument more stately than the best,
On which immensest treasures have been spent.
   Could you but into the hearts of thousands peep,
   There would you read his name engraven deep.

Oh! that my head were waters, and mine eyes
A flowing spring of tears, still issuing forth
In streams of bitterness, to solemnize
The *obits* of this man of matchless worth!
   Next to the tears our sins do need and crave,
   I would bestow my tears on *Shepard*'s grave.

2

We must not with our greatest Sovereign strive.
Who dare find fault with him that is most high,
That hath an absolute prerogative
And doth his pleasure? None may ask him, why.
   We're clay-lumps, dust-heaps, nothings in his sight;
   The Judge of all the Earth doth always right.

Ah! could not prayers and tears prevail with God?
Was there no warding off that dreadful blow?
And was there no averting of that rod?
Must *Shepard* die? and that good angel go?
   Alas! Our heinous sins (more than our hairs)
   It seems were louder, and outcried our prayers.

See what our sins have done! What ruins wrought!
And how they have plucked out our very eyes!
Our sins have slain our *Shepard*! We have bought,
And dearly paid for, our enormities.
   Ah cursèd sins! that strike at God, and kill
   His servants, and the blood of prophets spill.

As you would loathe the sword that's warm and red,
As you would hate the hands that are imbrued
I' th' hearts-blood of your dearest friends, so dread
And hate your sins. Oh! let them be pursued.
   Revenges take on bloody sins; for there's
   No refuge-city for these murderers.

In vain we build the prophets' sepulchres,
In vain bedew their tombs with tears, when dead;
In vain bewail the deaths of ministers
Whilst prophet-killing sins are harbourèd.
  Those that these murderous traitors' favour hide
  Are with the blood of prophets deeply dyed.

New England! Know thy heart-plague; feel this blow,
A blow that sorely wounds both head and heart,
A blow that reaches all, both high and low,
A blow that may be felt in every part.
  Mourn that this great man's fallen in Israel;
  Lest it be said, 'With him New England fell!'

JOHN DRYDEN
1631–1700

103   from *The State of Innocence*
(*1 Predestination and Free Will*)

Adam: Grant Heaven could once have given us liberty;
  Are we not bounded, now, by firm decree,
  Since whatsoe'er is pre-ordained, must be?
  Else Heaven, for man, events might pre-ordain,
  And man's free will might make those orders vain.
Gabriel: The Eternal, when he did the world create,
  All other agents did necessitate:
  So, what he ordered, they by nature do;
  Thus light things mount, and heavy downward go.
  Man only boasts an arbitrary state.
Adam: Yet causes their effects necessitate
  In willing agents: where is freedom then?
  Or who can break the chain which limits men
  To act what is unchangeably forecast,
  Since the first cause gives motion to the last?
Raphael: Heaven by fore-knowing what will surely be,
  Does only, first, effects in causes see;
  And finds, but does not make, necessity.
  Creation, is of power and will the effect,
  Foreknowledge, only of his Intellect;

His prescience makes not, but supposes, things;
Infers necessity to be; not brings.
Thus thou art not constrained to good or ill;
Causes which work the effect, force not the will.

(2 *Death the Consequence of the Fall*)

Adam: O wretched offspring! O unhappy state
    Of all mankind, by me betrayed to fate!
    Born, through my crime, to be offenders first;
    And, for those sins they could not shun, accurst.
Eve: Why is life forced on man; who, might he choose,
    Would not accept what he, with pain, must lose?
    Unknowing, he receives it, and, when known
    He thinks it his, and values it, 'tis gone.
Raphael: Behold of every age: ripe manhood see,
    Decrepit years, and helpless infancy:
    Those who, by lingering sickness, lose their breath;
    And those who, by despair, suborn their death.
    See yon mad fools who, for some trivial right,
    For love, or for mistaken honour, fight.
    See those, more mad, who throw their lives away
    In needless wars: the stakes which monarchs lay
    When for each other's provinces they play.
    Then as if earth too narrow were for fate,
    On open seas their quarrels they debate;
    In hollow wood they floating armies bear,
    And force imprisoned winds to bring 'em near.
Eve: Who would the miseries of man foreknow?
    Not knowing, we but share our part of woe.
    Now, we the fate of future ages bear;
    And ere the birth, behold our dead appear.
Adam: The deaths thou showest are forced and full of strife,
    Cast headlong from the precipice of life.
    Is there no smooth descent? no painless way
    Of kindly mixing with our native clay?
Raphael: There is; but rarely shall that path be trod
    Which, without horror, leads to death's abode.
    Some few, by temperance taught, approaching slow,
    To distant fate by easy journeys go.
    Gently they lay 'em down, as evening sheep
    On their own woolly fleeces softly sleep.

Adam:	So noiseless would I live, such death to find;
	Like timely fruit, not shaken by the wind
	But ripely dropping from the sapless bough,
	And, dying, nothing to myself would owe.
Eve:	Thus, daily changing, with a duller taste
	Of lessening joys I, by degrees, would waste;
	Still quitting ground by unperceived decay,
	And steal myself from life, and melt away.

104   from *Religio Laici*

1

Thus Man by his own strength to Heaven would soar:
And would not be obliged to God for more.
Vain, wretched creature, how art thou misled
To think thy Wit these God-like notions bred!
These truths are not the product of thy mind,
But dropped from Heaven, and of a nobler kind.
Revealed religion first informed thy sight,
And *Reason* saw not till *Faith* sprung the light.
Hence all thy Natural Worship takes the source:
'Tis *Revelation* what thou thinkst *Discourse*.

2

But if there be a *Power* too just and strong
To wink at crimes and bear unpunished wrong,
Look humbly upward, see his will disclose
The forfeit first, and then the fine impose,
A mulct thy poverty could never pay
Had not eternal wisdom found the way
And with cœlestial wealth supplied thy store;
His justice makes the fine, his mercy quits the score.
See God descending in thy human frame;
The offended, suffering in the offender's name.
All thy misdeeds to Him imputed see,
And all His righteousness devolved on thee.

105   ## *The Character of a Good Parson*
         ### *Imitated from Chaucer and Inlarg'd*

A parish-priest was of the pilgrim train;
An awful, reverend, and religious man.
His eyes diffused a venerable Grace,
And Charity itself was in his face.
Rich was his soul, though his attire was poor
(As God had clothed his own ambassador);
For such, on earth, his bless'd Redeemer bore.
Of sixty years he seemed; and well might last
To sixty more, but that he lived too fast;
Refined himself to soul, to curb the sense,
And made almost a sin of abstinence.
Yet had his aspect nothing of severe,
But such a face as promised him sincere.
Nothing reserved or sullen was to see
But sweet regards, and pleasing sanctity;
Mild was his accent, and his action free.
With eloquence innate his tongue was armed;
Though harsh the precept, yet the preacher charmed,
For, letting down the golden chain from high,
He drew his audience upward to the sky,
And oft with holy hymns he charmed their ears
(A music more melodious than the spheres).
For David left him, when he went to rest,
His lyre; and after him he sung the best.
He bore his great commission in his look
But sweetly tempered awe, and softened all he spoke.
He preached the joys of Heaven and pains of Hell,
And warned the sinner with becoming zeal,
But on eternal mercy loved to dwell.
He taught the Gospel rather than the Law
And forced himself to drive, but loved to draw.
For fear but freezes minds; but love, like heat,
Exhales the soul sublime to seek her native seat.
  To threats, the stubborn sinner oft is hard,
Wrapped in his crimes, against the storm prepared;
But when the milder beams of mercy play
He melts, and throws his cumbrous cloak away.
  Lightnings and thunder (Heaven's artillery)
As harbingers before the Almighty fly.
These but proclaim his style, and disappear;

The stiller sound succeeds, and God is there.
　　The tithes his parish freely paid, he took;
But never sued, or cursed with bell and book,
With patience bearing wrong, but offering none,
Since every man is free to lose his own.
The country churls, according to their kind
(Who grudge their dues, and love to be behind),
The less he sought his offerings, pinched the more,
And praised a priest contented to be poor.
　　Yet, of his little, he had some to spare
To feed the famished, and to clothe the bare,
For mortified he was to that degree,
A poorer than himself, he would not see.
True priests, he said, and preachers of the Word,
Were only stewards of their sovereign Lord.
Nothing was theirs, but all the public store
Entrusted riches to relieve the poor
Who, should they steal for want of his relief,
He judged himself accomplice with the thief.
　　Wide was his parish, not contracted close
In streets, but here and there a straggling house;
Yet still he was at hand, without request
To serve the sick, to succour the distressed;
Tempting, on foot, alone, without affright,
The dangers of a dark tempestuous night.
　　All this the good old man performed alone
Nor spared his pains, for curate he had none.
Nor durst he trust another with his care,
Nor rode himself to Paul's, the public fair,
To chaffer for preferment with his gold
Where bishoprics and sinecures are sold;
But duly watched his flock by night and day,
And from the prowling wolf redeemed the prey,
And hungry sent the wily fox away.
　　The proud he tamed, the penitent he cheered,
Nor to rebuke the rich offender feared.
His preaching much, but more his practice, wrought
(A living sermon of the truths he taught);
For this, by rules severe his life he squared
That all might see the doctrine which they heard.
For priests, he said, are patterns for the rest
(The gold of Heaven, who bear the God impressed);
But when the precious coin is kept unclean,

The Sovereign's image is no longer seen.
If they be foul on whom the people trust,
Well may the baser brass contract a rust.
　　The prelate for his holy life he prized,
The worldly pomp of prelacy despised.
His Saviour came not with a gaudy show,
Nor was His Kingdom of the world below.
Patience in want, and poverty of mind,
These marks of Church and Churchmen He designed
And living taught, and dying left behind.
The crown He wore was of the pointed thorn;
In purple He was crucified, not born.
They who contend for place and high degree
Are not His sons, but those of Zebedee.
　　Not but he knew the signs of earthly power
Might well become St Peter's successor.
The Holy Father holds a double reign:
The Prince may keep his pomp; the Fisher must be plain.
　　Such was the Saint, who shone with every grace
Reflecting, Moses-like, his maker's face.
God saw His image lively was expressed;
And His own work, as in Creation, blessed.
　　The Tempter saw him too, with envious eye,
And, as on Job, demanded leave to try.
He took the time when *Richard* was deposed,
And high and low with happy *Harry* closed.
This prince, though great in arms, the priest withstood,
Near though he was, yet not the next of blood.
Had *Richard* unconstrained resigned the throne,
A King can give no more than is his own;
The title stood entailed, had *Richard* had a son.
　　Conquest, an odious name, was laid aside
Where all submitted; none the battle tried.
The senseless plea of right by Providence
Was, by a flattering priest, invented since
And lasts no longer than the present sway,
But justifies the next who comes in play.
　　The People's Right remains: let those who dare
Dispute their power, when they the judges are.
　　He joined not in their choice, because he knew
Worse might, and often did, from change ensue.
Much to himself he thought, but little spoke;
And, undeprived, his benefice forsook.

Now through the land his cure of souls he stretched,
And like a primitive apostle preached,
Still cheerful; ever constant to his call;
By many followed; loved by most, admired by all.
With what he begged, his brethren he relieved,
And gave the charities himself received;
Gave, while he taught; and edified the more
Because he showed, by proof, 'twas easy to be poor.
    He went not with the crowd to see a shrine,
But fed us by the way with food divine.
    In deference to his virtues I forbear
To show you what the rest in orders were.
This brilliant is so spotless and so bright
He needs no foil, but shines by his own proper light.

THOMAS TRAHERNE
?1637–1674

106 *The Salutation*

These little limbs,
    These eyes and hands which here I find,
This panting heart wherewith my life begins,
        Where have ye been? Behind
What curtain were ye from me hid so long?
Where was, in what abyss, my new-made tongue?

        When silent I
    So many thousand thousand years
Beneath the dust did in a *Chaos* lie,
        How could I *Smiles*, or *Tears*,
Or *Lips*, or *Hands*, or *Eyes*, or *Ears* perceive?
Welcome ye treasures which I now receive.

        I that so long
    Was *Nothing* from eternity
Did little think such joys as ear and tongue
        To celebrate or see;
Such sounds to hear, such hands to feel, such feet,
Such eyes and objects, on the ground to meet.

New burnished joys!
Which finest gold and pearl excel!
Such sacred treasures are the limbs of boys
        In which a soul doth dwell;
Their organizèd joints and azure veins
More wealth include than the dead world contains.

        From dust I rise
    And out of Nothing now awake.
These brighter regions which salute mine eyes
        A gift from God I take.
The earth, the seas, the light, the lofty skies,
The sun and stars are mine; if these I prize.

        A stranger here
    Strange things doth meet, strange glory see,
Strange treasures lodg'd in this fair world appear,
        Strange all and new to me;
But that they *mine* should be who Nothing was,
That strangest is of all; yet brought to pass.

107   from *Christian Ethics*

For man to act as if his soul did see
The very brightness of eternity;
For man to act as if his love did burn
Above the spheres, even while it's in its urn;
For man to act even in the wilderness
As if he did those sovereign joys possess
Which do at once confirm, stir up, inflame
And perfect angels—having not the same!
It doth increase the value of his deeds;
In this a man a Seraphim exceeds.
    To act on obligations yet unknown,
To act upon rewards as yet unshown,
To keep commands whose beauty's yet unseen,
To cherish and retain a zeal between
Sleeping and waking, shows a constant care;
And that a deeper love, a love so rare
That no eye-service may with it compare.
    The angels, who are faithful while they view
His glory, know not what themselves would do,

Were they in our estate! A dimmer light
Perhaps would make them err as well as we;
And in the coldness of a darker night
Forgetful and lukewarm themselves might be.
Our very rust shall cover us with gold,
Our dust shall sparkle while their eyes behold
The glory springing from a feeble state,
Where mere belief doth, if not conquer fate,
Surmount, and pass what it doth antedate.

108   Ibid. (*Contentment*)

Contentment is a sleepy thing,
    If it in death alone must die;
A quiet mind is worse than poverty
    Unless it from enjoyment spring!
That's blessedness alone that makes a king
Wherein the joys and treasures are so great
They all the powers of the soul employ,
    And fill it with a work complete,
        While it doth all enjoy.
True joys alone contentment do inspire,
Enrich content, and make our courage higher.
    Content alone's a dead and silent stone:
        The real life of bliss
    Is glory reigning in a throne,
        Where all enjoyment is.
The soul of man is so inclined to see,
Without his treasures no man's soul can be,
    Nor rest content uncrowned!
        Desire and love
Must in the height of all their rapture move,
    Where there is true felicity.
Employment is the very life and ground
Of Life itself, whose pleasant motion is
    The form of Bliss;
All blessedness a life with glory crowned.
Life! life is all: in its most full extent
Stretched out to all things, and with all content!

THOMAS KEN
1637–1711

109   *'Glory to thee, my God, this night'*

Glory to thee, my God, this night
For all the blessings of the light;
Keep me, O keep me, King of kings,
Beneath thy own almighty wings.

Forgive me, Lord, for thy dear Son,
The ill that I this day have done,
That with the world, myself, and thee
I, ere I sleep, at peace may be.

Teach me to live, that I may dread
The grave as little as my bed;
Teach me to die, that so I may
Rise glorious at the awful day.

O may my soul on thee repose,
And with sweet sleep mine eyelids close,
Sleep that may me more vigorous make
To serve my God when I awake.

When in the night I sleepless lie,
My soul with heavenly thoughts supply;
Let no ill dreams disturb my rest,
No powers of darkness me molest.

Praise God, from whom all blessings flow,
Praise him, all creatures here below,
Praise him above, ye heavenly host,
Praise Father, Son, and Holy Ghost.

EDWARD TAYLOR
?1642–1729

110   *Upon a Wasp Chilled with Cold*

The Bear that breathes the northern blast
Did numb, torpedo-like, a wasp
Whose stiffened limbs encramped lay bathing
In Sol's warm breath and shine as saving,

Which with her hands she chafes, and stands
Rubbing her legs, shanks, thighs and hands.
Her petty toes, and fingers' ends
Nipped with this breath, she out extends
Unto the sun, in great desire
To warm her digits at that fire;
Doth hold her temples in this state
Where pulse doth beat, and head doth ache;
Doth turn and stretch her body small;
Doth comb her velvet capital,
As if her little brain-pan were
A volume of choice precepts clear;
As if her satin jacket hot
Contained apothecary's shop
Of Nature's receipts, that prevails
To remedy all her sad ails;
As if her velvet helmet high
Did turret rationality.
She fans her wing up to the wind
As if her petticoat were lined
With reason's fleece, and hoises sails
And humming flies in thankful gales
Unto her dun-curled palace hall,
Her warm thanks offering for all.

Lord, clear my misted sight that I
May hence view thy Divinity;
Some sparks whereof thou up dost hasp
Within this little downy wasp,
In whose small corporation we
A school and a schoolmaster see,
Where we may learn, and easily find
A nimble spirit bravely mind
Her work in every limb, and lace
It up neat with a vital grace,
Acting each part though ne'er so small
Here of this fustian animal;
Till I enravish'd climb into
The Godhead on this ladder do,
Where all my pipes inspir'd upraise
An Heavenly music furred with praise

111   from *Preparatory Meditations Before My*
                  Approach to the Lord's Supper

What love is this of thine, that cannot be
   In thine infinity, O Lord, confined,
Unless it in thy very person see
   Infinity, and finity, conjoined?
    What! Hath thy Godhead, as not satisfied,
    Married our manhood, making it its bride?

Oh, matchless love! Filling Heaven to the brim!
   O'er-running it; all running o'er beside
This world! Nay, overflowing hell, wherein
   For thine elect there rose a mighty tide,
    That there our veins might through thy person bleed
    To quench those flames that else would on us feed!

Oh, that thy love might overflow my heart,
   To fire the same with love! For love I would.
But oh, my straitened breast! My lifeless spark!
   My fireless flame! What, chilly, love, and cold?
    In measure small? In manner chilly? See!
    Lord, blow the coal. Thy love inflame in me.

112   *Ibid.*

   Meditation. Canticles 6:11. 'I went down
      into the Garden of Nuts, to see
      the fruits' etc.

Oh that I was the Bird of Paradise!
   Then in thy nutmeg garden, Lord, thy bower,
Celestial music blossom should my voice,
   Enchanted with thy garden's air and flower.
   This aromatic air would so inspire
   My ravish'd soul to sing with angels' choir.

What is thy church, my Lord, thy garden which
   Doth gain the best of soils? Such spots indeed
Are choicest plots empal'd with palings rich
   And set with slips, herbs best, and best of seed,
   As th' Hanging Gardens rare of Babylon
   And palace garden of King Solomon.

But that which doth excel all gardens here
    Was Eden's garden, Adam's palace bright.
The Tree of Life, and Knowledge too, were there,
    Sweet herbs and sweetest flowers, all sweet delight,
    A Paradise indeed of all perfume
    That to the nose, the eyes and ears doth tune.

But all these artificial gardens bright
    Enamelèd with bravest knots of pinks
And flowers enspangled with black, red and white,
    Compar'd with this are truly stinking sinks.
    As dunghills reek with stinking scents that dish
    Us out, so these, when balancèd with this.

For Zion's Paradise, Christ's garden dear,
    His church, enwalled with heavenly crystal fine,
Hath every bed beset with pearl all clear
    And alleys opal'd with gold, and silver shrine.
    The shining angels are its sentinels
    With flaming sword chanting out madrigals.

The sparkling plants, sweet spices, herbs and trees,
    The glorious shows of aromatic flowers,
The pleasing beauties soak'd in sweet breath lees
    Of Christ's rich garden ever upward towers.
    For Christ sweet showers of Grace makes on it fall.
    It therefore bears the bell away from all.

The nut of ev'ry kind is found to grow big
    With food, and physic, lodg'd within a tower,
A wooden wall with husky coverlid
    Or shell flesh'd o'er, or in an arching bower:
    Beech, hazel, walnut, cocho, almond brave,
    Pistick or chestnut in its prickly cave.

These all as meat and med'cine, emblems choice
    Of spiritual food and physic are, which sport
Up in Christ's garden. Yet the nutmeg's spice
    A leathern coat wears, and a macy shirt,
    Doth far excel them all. Aromatize
    My soul therewith, my Lord, and spiritual-wise.

Oh sweet, sweet Paradise, whose spicèd spring
    Will make the lips of him asleep to tune
Heart-ravishing tunes, sweet music for our king
    In aromatic air of blest perfume,

Open thy garden door. Me entrance give,
And in thy nut-tree garden make me live.

If, Lord, thou ope'st, and in thy garden bring
   Me, then thy linnet sweetly will
Upon thy nut-tree sit and sweetly sing,
   Will crack a nut and eat the kernel still.
     Thou wilt mine eyes, my nose and palate greet
     With curious flowers, sweet odours, viands sweet.

Thy garden's odoriferous air me make
   Suck in and out, to aromatize my lungs,
That I thy garden and its spicy state
   May breathe upon with such ensweetened songs,
     My lungs and breath ensweetened thus shall raise
     The glory of thy garden in its praise.

NAHUM TATE

1652–1715

113   *'While shepherds watched their flocks by night'*

While shepherds watched their flocks by night,
   All seated on the ground,
The angel of the Lord came down,
   And glory shone around.

Fear not! said he; for mighty dread
   Had seized their troubled mind:
Glad tidings of great joy I bring
   To you and all mankind.

To you, in David's town, this day
   Is born, of David's line,
A Saviour, who is Christ the Lord;
   And this shall be the sign:

The heavenly Babe you there shall find
   To human view displayed,
All meanly wrapped in swaddling bands
   And in a manger laid.

Thus spake the seraph; and forthwith
   Appeared a shining throng
Of angels praising God, and thus
   Addressed their joyful song:

All glory be to God on high,
   And to the earth be peace;
Good will henceforth from heaven to men
   Begin and never cease!

MATTHEW PRIOR
1664–1721

114   *On Exodus 3:14. 'I am that I am.'*
              An Ode

Man! Foolish Man!
Scarce know'st thou how thy self began;
Scarce has thou thought enough to prove thou art;
Yet steel'd with study'd boldness, thou dar'st try
To send thy doubting Reason's dazzled eye
Through the mysterious gulf of vast immensity.
Much thou canst there discern, much thence impart.
   Vain wretch! suppress thy knowing pride;
     Mortify thy learned lust:
Vain are thy thoughts, while thou thyself art dust.

Let wit her sails, her oars let wisdom lend;
The helm let politic experience guide:
Yet cease to hope thy short-liv'd bark shall ride
Down spreading Fate's unnavigable tide.
   What, tho' still it farther tend?
   Still 'tis farther from its End;
And in the bosom of that boundless sea,
Still finds its error lengthen with its way.

With daring pride and insolent delight
Your doubts resolv'd you boast, your labours crown'd;
And EUREKA! your God forsooth is found
Incomprehensible and Infinite.

How is He therefore found? Vain searcher! no:
Let your imperfect definition show
That nothing you, the weak definer, know.

Say, why should the collected Main
Itself within itself contain?
Why to its caverns should it sometimes creep,
And with delighted silence sleep
On the lov'd bosom of its parent's deep?
Why should its num'rous waters stay
In comely discipline, and fair array,
Till winds and tides exert their high commands?
Then, prompt and ready to obey,
Why do the rising surges spread
Their op'ning ranks o'er Earth's submissive head,
Marching thro' different paths to different lands?

Why does the constant sun
With measur'd steps his radiant journeys run?
Why does he order the diurnal hours
To leave Earth's other part, and rise in ours?
Why does he wake the correspondent moon,
And fill her willing lamp with liquid light,
Commanding her with delegated pow'rs
To beautify the world, and bless the night?
Why does each animated star
Love the just limits of its proper sphere?
Why does each consenting sign
With prudent harmony combine
In turns to move, and subsequent appear,
To gird the globe, and regulate the year?

Man does with dangerous curiosity
Those unfathom'd wonders try:
With fancied rules and arbitrary laws
Matter and motion he restrains;
And studied lines and fictious circles draws:
Then with imagin'd sovereignty
Lord of his new HYPOTHESIS he reigns.
He reigns: How long? 'till some usurper rise;
And he too, mighty thoughtful, mighty wise,
Studies new lines, and other circles feigns.
From this last toil again what knowledge flows?

Just as much, perhaps, as shows
  That all his predecessor's rules
Were empty cant, all JARGON of the schools;
  That he on t'other's ruin rears his throne;
And shows his friend's mistake, and thence confirms his own.

On earth, in air, amidst the seas and skies,
  Mountainous heaps of wonders rise;
  Whose tow'ring strength will ne'er submit
To Reason's batteries, or the mines of Wit:
Yet still enquiring, still mistaking Man,
Each hour repuls'd, each hour dare onward press;
And levelling at GOD his wandering guess
(That feeble engine of his reasoning war,
Which guides his doubts, and combats his despair),
Laws to his Maker the learn'd wretch can give:
Can bound that Nature, and prescribe that Will,
Whose pregnant Word did either ocean fill:
Can tell us whence all BEINGS are, and how they move and live.
  Thro' either ocean, foolish Man!
  That pregnant Word sent forth again,
Might to a world extend each ATOM there;
For every drop call forth a sea, a heav'n for every star.

Let cunning earth her fruitful wonders hide;
And only lift thy staggering Reason up
To trembling CALVARY's astonished top;
Then mock thy knowledge, and confound thy pride,
Explaining how Perfection suffer'd pain,
Almighty languish'd, and Eternal died:
How by her patient victor Death was slain;
And Earth profaned, yet bless'd, with deicide.
Then down with all thy boasted volumes, down;
  Only reserve the sacred one:
  Low, reverently low,
  Make thy stubborn knowledge bow;
Weep out thy Reason's, and thy body's, eyes;
  Deject thyself, that thou may'st rise;
To look to Heav'n, be blind to all below.

Then Faith, for Reason's glimmering light, shall give
  Her immortal perspective;
And Grace's presence Nature's loss retrieve:
Then thy enliven'd soul shall see

That all the volumes of philosophy,
With all their Comments, never could invent
   So politic an instrument
To reach the Heav'n of Heav'ns, the high abode
Where MOSES places his mysterious God,
As was that ladder which old JACOB rear'd,
When light divine had human darkness clear'd;
And his enlarg'd Ideas found the road
Which Faith had dictated, and angels trod.

JOSEPH ADDISON

1672–1719

115   *Ode*

The spacious firmament on high,
With all the blue ethereal sky,
And spangled heav'ns, a shining frame,
Their great original proclaim:
Th'unwearied sun, from day to day,
Does his creator's power display,
And publishes to every land
The work of an almighty hand.

Soon as the evening shades prevail,
The moon takes up the wondrous tale,
And nightly to the listening earth
Repeats the story of her birth:
Whilst all the stars that round her burn,
And all the planets, in their turn,
Confirm the tidings as they roll,
And spread the truth from pole to pole.

What though, in solemn silence, all
Move round the dark terrestrial ball?
What tho' nor real voice nor sound
Amid their radiant orbs be found?
In reason's ear they all rejoice,
And utter forth a glorious voice,
For ever singing, as they shine,
'The hand that made us is divine.'

ISAAC WATTS
1674–1748

116 *Crucifixion to the World by the Cross of Christ*

(*Galatians 6:14*)

When I survey the wondrous Cross
Where the young Prince of Glory died,
My richest gain I count but loss,
And pour contempt on all my pride.

Forbid it, Lord, that I should boast
Save in the death of Christ, my God;
All the vain things that charm me most,
I sacrifice them to his blood.

See from his head, his hands, his feet,
Sorrow and love flow mingled down;
Did e'er such love and sorrow meet?
Or thorns compose so rich a crown?

His dying crimson like a robe
Spreads o'er his body on the Tree,
Then am I dead to all the globe,
And all the globe is dead to me.

Were the whole realm of nature mine,
That were a present far too small;
Love so amazing, so divine,
Demands my soul, my life, my all.

117 *Submission to Afflictive Providences*

(*Job 1:21*)

Naked as from the earth we came,
    And crept to life at first,
We to the earth return again,
    And mingle with our dust.

The dear delights we here enjoy
  And fondly call our own
Are but short favours borrowed now
  To be repaid anon.

'Tis God that lifts our comforts high,
  Or sinks 'em in the grave.
He gives, and (blessed be his Name)
  He takes but what he gave.

Peace, all our angry passions then!
  Let each rebellious sigh
Be silent at his sovereign will,
  And every murmur die.

If smiling Mercy crown our lives
  Its praises shall be spread,
And we'll adore the Justice too
  That strikes our comforts dead.

118   *Look on him whom they pierced, and mourn*

Infinite grief! amazing woe!
  Behold my bleeding Lord:
Hell and the Jews conspired his death,
  And used the Roman sword.

Oh the sharp pangs of smarting pain
  My dear Redeemer bore,
When knotty whips, and ragged thorns
  His sacred body tore!

But knotty whips and ragged thorns
  In vain do I accuse,
In vain I blame the Roman bands,
  And the more spiteful Jews.

'Twere you, my sins, my cruel sins,
  His chief tormentors were;
Each of my crimes became a nail,
  And unbelief the spear.

'Twere you that pulled the vengeance down
   Upon his guiltless head:
Break, break my heart, oh burst mine eyes,
   And let my sorrows bleed.

Strike, mighty Grace, my flinty soul
   Till melting waters flow,
And deep repentance drown mine eyes
   In undissembled woe.

119   *The Church the Garden of Christ*

We are a Garden wall'd around,
Chosen and made peculiar Ground;
A little Spot inclos'd by Grace
Out of the World's wide Wilderness.

Like Trees of Myrrh and Spice we stand,
Planted by God the Father's Hand;
And all his Springs in Sion flow,
To make the young Plantation grow.

Awake, O heavenly Wind, and come,
Blow on this garden of Perfume;
Spirit Divine, descend and breathe
A gracious Gale on Plants beneath.

Make our best Spices flow abroad
To entertain our Saviour-God:
And faith, and Love, and Joy appear,
And every Grace be active here.

Let my Beloved come, and taste
His pleasant Fruits at his own Feast.
I come, my Spouse, I come, he cries,
With Love and Pleasure in his Eyes.

Our Lord into his Garden comes,
Well pleas'd to smell our poor Perfumes,
And calls us to a Feast divine,
Sweeter than Honey, Milk, or Wine.

Eat of the Tree of Life, my Friends,
The Blessings that my Father sends;
Your Taste shall all my Dainties prove,
And drink abundance of my Love.

Jesus, we will frequent thy Board,
And sing the Bounties of our Lord:
But the rich Food on which we live
Demands more Praise than Tongues can give.

120   *A Prospect of Heaven makes Death easy*

There is a land of pure delight
    Where saints immortal reign;
Infinite day excludes the night,
    And pleasures banish pain.

There everlasting spring abides,
    And never-withering flowers:
Death like a narrow sea divides
    This heavenly land from ours.

Sweet fields beyond the swelling flood
    Stand dressed in living green:
So to the Jews old Canaan stood,
    While Jordan rolled between.

But timorous mortals start and shrink
    To cross this narrow sea,
And linger shivering on the brink
    And fear to launch away.

O could we make our doubts remove,
    These gloomy doubts that rise,
And see the Canaan that we love
    With unbeclouded eyes,

Could we but climb where Moses stood,
    And view the landscape o'er,
Not Jordan's stream, nor Death's cold flood,
    Should fright us from the shore.

Man frail, and God eternal

1

O God, our help in ages past,
    Our hope for years to come,
Our shelter from the stormy blast,
    And our eternal home.

2

Under the shadow of thy throne
    Thy saints have dwelt secure;
Sufficient is thine arm alone,
    And our defence is sure.

3

Before the hills in order stood,
    Or earth receiv'd her frame,
From everlasting thou art God,
    To endless years the same.

4

Thy word commands our flesh to dust,
    'Return, ye sons of men':
All nations rose from earth at first,
    And turn to earth again.

5

A thousand ages in thy sight
    Are like an evening gone;
Short as the watch that ends the night
    Before the rising sun.

6

The busy tribes of flesh and blood,
    With all their lives and cares,
Are carried downwards by thy flood,
    And lost in following years.

7

Time like an ever-rolling stream
    Bears all its sons away;
They fly forgotten as a dream
    Dies at the opening day.

8

Like flowering fields the nations stand
  Pleas'd with the morning light;
The flowers beneath the mower's hand
  Lie withering ere 'tis night.

9

Our God, our help in ages past,
  Our hope for years to come,
Be thou our guard while troubles last,
  And our eternal home.

122   *Hosanna to Christ*

Hosanna to the royal son
  Of David's ancient line!
His natures two, his person one,
  Mysterious and divine.

The root of David, here we find,
  And offspring, are the same:
Eternity and time are joined
  In our Immanuel's name.

Blest he that comes to wretched man
  With peaceful news from Heaven!
Hosannas, of the highest strain,
  To Christ the Lord be given.

Let mortals ne'er refuse to take
  The Hosanna on their tongues,
Lest rocks and stones should rise and break
  Their silence into songs.

123   *The Shortness and Misery of Life*

Our days, alas! our mortal days
  Are short and wretched too;
Evil and few, the patriarch says,
  And well the patriarch knew.

'Tis but at best a narrow bound
 That Heaven allows to men,
And pains and sins run through the round
 Of threescore years and ten.

Well, if ye must be sad and few,
 Run on, my days, in haste.
Moments of sin, and months of woe,
 Ye cannot fly too fast.

Let Heavenly Love prepare my soul
 And call her to the skies,
Where years of long salvation roll,
 And glory never dies.

124   *Miracles at the Birth of Christ*

The King of Glory sends his Son
To make his entrance on this earth;
Behold the midnight bright as noon,
And heavenly hosts declare his birth.

About the young Redeemer's head
What wonders and what glories meet!
An unknown star arose, and led
The eastern sages to his feet.

Simeon and Anna both conspire
The infant-Saviour to proclaim;
Inward they felt the sacred fire,
And blessed the babe, and owned his name.

Let Jews and Greeks blaspheme aloud,
And treat the holy child with scorn;
Our souls adore the eternal God
Who condescended to be born.

125   *'Where-e'er my flatt'ring Passions rove'*

Where-e'er my flatt'ring Passions rove
 I find a lurking snare;
'Tis dangerous to let loose our love
 Beneath th'eternal fair.

Souls whom the tie of friendship binds,
   And partners of our blood,
Seize a large portion of our minds,
   And leave the less for God.

Nature has soft but powerful bands,
   And reason she controls;
While children with their little hands
   Hang closest to our souls.

Thoughtless they act th'old serpent's part;
   What tempting things they be!
Lord, how they twine about our heart,
   And draw it off from thee!

Dear Sovereign, break these fetters off,
   And set our spirits free;
God in himself is bliss enough,
   For we have all in Thee.

126   *The Passion and Exaltation of Christ*

Thus saith the Ruler of the Skies,
   Awake my dreadful Sword;
Awake my Wrath, and smite the Man
   My fellow, saith the Lord.

Vengeance receiv'd the dread command,
   And armèd down she flies,
Jesus submits to his Father's hand,
   And bows his head and dies.

But oh! the Wisdom and the Grace
   That join with Vengeance now!
He dies to save our Guilty Race,
   And yet he rises too.

A Person so divine was he
   Who yielded to be slain,
That he could give his Soul away,
   And take his Life again.

Live, glorious Lord, and reign on high,
    Let every Nation sing,
And Angels sound with endless Joy
    The Saviour and the King.

ISAAC HANN
1690–1778

127 (*After reading the life of Mrs Catherine Stubbs,
    in Isaac Ambrose's 'War with the Devils'*)

Devil! I tell thee without nubbs or jubbs,
Thou wert no match at all for Catherine Stubbs,
And if her God give grace to play the man,
Thou wilt come off as bad with Isaac Hann.
For all the arguments she used shall be
The arguments which he will use with thee:
And when thou canst those arguments repel
He must submit to go with thee to hell;
But while his Saviour God doth live and reign
He is secure—gang off with thy crack'd brain!
God is a sun and shield to every saint,
A cordial to their souls whene'er they faint;
He will give grace and glory we are told
And no good thing will He from them withhold.

JOHN BYROM
1692–1763

128 *A Hymn for Christmas Day*

Christians awake, salute the happy morn
Whereon the Saviour of the world was born;
Rise, to adore the Mystery of Love,
Which hosts of angels chanted from above.
With them the joyful tidings first begun
Of God incarnate and the Virgin's Son.
Then to the watchful shepherds it was told,
Who heard the angelic herald's voice: 'Behold!

JOHN BYROM

I bring good tidings of a Saviour's birth
To you, and all the nations upon earth;
This day hath God fulfilled his promised word;
This day is born a Saviour, Christ, the Lord:
In David's city, Shepherds, ye shall find
The long foretold Redeemer of mankind;
Wrapped up in swaddling clothes, the Babe divine
Lies in a manger; this shall be your sign.'
He spake, and straightway the celestial choir
In hymns of joy, unknown before, conspire.
The praises of redeeming Love they sung,
And Heaven's whole orb with Hallelujahs rung.
God's highest glory was their anthem still;
Peace upon earth, and mutual good will.
To Bethlehem straight the enlightened shepherds ran,
To see the wonder God had wrought for man;
And found, with Joseph and the blessed Maid,
Her Son, the Saviour, in a manger laid.
Amazed, the wondrous story they proclaim,
The first apostles of his infant fame.
While Mary keeps, and ponders in her heart
The heavenly vision, which the swains impart,
They to their flocks, still praising God, return,
And their glad hearts within their bosoms burn.
    Let us, like these good shepherds then, employ
Our grateful voices to proclaim the joy:
Like Mary, let us ponder in our mind
God's wondrous love in saving lost mankind.
Artless, and watchful, as these favoured swains,
While virgin meekness in the heart remains,
Trace we the Babe, who has retrieved our loss,
From his poor manger to his bitter cross;
Treading his steps, assisted by his grace,
Till man's first heavenly state again takes place.
Then may we hope, the angelic thrones among,
To sing, redeemed, a glad triumphal song.
He that was born, upon this joyful day,
Around us all his glory shall display;
Saved by his love, incessant we shall sing
Of angels, and of angel-men, the King.

PHILIP DODDRIDGE

1702–1751

129   *(Christ's Resurrection and Ascension)*

Ye humble souls that seek the Lord,
  Chase all your fears away;
And bow with rapture down to see
  The place where Jesus lay.

Thus low the Lord of Life was brought,
  Such wonders love can do;
Thus cold in death that bosom lay,
  Which throbbed and bled for you.

But raise your eyes and tune your songs;
  The Saviour lives again:
Not all the bolts and bars of death
  The Conqueror could detain.

High o'er the angelic bands He rears
  His once dishonoured head;
And through unnumbered years He reigns,
  Who dwelt among the dead.

With joy like His shall every saint
  His vacant tomb survey;
Then rise with his ascending Lord
  To realms of endless day.

130   *Meditations on the Sepulchre in the Garden*

(John 19:41)

The sepulchres, how thick they stand
Through all the road on either hand!
And burst upon the startling sight
In every garden of delight!

Thither the winding alleys tend;
There all the flowery borders end;
And forms, that charmed the eyes before,
Fragrance, and music are no more.

PHILIP DODDRIDGE

Deep in that damp and silent cell
My fathers and my brethren dwell;
Beneath its broad and gloomy shade
My kindred and my friends are laid.

But, while I tread the solemn way,
My faith that Saviour would survey
Who deigned to sojourn in the tomb,
And left behind a rich perfume.

My thoughts with extasy unknown,
While from his grave they view his throne,
Through mine own sepulchre can see
A paradise reserved for me.

CHARLES WESLEY
1707–1788

131   *'Love Divine, all loves excelling'*

Love Divine, all loves excelling,
    Joy of heaven, to earth come down,
Fix in us thy humble dwelling,
    All thy faithful mercies crown.
Jesu, thou art all compassion,
    Pure unbounded love thou art;
Visit us with thy salvation,
    Enter every trembling heart.

Breathe, O breathe thy loving Spirit
    Into every troubled breast,
Let us all in thee inherit,
    Let us find that second rest:
Take away our power of sinning,
    Alpha and Omega be,
End of faith as its beginning,
    Set our hearts at liberty.

Come, almighty to deliver,
    Let us all thy life receive;
Suddenly return, and never,
    Never more thy temples leave.

Thee we would be always blessing,
　　Serve thee as thy hosts above,
Pray, and praise thee without ceasing,
　　Glory in thy perfect love.

Finish then thy New Creation,
　　Pure and spotless let us be;
Let us see thy great salvation
　　Perfectly restored in thee,
Changed from glory into glory
　　Till in heaven we take our place,
Till we cast our crowns before thee,
　　Lost in wonder, love, and praise!

132　　　　　　　*Free Grace*

And can it be, that I should gain
　　An interest in the Saviour's blood?
Died he for me, who caused his pain,
　　For me, who him to death pursued?
Amazing Love! How can it be
That thou, my God, shouldst die for me?

'Tis Mystery all! the Immortal dies!
　　Who can explore his strange design?
In vain the first-born seraph tries
　　To sound the depths of Love divine.
'Tis Mercy all! Let earth adore;
Let angel minds enquire no more.

He left his Father's throne above,
　　(So free, so infinite his Grace!)
Emptied himself of all but Love,
　　And bled for Adam's helpless race:
'Tis Mercy all, immense and free!
For, O my God, it found out me!

Long my imprisoned spirit lay,
　　Fast bound in sin and nature's night.
Thine eye diffused a quickening ray;
　　I woke; the dungeon flamed with light;

My chains fell off, my heart was free,
I rose, went forth, and followed thee.

Still the small inward voice I hear
    That whispers all my sins forgiven;
Still the atoning blood is near
    That quenched the wrath of hostile heaven.
I feel the life his wounds impart;
I feel my Saviour in my heart.

No condemnation now I dread.
    Jesus, and all in him, is mine;
Alive in him, my living Head,
    And clothed in Righteousness divine,
Bold I approach the eternal throne,
And claim the crown, through Christ, my own.

133   *'O thou Eternal Victim slain'*

O thou Eternal Victim slain
A sacrifice for guilty man,
By the Eternal Spirit made
An offering in the sinner's stead;
Our everlasting Priest art thou,
And plead'st thy death for sinners now.

Thy Offering still continues new,
The vesture keeps its bloody hue,
Thou stand'st the ever-slaughter'd Lamb,
Thy Priesthood still remains the same,
Thy years, O God, can never fail,
Thy goodness is unchangeable.

O that our faith may never move,
But stand unshaken as thy love!
Sure evidence of things unseen,
Now let it pass the years between,
And view thee bleeding on the Tree,
My God, who dies for me, for me.

(*The Incarnation*)

Glory be to God on high,
   And Peace on Earth descend:
God comes down: He bows the Sky:
   He shows himself our Friend!
God th'Invisible *appears*,
   God the Blest, the Great I AM
Sojourns in this Vale of Tears,
And JESUS is his Name.

Him the Angels all ador'd
   Their Maker and their King:
Tidings of their Humbled LORD
   They now to Mortals bring:
Emptied of his Majesty,
   Of His dazzling Glories shorn,
Beings Source *begins to* BE
   And GOD himself is BORN!

See th'Eternal Son of GOD
   A Mortal Son of Man,
Dwelling in an Earthly Clod
   Whom Heaven cannot contain!
Stand amaz'd ye Heavens at This!
   See the LORD of Earth and Skies
Humbled to the Dust He is,
   And in a Manger lies!

We the Sons of Men rejoice,
   The Prince of Peace proclaim,
With Heaven's Host lift up our Voice,
   And shout *Immanuel*'s Name;
Knees and Hearts to Him we bow;
   Of our Flesh, and of our Bone
JESUS is our Brother now,
   And GOD is All our own!

135   from *The Horrible Decree*

Sinners, abhor the Fiend,
His *other* Gospel hear:
The God of Truth did not intend
The Thing his Words declare,
He offers Grace to All,
Which most cannot embrace
Mock'd with an ineffectual Call
And insufficient Grace.

The righteous God consign'd
Them over to their Doom,
And sent the Saviour of Mankind
To damn them from the Womb;
To damn for falling short
Of what they could not do,
For not believing the Report
Of that which was not true.

The God of Love pass'd by
The most of those that fell,
Ordain'd poor Reprobates to die,
And forc'd them into Hell.
He did not do the deed
(Some have more mildly rav'd,)
He did not damn *them—but decreed*
They never should be saved.

He did not them bereave
Of life, or stop their breath,
His Grace He only would not give,
And starv'd their Souls to Death.
Satanick Sophistry!
But still All-gracious God,
They charge the Sinner's Death on Thee,
Who bought'st him with thy Blood.

They think with Shrieks and Cries
To please the Lord of Hosts,
And offer Thee, in Sacrifice
Millions of slaughter'd Ghosts:

With New-born Babes they fill
The dire infernal Shade,
For such they say, was thy Great Will,
Before the World was made.

How long, O God, how long
Shall Satan's Rage proceed?
Wilt Thou not soon avenge the Wrong,
And crush the Serpent's Head?
Surely Thou shalt at last
Bruise him beneath our Feet:
The Devil, and his Doctrine, cast
Into the burning Pit.

Arise, O God, arise,
Thy glorious Truth maintain,
Hold forth the Bloody Sacrifice
For every Sinner slain!
Defend thy Mercy's Cause,
Thy Grace divinely free,
Lift up the Standard of thy Cross,
Draw all Men unto Thee.

136   (*During his Courtship*)

Christ, my Life, my Only Treasure,
Thou alone
Mould thine own,
After thy Good pleasure.

Thou, who paidst my Price, direct me!
Thine I am,
Holy Lamb,
Save, and always save me.

Order Thou my whole Condition,
Chuse my State,
Fix my Fate
By thy wise Decision.

From all Earthly Expectation
Set me free,
Seize for Thee
All my Strength of Passion.

Into absolute Subjection
  Be it brought,
  Every Thought,
Every fond Affection.

That which most my Soul requires
  For thy sake
  Hold it back
Purge my Best Desires.

Keep from me thy loveliest Creature,
  Till I prove
  JESUS' Love
Infinitely sweeter;

Till with purest Passion panting
  Cries my Heart
  'Where Thou art
Nothing more is wanting.'

Blest with thine Abiding Spirit,
  Fully blest
  Now I rest,
All in Thee inherit.

Heaven is now with Jesus given;
  Christ in me,
  Thou shalt be
Mine Eternal Heaven.

137   (*For his Wife, on her Birthday*)

    Come away to the skies,
    My beloved arise,
  And rejoice on the day thou wast born,
    On the festival day
    Come exulting away,
  To thy heavenly country return.

    We have laid up our love
    And treasure above,
  Though our bodies continue below;
    The redeem'd of the Lord
    We remember his word,
  And with singing to Sion we go.

With singing we praise
The original grace
By our heavenly Father bestow'd,
Our being receive
From his bounty, and live
To the honour and glory of God.

For thy glory we are,
Created to share
Both the nature and kingdom divine:
Created again
That our souls may remain
In time and eternity thine.

With thanks we approve
The design of thy love
Which hath join'd us, in Jesus his name,
So united in heart,
That we never can part,
Till we meet at the feast of the Lamb.

There, there at his seat
We shall suddenly meet,
And be parted in body no more,
We shall sing to our lyres
With the heavenly quires,
And our Saviour in glory adore.

Hallelujah we sing
To our Father and King,
And his rapturous praises repeat;
To the Lamb that was slain
Hallelujah again
Sing all heaven, and fall at his feet.

In assurance of hope
We to Jesus look up,
Till his banner unfurl'd in the air
From our grave we both see,
And cry out IT IS HE,
And fly up to acknowledge him there!

138   *(On the Death of his Son)*

Dead! dead! the Child I lov'd so well!
    Transported to the world above!
I need no more my heart conceal.
    I never dar'd indulge my love;
But may I not indulge my grief,
And seek in tears a sad relief?

Mine earthly happiness is fled,
    His mother's joy, his father's hope,
(O had I dy'd in *Isaac*'s stead!)
    He *should* have liv'd, my age's prop,
He should have clos'd his father's eyes,
And follow'd me to paradise.

But hath not heaven, who first bestowed,
    A right to take his gifts away?
I bow me to the sovereign GOD,
    Who snatched him from the evil day!
Yet nature *will* repeat her moan,
And fondly cry, 'My son, my son!'

Turn from him, turn, officious thought!
    Officious thought presents again
The thousand little acts he wrought,
    Which wound my heart with soothing pain:
His looks, his winning gestures rise,
His waving hands, and laughing eyes!

Those waving hands no more shall move,
    Those laughing eyes shall smile no more:
He cannot now engage our love,
    With sweet insinuating power
Our weak unguarded hearts insnare,
And rival his Creator there.

From us, as we from him, secure,
    Caught to his heavenly Father's breast,
He waits, till we the bliss insure,
    From all these stormy sorrows rest,
And see him with our Angel stand,
To waft, and welcome us to land.

139 (*On Sympathisers with the American Revolution*)

What hope of safety for our Realm,
From men who by destruction thrive,
By violence seize the shatter'd Helm,
And madly let the Vessel drive,
Till dash'd against the rocks it break
And then they gather up the wreck.

Makers of wrecks, a desperate race
Who treason and rebellion love,
Who spit in a mild Monarch's face,
Can they the public ills remove
Or, plung'd themselves in depths of vice,
Assist our sinking State to rise?

Proud, profligate, to evil sold,
Their Country's curse, reproach, and shame,
Their lust of power, and thirst of gold
Cloaking beneath the patriot's name,
Shall These our liberties defend,
Shall These, who caus'd, our troubles end?

Who their own Countrymen destroy'd,
Kindled and fed Rebellion's fire,
And all their hellish arts employ'd
To raise the civil discord higher,
Will These restore our happiness
Or give us back a lasting peace?

Order and government they scorn,
Forbid the slighted laws to reign,
And while their injur'd King they spurn,
The Rabble's Majesty maintain,
Those abject instruments of ill,
Those tools of every tyrant's will.

First for themselves the Patriots care,
And each sincerely seeks his own,
Eager the public spoils to share,
(Now they have pull'd their Rivals down)
And all into their hands to seize,
The meed of prosperous wickedness.

Thro' avarice and ambition blind,
  Their schemes, bewilder'd, they pursue,
Grasping at what they cannot find,
  Still undetermin'd what to do,
Till some superior Fiend appear,
And claim the Sovereign Character.

Daring as Charles's spurious brood,
  Hardened as Wilkes in wickedness,
As dissolute as Fox and lewd,
  Worthy of the Protector's place,
Worthy the Place by right his own
When Cromwell fills a burning throne.

Such is the crooked Statesman's hire,
  The Traitors who their Country sell,
Or in Rebellion's cause expire,
  They claim the hottest place in hell,
Unless the Saviour interpose,
To snatch them from eternal woes.

Saviour, the human Fiends convince,
  Persuade them from their sins to part,
And when they cast away their sins
  And turn to Thee with all their heart,
O let them all thy love receive,
And saved, with us, for ever live!

140   *Wrestling Jacob*

Come, O thou Traveller unknown
  Whom still I hold, but cannot see,
My company before is gone,
  And I am left alone with thee,
With thee all night I mean to stay,
And wrestle till the break of day.

I need not tell thee who I am,
  My misery, or sin declare,
Thyself hast called me by my name,
  Look on thy hands, and read it there,
But who, I ask thee, who art thou?
Tell me thy name, and tell me now.

In vain thou strugglest to get free,
  I never will unloose my hold:
Art thou the Man that died for me?
  The secret of thy love unfold.
Wrestling I will not let thee go,
Till I thy name, thy nature know.

Wilt thou not yet to me reveal
  Thy new, unutterable name?
Tell me, I still beseech thee, tell;
  To know it now resolved I am.
Wrestling I will not let thee go,
Till I thy name, thy nature know.

'Tis all in vain to hold thy tongue,
  Or touch the hollow of my thigh:
Though every sinew be unstrung,
  Out of my arms thou shalt not fly.
Wrestling I will not let thee go,
Till I thy name, thy nature know.

What though my shrinking flesh complain,
  And murmur to contend so long,
I rise superior to my pain,
  When I am weak then I am strong,
And when my all of strength shall fail,
I shall with the God-Man prevail.

My strength is gone, my nature dies,
  I sink beneath thy weighty hand,
Faint to revive, and fall to rise;
  I fall, and yet by faith I stand,
I stand, and will not let thee go,
Till I thy name, thy nature know.

Yield to me now—for I am weak;
  But confident in self-despair:
Speak to my heart, in blessings speak,
  Be conquered by my instant prayer,
Speak, or thou never hence shalt move,
And tell me, if thy name is Love.

'Tis Love, 'tis Love! Thou died'st for me,
 I hear thy whisper in my heart.
The morning breaks, the shadows flee:
 Pure Universal Love thou art;
To me, to all, thy bowels move,
Thy nature and thy name is Love.

My prayer hath power with God; the Grace
 Unspeakable I now receive,
Through Faith I see thee face to face,
 I see thee face to face, and live:
In vain I have not wept, and strove,
Thy nature and thy name is Love.

I know thee, Saviour, who thou art,
 Jesus, the feeble sinner's friend;
Nor wilt thou with the night depart,
 But stay, and love me to the end;
Thy mercies never shall remove,
Thy nature and thy name is Love.

The Sun of Righteousness on me
 Hath rose with healing in his wings.
Withered my nature's strength; from thee
 My soul its life and succour brings,
My help is all laid up above;
Thy nature and thy name is Love.

Contented now upon my thigh
 I halt, till life's short journey end;
All helplessness, all weakness I
 On thee alone for strength depend,
Nor have I power from thee to move;
Thy nature and thy name is Love.

Lame as I am, I take the prey,
 Hell, earth and sin with ease o'ercome;
I leap for joy, pursue my way,
 And as a bounding hart fly home,
Through all eternity to prove
Thy nature and thy name is Love.

141 ## *The Whole Armour of God*

Soldiers of Christ, arise
And put your Armour on,
Strong in the Strength which God supplies
Thro' his Eternal Son;
Strong in the Lord of Hosts,
And in his mighty Power,
Who in the Strength of Jesus trusts
Is more than Conqueror.

Stand then in His great Might,
With all his Strength endu'd,
And take, to arm you for the Fight,
The Panoply of God;
That having all Things done,
And all your Conflicts past,
Ye may o'ercome thro' Christ alone,
And stand entire at last.

Stand then against your Foes,
In close and firm Array,
Legions of wily Fiends oppose
Throughout the Evil Day;
But meet the Sons of Night,
But mock their vain Design,
Arm'd in the Arms of Heavenly Light
And Righteousness Divine.

Leave no Unguarded Place,
No Weakness of the Soul,
Take every Virtue, every Grace,
And fortify the Whole;
Indissolubly join'd,
To Battle all proceed,
But arm yourself with all the Mind
That was in Christ your Head.

Let Truth the Girdle be
That binds your Armour on,
In Faithful firm Sincerity
To Jesus cleave alone;

Let Faith and Love combine
To guard your Valiant Breast,
The Plate be Righteousness Divine,
Imputed and Imprest.

Still let your Feet be shod,
Ready His Will to do,
Ready in all the Ways of God
His Glory to pursue:
Ruin is spread beneath,
The Gospel Greaves put on,
And safe thro' all the Snares of Death
To Life Eternal run.

But above all, lay hold
On Faith's victorious Shield,
Arm'd with that Adamant and Gold
Be sure to win the Field;
If Faith surround your Heart,
Satan shall be subdu'd,
Repell'd his ev'ry Fiery Dart
And quench'd with Jesu's Blood.

Jesus hath died for You!
What can his Love withstand?
Believe; hold fast your Shield; and who
Shall pluck you from His Hand?
Believe that Jesus reigns,
All Power to Him is giv'n,
Believe, 'till freed from Sin's Remains,
Believe yourselves to Heaven.

Your Rock can never shake:
Hither, He saith, come up!
The Helmet of Salvation take,
The Confidence of Hope:
Hope for His Perfect Love,
Hope for His People's Rest,
Hope to sit down with Christ above
And share the Marriage Feast.

Brandish in Faith 'till then
The Spirit's two-edg'd Sword,

Hew all the Snares of Fiends and Men
   In Pieces with the Word;
    'TIS WRITTEN. This applied
   Baffles their Strength and Art;
Spirit and Soul with this divide,
   And Joints and Marrow part.

   To keep your Armour bright
   Attend with constant Care,
Still walking in your Captain's Sight,
   And watching unto Prayer;
   Ready for all Alarms,
   Stedfastly set your Face,
And always exercise your Arms,
   And use your every Grace.

   Pray, without ceasing pray,
   (Your Captain gives the Word)
His Summons chearfully obey,
   And call upon the Lord;
   To God your every Want
   In Instant Prayer display,
Pray always; pray, and never faint;
   Pray, without ceasing Pray.

   In Fellowship; alone
   To God with Faith draw near,
Approach His Courts, besiege His Throne
   With all the power of Prayer:
   Go to His Temple, go,
   Nor from His Altar move;
Let every House His Worship know,
   And every Heart His Love.

   To God your Spirits dart,
   Your Souls in Words declare,
Or groan, to Him who reads the Heart,
   Th'unutterable Prayer.
   His Mercy now implore,
   And now shew forth His Praise,
In Shouts, or silent Awe, adore
   His Miracles of Grace.

Pour out your Souls to God,
　And bow them with your Knees,
And spread your Hearts and Hands abroad
　And pray for *Sion's* Peace;
　Your Guides and Brethren, bear
　For ever on your Mind;
Extend the Arms of mighty Prayer
　Ingrasping all Mankind.

From Strength to Strength go on,
　Wrestle, and fight, and pray,
Tread all the Powers of Darkness down,
　And win the well-fought Day;
　Still let the Spirit cry
　In all His Soldiers, 'Come'
Till Christ the Lord descends from High
　And takes the Conqu'rors Home.

CHRISTOPHER SMART

1722–1771

142　　　*Psalm 147. 'Praise ye the Lord'*

HOSANNA—musick is divine,
When in the praise the psalmists join,
　And each good heart is warm;
Yea, joy is sweetest so renew'd,
And all the rites of gratitude
　Are rapture to perform.

The Lord fair Salem shall replace,
And set upon his ancient base
　Hananiel's goodly tow'r;
Make captives free, the barren big,
And under his own vine and fig
　All Jacob re-embow'r.

He shall the broken heart repair,
And for all sickness and despair
　A cure in Christ provide;
And heal the wounded and the bruis'd,

His oil into their sores infus'd,
  And soothing balm applied.

Tho' their bright swarms the sand surpass,
Of every magnitude and class
  He knows th'ethereal flames;
The numb'rer of their host is He,
And to his summons 'here we be',
  They answer by their names.

For God is magnitude immense,
His prowess is omnipotence
  That knows no date or end;
His wisdom infinitely great,
And all duration, depth and height,
  His mysteries transcend.

The Lord with approbation sees
The meek, and from his faithful knees
  He lifts him up on high;
But spurns the sinner and unjust,
And leaves low luxury and lust
  To worms that never die.

Sing praises all degrees and ranks,
As in the pray'r of general thanks
  The holy church commune;
As to the touch the harp revives,
Sing praises with your lips and lives
  To Christ the word and tune.

He the blue heav'n in beauty shrouds,
And balances the plumy clouds
  Which for the rain he wrings;
He causes the mild dew to drop,
And grass upon the mountain top
  In tufted verdure springs.

For every thing that moves and lives,
Foot, fin, or feather meat he gives,
  He deals the beasts their food
Both in the wilderness and stall,
And hears the raven's urgent call,
  And stills her clam'rous brood.

And yet his maker has no need
Of the train'd ox, or prancing steed,
 Tho' thunder cloath his chest;
And man that manages the rein,
Is but a creature brief and vain
 With such proportion blest.

But God is pleas'd with duteous fear,
Men with clean hands and conscience clear,
 Which at thy mercy-gate
With ceaseless application knock,
And patient on him as their rock
 For sure redemption wait.

O Sion, praise the Lord, and thou,
Fair Salem, to his praises bow
 Thine olives and thy palms;
Are there afflicted? let them pray,
But mirth shall dedicate her day
 To hymns and festive psalms.

For by his might the Lord supports
Thy mounds, and fortifies thy forts,
 Thy brazen bars he nails;
Thy sportive children fill the streets,
Thy foe without the wall retreats,
 Nor want within prevails.

He sheathes the sword and blunts the spears,
And thy redoubtable frontiers
 Barbarian inroads scorn;
That thou may'st in thy peace possess
The blessings of a social mess,
 And flour of choicest corn.

He sends his word upon the earth
To call conception into birth,
 And kind with kind to match;
And to sustain all human race,
The blessed angels of his grace
 Make infinite dispatch.

His snow upon the ground he teems,
Like bleaching wool beside the streams,
　To warm the tender blade;
Like ashes from the furnace cast,
His frost comes with the northern blast
　To pinch and to pervade.

Like vitreous fragments o'er the field,
In ice the waters are congeal'd,
　Their liquid swiftness lost;
The breath steams on the sharpen'd air,
And who so hardy as to bear
　The quickness of his frost!

He sends the word of his command
To melt and loosen all the land,
　And let the floods at large;
He blows, and with the genial breeze,
The fount and river by degrees
　Their usual tale discharge.

His word to Jacob he disclos'd,
When he upon the stones repos'd
　And worship'd in a trance;
And laws to Israel enjoin'd
When o'er the nations of mankind
　He bade his tribes advance.

Such wond'rous love has not been shown,
But to the patriarch's seed alone
　His duty to requite;
And judgements on the rest impend,
Till Jesus make them comprehend
　His ways, his truth and light.

143　from *Hymns and Spiritual Songs for the Fasts and Festivals of the Church of England*

Hymn 3
Epiphany

GRACE, thou source of each perfection,
　Favour from the height thy ray;
Thou the star of all direction,
　Child of endless truth and day.

CHRISTOPHER SMART

Thou that bidst my cares be calmer,
　Lectur'd what to seek and shun,
Come, and guide a western palmer
　To the Virgin and her Son.

Lo! I travel in the spirit,
　On my knees my course I steer
To the house of might and merit
　With humility and fear.

Poor at least as John or Peter
　I my vows alone prefer;
But the strains of love are sweeter
　Than the frankincense and myrrh.

Neither purse nor scrip I carry,
　But the books of life and pray'r;
Nor a staff my foe to parry,
　'Tis the cross of Christ I bear.

From a heart serene and pleasant
　'Midst unnumber'd ills I feel,
I will meekly bring my present,
　And with sacred verses kneel.

Muse, through Christ the Word, inventive
　Of the praise so greatly due;
Heav'nly gratitude retentive
　Of the bounties ever new,

Fill my heart with genuine treasures,
　Pour them out before his feet,
High conceptions, mystic measures,
　Springing strong and flowing sweet.

Come, ye creatures of thanksgiving,
　Which are harmoniz'd to bless,
Birds that warble for your living,
　Beasts with ways of love express.

Thou the shepherd's faithful fellow,
　As he lies by Cedron's stream,
Where soft airs and waters mellow
　Take their Saviour for their theme;

Thou too gaily grave domestic,
   With whose young fond childhood plays,
Held too mean for verse majestic,
   First with me thy Maker praise.

Brousing kids, and lambkins grazing,
   Colts and younglings of the drove,
Come with all your modes of praising,
   Bounding through the leafless grove.

Ye that skill the flow'rs to fancy,
   And in just assemblage sort,
Pluck the primrose, pluck the pansy,
   And your prattling troop exhort:

'Little men, in Jesus mighty,
   And ye maids that go alone,
Bodies chaste, and spirits flighty,
   Ere the world and guilt are known,

'Breath so sweet, and cheeks so rosy—
   Put your little hands to pray,
Take ye ev'ry one a posy,
   And away to Christ, away.' –

Youth, benevolence, and beauty,
   In your Saviour's praise agree,
Which this day receives our duty,
   Sitting on the virgin's knee;

That from this day's institution
   Ev'ry penitent in deed,
At his hour of retribution,
   As a child, through him may speed.

144   # Hymn 13
St Philip and St James

Now the winds are all composure,
   But the breath upon the bloom,
Blowing sweet o'er each inclosure,
   Grateful off'rings of perfume.

CHRISTOPHER SMART

Tansy, calaminth and daisies,
　　On the river's margin thrive;
And accompany the mazes
　　Of the stream that leaps alive.

Muse, accordant to the season,
　　Give the numbers life and air;
When the sounds and objects reason
　　In behalf of praise and pray'r.

All the scenes of nature quicken,
　　By the genial spirit fann'd;
And the painted beauties thicken
　　Colour'd by the master's hand.

Earth her vigour repossessing
　　As the blasts are held in ward;
Blessing heap'd and press'd on blessing,
　　Yield the measure of the Lord.

Beeches, without order seemly,
　　Shade the flow'rs of annual birth,
And the lily smiles supremely
　　Mention'd by the Lord on earth.

Cowslips seize upon the fallow,
　　And the cardamine in white,
Where the corn-flow'rs join the mallow,
　　Joy and health, and thrift unite.

Study sits beneath her arbour,
　　By the bason's glossy side;
While the boat from out its harbour
　　Exercise and pleasure guide.

Pray'r and praise be mine employment,
　　Without grudging or regret;
Lasting life, and long enjoyment,
　　Are not here, and are not yet.

Hark! aloud, the black-bird whistles,
　　With surrounding fragrance blest,
And the goldfinch in the thistles
　　Makes provision for her nest.

Ev'n the hornet hives his honey,
　　Bluecap builds his stately dome,
And the rocks supply the coney
　　With a fortress and an home.

But the servants of their Saviour,
　　Which with gospel peace are shod,
Have no bed but what the paviour
　　Makes them in the porch of God.

O thou house that hold'st the charter
　　Of salvation from on high,
Fraught with prophet, saint, and martyr,
　　Born to weep, to starve and die!

Great today thy song and rapture
　　In the choir of Christ and WREN
When two prizes were the capture
　　Of the hand that fish'd for men.

To the man of quick compliance
　　Jesus call'd, and Philip came;
And began to make alliance
　　For his master's cause and name.

James, of title most illustrious,
　　Brother of the Lord, allow'd;
In the vineyard how industrious,
　　Nor by years nor hardship bow'd!

Each accepted in his trial,
　　One the CHEERFUL one the JUST;
Both of love and self-denial,
　　Both of everlasting trust.

Living they dispens'd salvation,
　　Heav'n-endow'd with grace and pow'r;
And they dy'd in imitation
　　Of their Saviour's final hour,

Who, for cruel traitors pleading,
　　Triumph'd in his parting breath;
O'er all miracles preceding
　　His inestimable death.

145

Hymn 14

The Ascension of Our Lord Jesus Christ

'AND other wond'rous works were done
    No mem'ry can recall;
Which were they number'd every one,
Not all the space beneath the sun
    Cou'd hold the fair detail of all.'

The text is full, and strong to do
    The glorious subject right;
But on the working mind's review
The letter's like the spirit true,
    And clear and evident as light.

For not a particle of space
    Where'er his glory beam'd,
With all the modes of site and place,
But were the better for his grace,
    And up to higher lot redeem'd.

For all the motley tribe that pair,
    And to their cover skim,
Became his more immediate care,
The raven urgent in his pray'r,
    And those that make the woodland hymn.

For every creature left at will
    The howling WASTE to roam,
Which live upon the blood they spill,
From his own hands receive their fill,
    What time the desert was his home.

They knew him well, and could not err,
    To him they all appeal'd;
The beast of sleek or shaggy fur,
And found their natures to recur
    To what they were in Eden's field.

For all that dwell in depth or wave,
    And ocean—every drop—
Confess'd his mighty pow'r to save,
When to the floods his peace he gave,
    And bade careering whirlwinds stop.

And all things meaner from the worm
    Probationer to fly;
To him that creeps his little term,
And countless rising from the sperm
    Shed by sea-reptiles, where they ply.

These all were bless'd beneath his feet,
    Approaching them so near;
Vast flocks that have no mouths to bleat,
With yet a spirit to intreat,
    And in their rank divinely dear.

For on some special good intent,
    Advancement or relief,
Or some great evil to prevent,
Or some perfection to augment,
    He held his life of tears and grief.

'Twas his the pow'rs of hell to curb,
    And men possess'd to free;
And all the blasting fiends disturb
From seed of bread, from flow'r and herb,
    From fragrant shrub and stately tree.

The song can never be pursu'd
    When Infinite's the theme—
For all to crown, and to conclude,
He bore and bless'd ingratitude,
    And insult in its worst extreme.

And having then such deeds achiev'd
    As never man before,
From scorn and cruelty repriev'd,
In highest heav'n he was receiv'd,
    To reign with God for evermore.

146   Hymn 32

The Nativity of Our Lord and Saviour Jesus Christ

WHERE is this stupendous stranger,
    Swains of Solyma, advise,
Lead me to my Master's manger,
    Show me where my Saviour lies?

CHRISTOPHER SMART

O MOST Mighty!   O MOST HOLY!
   Far beyond the seraph's thought,
Art thou then so mean and lowly
   As unheeded prophets taught?

O the magnitude of meekness!
   Worth from worth immortal sprung;
O the strength of infant weakness,
   If eternal is so young!

If so young and thus eternal,
   Michael tune the shepherd's reed,
Where the scenes are ever vernal,
   And the loves be love indeed!

See the God blasphem'd and doubted
   In the schools of Greece and Rome;
See the pow'rs of darkness routed,
   Taken at their utmost gloom.

Nature's decorations glisten
   Far above their usual trim;
Birds on box and laurels listen,
   As so near the cherubs hymn.

Boreas now no longer winters
   On the desolated coast;
Oaks no more are riv'n in splinters
   By the whirlwind and his host.

Spinks and ouzles sing sublimely,
   'We too have a Saviour born,'
Whiter blossoms burst untimely
   On the blest Mosaic thorn.

God all-bounteous, all-creative,
   Whom no ills from good dissuade,
Is incarnate, and a native
   Of the very world he made.

CHRISTOPHER SMART

147 from *Hymns for the Amusement of Children*
Hymn 9
Moderation

1
THO' I my party long have chose,
And claim Christ Jesus on my side,
Yet will I not my peace oppose,
By pique, by prejudice, or pride.

2
Blessed be God, that at the font
My sponsors bound me to the call
Of Christ, in England, to confront
The world, the flesh, the fiend and all.

3
And yet I will my thoughts suppress,
And keep my tongue from censure clear;
The Jew, the Turk, the Heathen bless,
And hold the plough and persevere.

4
There's God in ev'ry man most sure,
And ev'ry soul's to Christ allied:
If fears deject, if hopes allure,
If Jesus wept, and pray'd and died.

148 ## Hymn 13
Elegance

1
'Tis in the spirit that attire,
Th'investiture of saints in heav'n,
Those robes of intellectual fire,
Which to the great elect are giv'n.

2
'Bring out to my returning son
The robes for elegance the best';
Thus in the height it shall be done,
And thus the penitent be blest.

3

'Tis in the body, that sweet mien,
  Ingenuous Christians all possess,
Grace, easy motions, smiles serene,
  Clean hands and seemliness of dress.

4

Whoever has thy charming pow'rs
  Is amiable as Kidron's swan,
Like holy Esdras feeds on flow'rs,
  And lives on honey like St John.

149

Hymn 14
Loveliness

1

'Good-nature' is thy sterling name,
  Yet 'loveliness' is English too;
Sweet disposition, whose bright aim
  Is to the mark of Jesus true.

2

I've seen thee in an homely face
  Excel by pulchritude of mind;
To ill-form'd features give a grace
  Serene, benevolent and kind.

3

'Tis when the spirit is so great
  That it the body still controuls,
As godly inclinations meet
  In sweet society of souls.

4

It is that condescending air,
  Where perfect willingness is plain
To smile assent, to join in pray'r
  And, urg'd a mile, to go it twain.

5

To grant at once the boon preferr'd,
  By contrite foe, or needy friend;

To be obliging is the word,
    And God's good blessing is the end.

150   # Hymn 15
Taste

1

O GUIDE my judgement and my taste,
    Sweet SPIRIT, author of the book
Of wonders, told in language chaste
    And plainness, not to be mistook.

2

O let me muse, and yet at sight
    The page admire, the page believe;
'Let there be light, and there was light,
    Let there be Paradise and Eve!'

3

Who his soul's rapture can refrain?
    At Joseph's ever-pleasing tale
Of marvels, the prodigious train,
    To Sinai's hill from Goshen's vale.

4

The Psalmist and proverbial Seer,
    And all the prophets sons of song,
Make all things precious, all things dear,
    And bear the brilliant word along.

5

O take the book from off the shelf,
    And con it meekly on thy knees;
Best panegyric on itself,
    And self-avouch'd to teach and please.

6

Respect, adore it heart and mind.
    How greatly sweet, how sweetly grand,
Who reads the most, is most refin'd,
    And polish'd by the Master's hand.

Hymn 26
Mutual Subjection

1

SOME think that in the Christian scheme
    Politeness has no part;
That manners we should disesteem,
    And look upon the heart.

2

The heart the Lord alone can read,
    Which left us this decree,
That men alternate take the lead
    In sweet complacency.

3

When his Disciples great dispute
    Christ Jesus reconcil'd,
He made their sharp contention mute,
    By shewing them a child.

4

If I have got the greater share
    Of talents—I shou'd bow
To Christ, and take the greater care
    To serve and to allow.

5

This union with thy grace empow'r
    More influence to supply;
Hereafter, he that lacks this hour,
    May be as great as I.

152

Hymn 29
Long-suffering of God

1

One hundred feet from off the ground
    That noble Aloe blows;
But mark ye by what skill profound
    His charming grandeur rose.

2

One hundred years of patient care
   The gardners did bestow,
Toil and hereditary pray'r
   Made all this glorious show.

3

Thus man goes on from year to year,
   And bears no fruit at all;
But gracious God, still unsevere,
   Bids show'rs of blessings fall.

4

The beams of mercy, dews of grace,
   Our Saviour still supplies—
Ha! ha! the soul regains her place,
   And sweetens all the skies.

EDWARD PERRONET

1725–1792

153   *'All hail the power of Jesus' name'*

All hail the power of Jesus' name;
   Let angels prostrate fall;
Bring forth the royal diadem
   To crown him Lord of all.

Crown him, ye morning stars of light,
   Who fixed this floating ball;
Now hail the strength of Israel's might,
   And crown him Lord of all.

Crown him, ye martyrs of your God,
   Who from his altar call;
Extol the Stem-of-Jesse's Rod,
   And crown him Lord of all.

Ye seed of Israel's chosen race,
   Ye ransomed of the fall,
Hail him who saves you by his grace,
   And crown him Lord of all.

Hail him, ye heirs of David's line,
    Whom David Lord did call,
The God incarnate, Man divine,
    And crown him Lord of all.

Sinners, whose love can ne'er forget
    The wormwood and the gall,
Go, spread your trophies at his feet,
    And crown him Lord of all.

Let every tribe and every tongue
    That bound creation's call,
Now shout in universal song
    The crownèd Lord of all.

JOHN NEWTON
1725–1807

154   *'How sweet the Name of Jesus sounds'*

How sweet the Name of Jesus sounds
    In a believer's ear!
It soothes his sorrows, heals his wounds,
    And drives away his fear!

It makes the wounded spirit whole
    And calms the troubled breast;
'Tis manna to the hungry soul,
    And to the weary, rest.

Dear Name! the rock on which I build,
    My shield and hiding-place,
My never-failing treasury, fill'd
    With boundless stores of grace,—

By Thee my prayers acceptance gain,
    Although with sin defiled;
Satan accuses me in vain,
    And I am own'd a Child.

Weak is the effort of my heart,
    And cold my warmest thought;
But, when I see Thee as Thou art,
    I'll praise Thee as I ought.

Till then, I would Thy love proclaim
    With every fleeting breath;
And may the music of Thy Name
    Refresh my soul in death!

155   *'Glorious things of thee are spoken'*

Glorious things of thee are spoken,
    Zion, city of our God;
He, whose word cannot be broken,
    Formed thee for his own abode:
On the Rock of Ages founded,
    What can shake thy sure repose?
With salvation's walls surrounded,
    Thou mayst smile at all thy foes.

See, the streams of living waters,
    Springing from eternal love,
Well supply thy sons and daughters,
    And all fear of want remove:
Who can faint, while such a river
    Ever flows their thirst to assuage—
Grace, which, like the Lord the giver,
    Never fails from age to age?

Blest inhabitants of Zion,
    Washed in the Redeemer's blood;
Jesus, whom their souls rely on,
    Makes them kings and priests to God.
'Tis his love his people raises
    Over self to reign as kings;
And as priests, his solemn praises
    Each for a thankoffering brings.

Saviour, if of Zion's city
    I, through grace, a member am,

JOHN NEWTON

Let the world deride or pity,
　　I will glory in thy name:
Fading is the worldling's pleasure,
　　All his boasted pomp and show;
Solid joys and lasting treasure
　　None but Zion's children know.

WILLIAM COWPER

1731–1800

156　　　　　　　　from *Truth*

Man on the dubious waves of error toss'd,
His ship half-founder'd and his compass lost,
Sees, far as human optics may command,
A sleeping fog, and fancies it dry land;
Spreads all his canvas, every sinew plies,
Pants for it, aims at it, enters it, and dies.
Then farewell all self-satisfying schemes,
His well-built systems, philosophic dreams,
Deceitful views of future bliss, farewell!
He reads his sentence at the flames of hell.
　　Hard lot of man! to toil for the reward
Of virtue, and yet lose it!—Wherefore hard?
He that would win the race must guide his horse
Obedient to the customs of the course,
Else, though unequall'd to the goal he flies,
A meaner than himself shall gain the prize.
Grace leads the right way,—if you choose the wrong,
Take it, and perish, but restrain your tongue;
Charge not, with light sufficient and left free,
Your wilful suicide on God's decree.

*

　　Who judged the Pharisee? What odious cause
Exposed him to the vengeance of the laws?
Had he seduced a virgin, wrong'd a friend,
Or stabb'd a man to serve some private end?
Was blasphemy his sin? Or did he stray
From the strict duties of the sacred day?
Sit long and late at the carousing board?
(Such were the sins with which he charged his Lord.)

No—the man's morals were exact. What then?
'Twas his ambition to be seen of men.
His virtues were his pride; and that one vice
Made all his virtues gewgaws of no price;
He wore them as fine trappings for a show,
A praying, synagogue-frequenting beau.

  The self-applauding bird, the peacock, see—
Mark what a sumptuous pharisee is he!
Meridian sunbeams tempt him to unfold
His radiant glories, azure, green, and gold:
He treads as if, some solemn music near,
His measured step were govern'd by his ear,
And seems to say—'Ye meaner fowl, give place;
I am all splendour, dignity, and grace!'

  Not so the pheasant on his charms presumes,
Though he, too, has a glory in his plumes.
He, Christian-like, retreats with modest mien
To the close copse or far-sequester'd green,
And shines without desiring to be seen.
The plea of works, as arrogant and vain,
Heaven turns from with abhorrence and disdain;
Not more affronted by avow'd neglect
Than by the mere dissembler's feigned respect.
What is all righteousness that men devise,
What, but a sordid bargain for the skies?
But Christ as soon would abdicate His own,
As stoop from heaven to sell the proud a throne.

*

  Some lead a life unblameable and just,
Their own dear virtue their unshaken trust:
They never sin—or if (as all offend)
Some trivial slips their daily walk attend,
The poor are near at hand, the charge is small,
A light gratuity atones for all.
For though the Pope has lost his interest here
And pardons are not sold as once they were,
No Papist more desirous to compound
Than some grave sinners upon English ground.

  That plea refuted, other quirks they seek—
Mercy is infinite, and man is weak;
The future shall obliterate the past,
And Heaven no doubt shall be their home at last.

Come, then—a still, small whisper in your ear—
He has no hope that never had a fear;
And he that never doubted of his state,
He may perhaps—perhaps he may—too late.

*

Not that the Former of us all in this,
Or aught He does, is govern'd by caprice;
The supposition is replete with sin,
And bears the brand of blasphemy burnt in.
Not so—the silver trumpet's heavenly call
Sounds for the poor, but sounds alike for all;
Kings are invited and, would kings obey,
No slaves on earth more welcome were than they;
But royalty, nobility, and state
Are such a dead preponderating weight
That endless bliss (how strange soe'er it seem)
In counterpoise flies up, and kicks the beam.

*

How readily, upon the gospel plan,
That question has its answer—'What is man?'
Sinful and weak, in every sense a wretch,
An instrument whose chords upon the stretch
And strain'd to the last screw that he can bear
Yield only discord in his Maker's ear;
Once the blest residence of truth divine,
Glorious as Solyma's interior shrine,
Where in His own oracular abode
Dwelt visibly the light-creating God;
But made long since, like Babylon of old,
A den of mischiefs never to be told.
And she, once mistress of the realms around
Now scatter'd wide and nowhere to be found,
As soon shall rise and reascend the throne
By native power and energy her own,
As Nature, at her own peculiar cost,
Restore to man the glories he has lost.
Go, bid the winter cease to chill the year,
Replace the wandering comet in his sphere,
Then boast—but wait for that unhoped-for hour—
The self-restoring arm of human power.
But what is man in his own proud esteem?

Hear him, himself the poet and the theme:
'A monarch clothed with majesty and awe,
His mind his kingdom, and his will his law;
Grace in his mien, and glory in his eyes,
Supreme on earth, and worthy of the skies,
Strength in his heart, dominion in his nod
And, thunderbolts excepted, quite a god!'
    So sings he, charm'd with his own mind and form,
The song magnificent—the theme a worm!
Himself so much the source of his delight,
His Maker has no beauty in his sight.
See where he sits, contemplative and fixed,
Pleasure and wonder in his features mix'd,
His passions tamed and all at his control,
How perfect the composure of his soul!
Complacency has breathed a gentle gale
O'er all his thoughts, and swell'd his easy sail.
His books well trimm'd and in the gayest style,
Like regimental coxcombs rank and file,
Adorn his intellects as well as shelves
And teach him notions splendid as themselves;
The Bible only stands neglected there,
Though that of all most worthy of his care,
And, like an infant troublesome awake,
Is left to sleep for peace and quiet sake.

*

Oh, that unwelcome voice of heavenly love,
Sad messenger of mercy from above,
How does it grate upon his thankless ear,
Crippling his pleasures with the cramp of fear!
His wit and judgement at continual strife,
That civil war embitters all his life;
In vain he points his powers against the skies,
In vain he closes or averts his eyes,
Truth will intrude—she bids him yet beware—
And shakes the sceptic in the scorner's chair.
    Though various foes against the Truth combine,
Pride above all opposes her design;
Pride, of a growth superior to the rest,
The subtlest serpent with the loftiest crest,
Swells at the thought and, kindling into rage,
Would hiss the cherub Mercy from the stage.

'And is the soul indeed so lost?' she cries,
'Fallen from her glory, and too weak to rise?
Torpid and dull beneath a frozen zone,
Has she no spark that may be deem'd her own?
Grant her indebted to what zealots call
Grace undeserved, yet surely not for all;
Some beams of rectitude she yet displays,
Some love of virtue, and some power to praise;
Can lift herself above corporeal things
And, soaring on her own unborrow'd wings,
Possess herself of all that's good or true,
Assert the skies, and vindicate her due.
Past indiscretion is a venial crime;
And if the youth, unmellow'd yet by time,
Bore on his branch, luxuriant then and rude,
Fruits of a blighted size, austere and crude,
Maturer years shall happier stores produce
And meliorate the well-concocted juice.
Then, conscious of her meritorious zeal,
To Justice she may make her bold appeal
And leave to Mercy, with a tranquil mind,
The worthless and unfruitful of mankind.'
   Hear then how Mercy, slighted and defied,
Retorts the affront against the crown of Pride:
'Perish the virtue, as it ought, abhorr'd,
And the fool with it that insults his Lord.
The atonement a Redeemer's love has wrought
Is not for you—the righteous need it not.
Seest thou yon harlot, wooing all she meets,
The worn-out nuisance of the public streets,
Herself from morn to night, from night to morn,
Her own abhorrence, and as much your scorn?
The gracious shower, unlimited and free,
Shall fall on her, when Heaven denies it thee.
Of all that wisdom dictates, this the drift—
That man is dead in sin, and life a gift.'

157   *Love Constraining to Obedience*

        No strength of Nature can suffice
           To serve the Lord aright:
        And what she has she misapplies,
           For want of clearer light.

How long beneath the Law I lay
   In bondage and distress;
I toiled the precept to obey,
   But toiled without success.

Then to abstain from outward sin
   Was more than I could do;
Now, if I feel its power within,
   I feel I hate it too.

Then all my servile works were done
   A righteousness to raise;
Now, freely chosen in the Son,
   I freely choose His ways.

'What shall I do,' was then the word
   'That I may worthier grow?'
'What shall I render to the Lord?'
   Is my inquiry now.

To see the law by Christ fulfilled,
   And hear His pardoning voice,
Changes a slave into a child,
   And duty into choice.

158   *Self-Acquaintance*

Dear Lord! accept a sinful heart,
   Which of itself complains,
And mourns, with much and frequent smart,
   The evil it contains.

There fiery seeds of anger lurk,
   Which often hurt my frame;
And wait but for the tempter's work
   To fan them to a flame.

Legality holds out a bribe
   To purchase life from Thee;
And discontent would fain prescribe
   How Thou shalt deal with me.

While unbelief withstands thy grace,
   And puts the mercy by,
Presumption, with a brow of brass,
   Says, 'Give me, or I die!'

How eager are my thoughts to roam
   In quest of what they love!
But ah! when duty calls them home,
   How heavily they move!

Oh, cleanse me in a Saviour's blood,
   Transform me by thy power,
And make me Thy belov'd abode,
   And let me roam no more.

159   *'The Lord will Happiness divine'*

The Lord will happiness divine
   On contrite hearts bestow;
Then tell me, gracious God, is mine
   A contrite heart, or no?

I hear, but seem to hear in vain,
   Insensible as steel;
If aught is felt, 'tis only pain
   To find I cannot feel.

I sometimes think myself inclined
   To love Thee, if I could;
But often feel another mind,
   Averse to all that's good.

My best desires are faint and few,
   I fain would strive for more;
But when I cry, 'My strength renew',
   Seem weaker than before.

Thy saints are comforted, I know,
   And love Thy house of prayer;
I therefore go where others go,
   But find no comfort there.

Oh make this heart rejoice, or ache;
　　Decide this doubt for me;
And if it be not broken, break,
　　And heal it, if it be.

160　　　　　　*Walking with God*

Oh! for a closer walk with God,
　　A calm and heavenly frame;
A light to shine upon the road
　　That leads me to the Lamb!

Where is the blessedness I knew
　　When first I saw the Lord?
Where is the soul–refreshing view
　　Of Jesus and his word?

What peaceful hours I once enjoyed!
　　How sweet their memory still!
But they have left an aching void
　　The world can never fill.

Return, O holy Dove, return,
　　Sweet messenger of rest;
I hate the sins that made thee mourn,
　　And drove thee from my breast.

The dearest idol I have known,
　　Whate'er that idol be,
Help me to tear it from thy throne,
　　And worship only Thee.

So shall my walk be close with God,
　　Calm and serene my frame;
So purer light shall mark the road
　　That leads me to the Lamb.

161　　　　　*Light Shining out of Darkness*

God moves in a mysterious way
　　His wonders to perform;
He plants His footsteps in the sea,
　　And rides upon the storm.

Deep in unfathomable mines
   Of never failing skill
His treasures up His bright designs,
   And works His sovereign will.

Ye fearful saints, fresh courage take:
   The clouds ye so much dread
Are big with mercy, and shall break
   In blessings on your head.

Judge not the Lord by feeble sense,
   But trust Him for His grace;
Behind a frowning providence
   He hides a smiling face.

His purposes will ripen fast,
   Unfolding ev'ry hour;
The bud may have a bitter taste,
   But sweet will be the flow'r.

Blind unbelief is sure to err,
   And scan His work in vain;
God is His own interpreter,
   And He will make it plain.

162   *Joy and Peace in Believing*

Sometimes a light surprises
   The Christian while he sings;
It is the Lord who rises
   With healing on His wings.
When comforts are declining,
   He grants the soul again
A season of clear shining
   To cheer it after rain.

In holy contemplation
   We sweetly then pursue
The theme of God's salvation,
   And find it ever new.
Set free from present sorrow,
   We cheerfully can say,

'E'en let th'unknown tomorrow
    Bring with it what it may!

It can bring with it nothing
    But He will bear us thro';
Who gives the lilies clothing
    Will clothe His people too.
Beneath the spreading heavens
    No creature but is fed;
And he who feeds the ravens
    Will give His children bread.

Though vine, nor fig-tree neither,
    Their wonted fruit should bear,
Tho' all the field should wither,
    Nor flocks, nor herds, be there,
Yet God the same abiding,
    His praise shall tune my voice
For while in him confiding,
    I cannot but rejoice.'

163   *Jehovah our Righteousness*
                              (*Jeremiah 23:6*)

My God, how perfect are thy ways!
    But mine polluted are;
Sin twines itself about my praise,
    And slides into my pray'r.

When I would speak what thou hast done
    To save me from my sin,
I cannot make Thy mercies known
    But self-applause creeps in.

Divine desire, that holy flame
    Thy grace creates in me,
Alas! impatience is its name
    When it returns to Thee.

This heart, a fountain of vile thoughts,
    How does it overflow,
While self upon the surface floats
    Still bubbling from below!

Let others in the gaudy dress
   Of fancied merit shine;
The Lord shall be my righteousness;
   The Lord for ever mine.

164   *Exhortation to Prayer*

What various hindrances we meet
In coming to a mercy-seat!
Yet who that knows the worth of pray'r
But wishes to be often there?

Pray'r makes the dark'ned cloud withdraw,
Pray'r climbs the ladder Jacob saw,
Gives exercise to faith and love,
Brings ev'ry blessing from above.

Restraining pray'r, we cease to fight;
Pray'r makes the Christian's armour bright;
And Satan trembles, when he sees
The weakest saint upon his knees.

While Moses stood with arms spread wide,
Success was found on Israel's side;
But when thro' weariness they fail'd,
That moment Amalek prevail'd.

Have you no words? Ah, think again!
Words flow apace when you complain
And fill your fellow-creature's ear
With the sad tale of all your care.

Were half the breath thus vainly spent
To heav'n in supplication sent,
Your cheerful song would oft'ner be:
'Hear what the Lord has done for me!'

165

Stanzas

*Subjoined to the Yearly Bill of Mortality
of the Parish of All Saints, Northampton:
for the year 1787*

While thirteen moons saw smoothly run
    The Nen's barge-laden wave,
All these, life's rambling journey done,
    Have found their home, the grave.

Was man (frail always) made more frail
    Than in foregoing years?
Did famine or did plague prevail,
    That so much death appears?

No: these were vigorous as their sires,
    Nor plague nor famine came;
This annual tribute Death requires,
    And never waives his claim.

Like crowded forest-trees we stand,
    And some are marked to fall;
The axe will smite at God's command,
    And soon shall smite us all.

Green as the bay-tree, ever green,
    With its new foliage on,
The gay, the thoughtless, have I seen;
    I passed—and they were gone.

Read, ye that run, the awful truth
    With which I charge my page;
A worm is in the bud of youth,
    And at the root of age.

No present health can health ensure
    For yet an hour to come;
No medicine, though it oft can cure,
    Can always balk the tomb.

Nen] River Nene

And oh! that humble as my lot,
  And scorned as is my strain,
These truths, though known, too much forgot,
  I may not teach in vain.

So prays your Clerk with all his heart,
  And ere he quits the pen,
Bégs *you* for once to take *his* part,
  And answer all—'Amen!'

166   *On a Similar Occasion*
            for the year 1790

He who sits from day to day,
  Where the prisoned lark is hung,
Heedless of his loudest lay,
  Hardly knows that he has sung.

Where the watchman in his round
  Nightly lifts his voice on high,
None, accustomed to the sound,
  Wakes the sooner for his cry.

So your verse-man I, and clerk,
  Yearly in my song proclaim
Death at hand—yourselves his mark—
  And the foe's unerring aim.

Duly at my time I come,
  Publishing to all aloud—
'Soon the grave must be your home,
  And your only suit a shroud.'

But the monitory strain,
  Oft repeated in your ears,
Seems to sound too much in vain,
  Wins no notice, wakes no fears.

Can a truth, by all confessed
  Of such magnitude and weight,
Grow, by being oft expressed,
  Trivial as a parrot's prate?

Pleasure's call attention wins,
   Hear it often as we may;
New as ever seem our sins,
   Though committed every day.

Death and Judgement, Heaven and Hell—
   These alone, so often heard,
No more move us than the bell
   When some stranger is interred.

Oh then, ere the turf or tomb
   Cover us from every eye,
Spirit of instruction, come;
   Make us learn that we must die.

167   *On a Similar Occasion*
                   for the year 1792

Thankless for favours from on high,
   Man thinks he fades too soon;
Though 'tis his privilege to die,
   Would he improve the boon.

But he, not wise enough to scan
   His best concerns aright,
Would gladly stretch life's little span
   To ages, if he might.

To ages in a world of pain,
   To ages, where he goes
Galled by affliction's heavy chain,
   And hopeless of repose.

Strange fondness of the human heart,
   Enamoured of its harm!
Strange world, that costs it so much smart,
   And still has power to charm.

Whence has the world her magic power?
   Why deem we Death a foe?
Recoil from weary life's best hour,
   And covet longer woe?

The cause is Conscience;—Conscience oft
   Her tale of guilt renews:
Her voice is terrible, though soft,
   And dread of Death ensues.

Then, anxious to be longer spared,
   Man mourns his fleeting breath:
And evils then seem light, compared
   With the approach of Death.

'Tis judgement shakes him; there's the fear
   That prompts the wish to stay:
He has incurred a long arrear,
   And must despair to pay.

Pay?—follow Christ, and all is paid:
   His death your peace ensures;
Think on the grave where *He* was laid,
   And calm descend to *yours*.

AUGUSTUS MONTAGUE TOPLADY

1740–1778

168   *'Rock of Ages'*

Rock of Ages, cleft for me,
Let me hide myself in Thee!
Let the water and the blood
From Thy riven side which flow'd,
Be of sin the double cure,
Cleanse me from its guilt and power.

Not the labours of my hands
Can fulfil Thy law's demands;
Could my zeal no respite know,
Could my tears for ever flow,
All for sin could not atone;
Thou must save, and Thou alone.

Nothing in my hand I bring;
Simply to Thy Cross I cling;
Naked, come to Thee for dress;
Helpless, look to Thee for grace;
Foul, I to the Fountain fly;
Wash me, Saviour, or I die!

While I draw this fleeting breath,
When my eyestrings break in death,
When I soar through tracts unknown,
See Thee on Thy Judgement-throne;
Rock of Ages, cleft for me,
Let me hide myself in Thee!

TIMOTHY DWIGHT

1752–1817

169   from *The Triumph of Infidelity*

Here stood Hypocrisy, in sober brown,
His sabbath face all sorrow'd with a frown.
A dismal tale he told of dismal times,
And this sad world brimfull of saddest crimes;
Furrowed his cheeks with tears for others' sin,
But closed his eyelids on the hell within.
There smiled the smooth Divine, unused to wound
The sinner's heart with hell's alarming sound.
No terrors on his gentle tongue attend,
No grating truths the nicest ear offend.
That strange 'New Birth', that methodistic 'Grace'
Nor in his heart, nor sermons, found a place.
Plato's fine tales he clumsily retold,
Trite, fireside, moral see-saws, dull as old;
His Christ and Bible placed at good remove
Guilt hell-deserving, and forgiving love.
'Twas best, he said, mankind should cease to sin;
Good fame required it; so did peace within.
Their honours, well he knew, would ne'er be driven;
But hoped they still would please to go to heaven.
Each week, he paid his visitation dues;
Coaxed, jested, laughed; rehearsed the private news;

Smoked with each goody, thought her cheese excelled;
Her pipe he lighted, and her baby held.
Or placed in some great town, with lacquered shoes,
Trim wig, and trimmer gown, and glistening hose,
He bowed, talked politics, learned manners mild;
Most meekly questioned, and most smoothly smiled;
At rich men's jests laughed loud, their stories praised;
Their wives' new patterns gazed, and gazed, and gazed;
Most daintily on pampered turkeys dined;
Nor shrunk with fasting, nor with study pined:
Yet from their churches saw his brethren driven
Who thundered truth and spoke the voice of heaven,
Chilled trembling guilt, in Satan's headlong path
Charmed the feet back, and roused the ear of death.
'Let fools', he cried, 'starve on, while prudent I
Snug in my nest shall live, and snug shall die.'
    There stood the infidel of modern breed,
Blest vegetation of infernal seed.
Alike no Deist, and no Christian, he;
But from all principle, all virtue, free.
To him all things the same, as good or evil:
Jehovah, Jove, the Lama, or the Devil;
Mohammed's braying, or Isaiah's lays;
The Indian's pow-wows, or the Christian's praise.
With him all *natural* desires are good:
His thirst for stews; the Mohawk's thirst for blood,
Made not to know, or love, the all-beauteous mind
Or wing through heaven his path to bliss refined
But his dear self, choice Dagon! to adore;
To dress, to game, to swear, to drink, to whore;
To race his steeds; or cheat, when others run;
Pit tortured cocks, and swear 'tis glorious fun.
His soul not clothed with attributes divine
But a nice watch-spring to that grand machine,
That work more nice than Rittenhouse can plan,
The body; man's chief part; himself, the man;
Man, that illustrious brute of noblest shape,
A swine unbristled, and an untailed ape.
To couple, eat, and die—his glorious doom:
The oyster's churchyard, and the capon's tomb.

WILLIAM BLAKE
1757–1827

170   *Jerusalem*

And did those feet in ancient time
Walk upon England's mountains green?
And was the holy Lamb of God
On England's pleasant pastures seen?

And did the Countenance Divine
Shine forth upon our clouded hills?
And was Jerusalem builded here
Among these dark Satanic Mills?

Bring me my Bow of burning gold!
Bring me my Arrows of desire!
Bring me my Spear! O clouds, unfold!
Bring me my Chariot of fire!

I will not cease from Mental Fight,
Nor shall my Sword sleep in my hand,
Till we have built Jerusalem
In England's green and pleasant land.

ROBERT BURNS
1759–1796

171   *Address to the Unco Guid*

O ye wha are sae guid yoursel,
    Sae pious and sae holy,
Ye've nought to do but mark and tell
    Your neebour's fauts and folly!
Whase life is like a weel-gaun mill,
    Supplied wi' store o' water,
The heaped happer's ebbing still,
    And still the clap plays clatter.

171   *Unco Guid*] Uncommonly Righteous

Hear me, ye venerable Core,
 As counsel for poor mortals,
That frequent pass douce Wisdom's door
 For glaikit Folly's portals;
I, for their thoughtless, careless sakes,
 Would here propone defences,
Their donsie tricks, their black mistakes,
 Their failings and mischances.

Ye see your state wi' theirs compared,
 And shudder at the niffer,
But cast a moment's fair regard
 What maks the mighty differ;
Discount what scant occasion gave,
 That purity ye pride in,
And (what's aft mair than a' the lave)
 Your better art o' hiding.

Think, when your castigated pulse
 Gies now and then a wallop,
What ragings must his veins convulse,
 That still eternal gallop:
Wi' wind and tide fair i' your tail,
 Right on ye scud your sea-way;
But in the teeth o' baith to sail,
 It maks an unco leeway.

See Social-life and Glee sit down,
 All joyous and unthinking,
Till, quite transmugrified, they're grown
 Debauchery and Drinking:
O would they stay to calculate
 The eternal consequences;
Or your more dreaded hell to state,
 Damnation of expenses!

Ye high, exalted, virtuous dames,
 Tied up in godly laces,
Before ye gie poor Frailty names,
 Suppose a change o' cases;

   douce] sober   *glaikit*] giddy
   donsie] unlucky *niffer*] exchange

A dear-loved lad, convenience snug,
  A treacherous inclination—
But, let me whisper i' your lug,
  Ye're aiblins nae temptation.

Then gently scan your brother Man,
  Still gentler sister Woman;
Though they may gang a kennin wrang,
  To step aside is human:
One point must still be greatly dark,
  The moving *Why* they do it;
And just as lamely can ye mark,
  How far perhaps they rue it.

Who made the heart, 'tis *He* alone
  Decidedly can try us,
He knows each chord, its various tone,
  Each string, its various bias:
Then at the balance let's be mute,
  We never can adjust it;
What's *done* we partly may compute,
  But know not what's resisted.

WILLIAM WORDSWORTH
1770–1850

172   *Resolution and Independence*

There was a roaring in the wind all night;
The rain came heavily and fell in floods;
But now the sun is rising calm and bright;
The birds are singing in the distant woods;
Over his own sweet voice the stock-dove broods;
The jay makes answer as the magpie chatters;
And all the air is filled with pleasant noise of waters.

All things that love the sun are out of doors;
The sky rejoices in the morning's birth;
The grass is bright with rain-drops;—on the moors
The hare is running races in her mirth;

171   *aiblins*] perhaps   *a kennin*] a little

And with her feet she from the plashy earth
Raises a mist that, glittering in the sun,
Runs with her all the way, wherever she doth run.

I was a Traveller then upon the moor;
I saw the hare that raced about with joy;
I heard the woods and distant waters roar;
Or heard them not, as happy as a boy:
The pleasant season did my heart employ:
My old remembrances went from me wholly;
And all the ways of men, so vain and melancholy.

But, as it sometimes chanceth, from the might
Of joy in minds that can no further go,
As high as we have mounted in delight
In our dejection do we sink as low;
To me that morning did it happen so;
And fears and fancies thick upon me came;
Dim sadness—and blind thoughts, I knew not, nor could name.

I heard the sky-lark warbling in the sky;
And I bethought me of the playful hare:
Even such a happy Child of earth am I;
Even as these blissful creatures do I fare;
Far from the world I walk, and from all care;
But there may come another day to me—
Solitude, pain of heart, distress, and poverty.

My whole life I have lived in pleasant thought,
As if life's business were a summer mood;
As if all needful things would come unsought
To genial faith, still rich in genial good;
But how can he expect that others should
Build for him, sow for him, and at his call
Love him, who for himself will take no heed at all?

I thought of Chatterton, the marvellous Boy,
The sleepless Soul that perished in his pride;
Of Him who walked in glory and in joy
Following his plough, along the mountain-side:
By our own spirits are we deified:
We Poets in our youth begin in gladness;
But thereof come in the end despondency and madness.

Now, whether it were by peculiar grace,
A leading from above, a something given,
Yet it befell that, in this lonely place,
When I with these untoward thoughts had striven,
Beside a pool bare to the eye of heaven
I saw a Man before me unawares:
The oldest man he seemed that ever wore grey hairs.

As a huge stone is sometimes seen to lie
Couched on the bald top of an eminence;
Wonder to all who do the same espy,
By what means it could thither come, and whence;
So that it seems a thing endued with sense:
Like a sea-beast crawled forth, that on a shelf
Of rock or sand reposeth, there to sun itself;

Such seemed this Man, not all alive nor dead,
Nor all asleep—in his extreme old age:
His body was bent double, feet and head
Coming together in life's pilgrimage;
As if some dire constraint of pain, or rage
Of sickness felt by him in times long past,
A more than human weight upon his frame had cast.

Himself he propped, limbs, body, and pale face,
Upon a long grey staff of shaven wood:
And, still as I drew near with gentle pace,
Upon the margin of that moorish flood
Motionless as a cloud the old Man stood,
That heareth not the loud winds when they call;
And moveth all together, if it move at all.

At length, himself unsettling, he the pond
Stirred with his staff, and fixedly did look
Upon the muddy water, which he conned,
As if he had been reading in a book:
And now a stranger's privilege I took;
And, drawing to his side, to him did say,
'This morning gives us promise of a glorious day.'

A gentle answer did the old Man make,
In courteous speech which forth he slowly drew:
And him with further words I thus bespake,

'What occupation do you there pursue?
This is a lonesome place for one like you.'
Ere he replied, a flash of mild surprise
Broke from the sable orbs of his yet-vivid eyes.

His words came feebly, from a feeble chest,
But each in solemn order followed each,
With something of a lofty utterance drest—
Choice word and measured phrase, above the reach
Of ordinary men; a stately speech;
Such as grave Livers do in Scotland use,
Religious men, who give to God and man their dues.

He told, that to these waters he had come
To gather leeches, being old and poor:
Employment hazardous and wearisome!
And he had many hardships to endure:
From pond to pond he roamed, from moor to moor;
Housing, with God's good help, by choice or chance;
And in this way he gained an honest maintenance.

The old Man still stood talking by my side;
But now his voice to me was like a stream
Scarce heard; nor word from word could I divide;
And the whole body of the Man did seem
Like one whom I had met with in a dream;
Or like a man from some far region sent,
To give me human strength, by apt admonishment.

My former thoughts returned: the fear that kills;
And hope that is unwilling to be fed;
Cold, pain, and labour, and all fleshly ills;
And mighty Poets in their misery dead.
—Perplexed, and longing to be comforted,
My question eagerly did I renew,
'How is it that you live, and what is it you do?'

He with a smile did then his words repeat;
And said that, gathering leeches, far and wide
He travelled; stirring thus about his feet
The waters of the pools where they abide.
'Once I could meet with them on every side;
But they have dwindled long by slow decay;
Yet still I persevere, and find them where I may.'

While he was talking thus, the lonely place,
The old Man's shape, and speech—all troubled me:
In my mind's eye I seemed to see him pace
About the weary moors continually,
Wandering about alone and silently.
While I these thoughts within myself pursued,
He, having made a pause, the same discourse renewed.

And soon with this he other matter blended,
Cheerfully uttered, with demeanour kind,
But stately in the main; and when he ended,
I could have laughed myself to scorn to find
In that decrepit Man so firm a mind.
'God,' said I, 'be my help and stay secure;
I'll think of the Leech-gatherer on the lonely moor!'

JAMES MONTGOMERY
1771–1854

173   *Nativity*

Angels, from the realms of glory,
   Wing your flight o'er all the earth,
Ye who sang creation's story,
   Now proclaim Messiah's birth;
     Come and worship,
Worship Christ the new-born King.

Shepherds, in the field abiding,
   Watching o'er your flocks by night,
God with man is now residing,
   Yonder shines the infant-light;
     Come and worship,
Worship Christ the new-born King.

Sages, leave your contemplations,
   Brighter visions beam afar;
Seek the great Desire of nations;
   Ye have seen His natal star;
     Come and worship,
Worship Christ the new-born King.

Saints before the altar bending,
   Watching long in hope and fear,
Suddenly the Lord, descending,
   In His temple shall appear;
      Come and worship,
Worship Christ the new-born King.

Sinners, wrung with true repentance,
   Doom'd for guilt to endless pains,
Justice now revokes the sentence,
   Mercy calls you,—break your chains;
      Come and worship,
Worship Christ the new-born King.

SAMUEL TAYLOR COLERIDGE
1772–1834

174

My Baptismal Birthday

God's child in Christ adopted,—Christ my all,—
What that earth boasts were not lost cheaply, rather
Than forfeit that blest name, by which I call
The Holy One, the Almighty God, my Father?—
Father! in Christ we live, and Christ in Thee—
Eternal Thou, and everlasting we.
The heir of heaven, henceforth I fear not death:
In Christ I live! in Christ I draw the breath
Of the true life!—Let, then, earth, sea, and sky
Make war against me! On my front I show
Their mighty Master's seal. In vain they try
To end my life, that can but end its woe.—
Is that a deathbed where a Christian lies?—
Yes! but not his—'tis Death itself that dies.

175

*Epitaph**

Stop, Christian Passer-by!—Stop, child of God,
And read with gentle breast. Beneath this sod
A poet lies, or that which once seem'd he.—
Oh! lift one thought in prayer for S.T.C.;

* dated 9 November 1833.

That he who many a year with toil of breath
Found death in life, may here find life in death!
Mercy for praise—to be forgiven for fame
He ask'd, and hoped, through Christ. Do thou the same!

REGINALD HEBER

1783–1826

176   *'By Cool Siloam's shady Rill'*

By cool Siloam's shady rill
    How sweet the lily grows!
How sweet the breath beneath the hill
    Of Sharon's dewy rose!

Lo, such the child whose early feet
    The paths of peace have trod;
Whose secret heart, with influence sweet,
    Is upward drawn to God!

By cool Siloam's shady rill
    The lily must decay;
The rose that blooms beneath the hill
    Must shortly fade away.

And soon, too soon, the wintry hour
    Of man's maturer age
Will shake the soul with sorrow's power,
    And stormy passion's rage.

O Thou, Whose infant feet were found
    Within Thy Father's shrine!
Whose years, with changeless virtue crown'd,
    Were all alike Divine;

Dependent on Thy bounteous breath,
    We seek Thy grace alone,
In childhood, manhood, age, and death,
    To keep us still Thine own!

JOHN KEBLE
1792–1866

177

(*Morning Hymn*)

New every morning is the love
Our wakening and uprising prove;
Through sleep and darkness safely brought,
Restored to life, and power, and thought.

New mercies, each returning day,
Hover around us while we pray;
New perils past, new sins forgiven,
New thoughts of God, new hopes of heaven.

If, on our daily course, our mind
Be set to hallow all we find,
New treasures still, of countless price,
God will provide for sacrifice.

The trivial round, the common task,
Will furnish all we ought to ask;
Room to deny ourselves, a road
To bring us daily nearer God.

Only, O Lord, in thy dear love
Fit us for perfect rest above;
And help us this and every day
To live more nearly as we pray.

178

'*Fill high the bowl*'

'Fill high the bowl, and spice it well, and pour
The dews oblivious: for the Cross is sharp,
    The Cross is sharp, and He
    Is tenderer than a lamb.

'He wept by Lazarus' grave—how will He bear
This bed of anguish? and His pale weak form
    Is worn with many a watch
    Of sorrow and unrest.

'His sweat last night was as great drops of blood,
And the sad burden pressed Him so to earth,
    The very torturers paused
    To help Him on His way.

'Fill high the bowl, benumb His aching sense
With medicined sleep.'—O awful in Thy woe!
    The parching thirst of death
    Is on Thee, and Thou triest

The slumberous potion bland, and wilt not drink:
Not sullen, nor in scorn, like haughty man
    With suicidal hand
    Putting his solace by:

But as at first Thine all-pervading look
Saw from Thy Father's bosom to the abyss,
    Measuring in calm presage
    The infinite descent;

So to the end, though now of mortal pangs
Made heir, and emptied of Thy glory awhile,
    With unaverted eye
    Thou meetest all the storm.

Thou wilt feel all, that Thou mayst pity all;
And rather wouldst Thou wrestle with strong pain,
    Than overcloud Thy soul,
    So clear in agony,

Or lose one glimpse of Heaven before the time.
O most entire and perfect sacrifice,
    Renewed in every pulse
    That on the tedious Cross

Told the long hours of death, as, one by one,
The life-strings of that tender heart gave way:
    E'en sinners, taught by Thee,
    Look sorrow in the face,

And bid her freely welcome, unbeguiled
By false kind solaces, and spells of earth:—
    And yet not all unsoothed:
    For when was Joy so dear

As the deep calm that breathed '*Father, forgive*',
Or, '*Be with Me in Paradise today*'?
    And, though the strife be sore,
    Yet in His parting breath

Love masters Agony; the soul that seemed
Forsaken, feels her present God again,
    And in her Father's arms
    Contented dies away.

179   (*Epithalamium*)

    The voice that breathed o'er Eden,
      That earliest wedding-day,
    The primal marriage blessing,
      It hath not passed away.

    Still in the pure espousal
      Of Christian man and maid
    The Holy Three are with us,
      The threefold grace is said,

    For dower of blessed children,
      For love and faith's sweet sake,
    For high mysterious union
      Which naught on earth may break.

    Be present, Holy Father,
      To give away this bride,
    As Eve Thou gav'st to Adam
      Out of his piercèd side.

    Be present, Holy Jesus,
      To join their loving hands,
    As Thou didst bind two natures
      In Thine eternal bands.

    Be present, Holy Spirit,
      To bless them as they kneel,
    As Thou for Christ the Bridegroom
      The heavenly spouse dost seal.

O spread Thy pure wings o'er them!
  Let no ill power find place,
When onward through life's journey
  The hallowed path they trace,

To cast their crowns before Thee,
  In perfect sacrifice,
Till to the home of gladness
  With Christ's own bride they rise.

HENRY FRANCIS LYTE
1793–1847

180   *'Abide with me'*

Abide with me; fast falls the eventide;
The darkness deepens; Lord, with me abide:
When other helpers fail, and comforts flee,
Help of the helpless, oh abide with me.

Swift to its close ebbs out life's little day;
Earth's joys grow dim, its glories pass away;
Change and decay in all around I see;
O thou who changest not, abide with me.

I need thy presence every passing hour;
What but thy grace can foil the tempter's power?
Who like thyself my guide and stay can be?
Through cloud and sunshine, Lord, abide with me.

I fear no foe with thee at hand to bless;
Ills have no weight, and tears no bitterness;
Where is death's sting? where, grave, thy victory?
I triumph still, if thou abide with me.

Hold thou thy cross before my closing eyes;
Shine through the gloom, and point me to the skies;
Heaven's morning breaks, and earth's vain shadows flee;
In life, in death, O Lord, abide with me.

181 *Psalm 103. 'Praise the Lord, O my soul'*

Praise, my soul, the King of heaven;
    To his feet thy tribute bring;
Ransomed, healed, restored, forgiven,
    Who like thee his praise should sing?
        Praise him, praise him,
    Praise the everlasting King.

Praise him for his grace and favour
    To our fathers in distress;
Praise him still the same for ever,
    Slow to chide, and swift to bless:
        Praise him, praise him,
    Glorious in his faithfulness.

Father-like he tends and spares us;
    Well our feeble frame he knows;
In his hands he gently bears us,
    Rescues us from all our foes:
        Praise him, praise him,
    Widely as his mercy flows.

Angels, help us to adore him,
    Ye behold him face to face;
Sun and moon, bow down before him;
    Dwellers all in time and space,
        Praise him, praise him.
    Praise with us the God of grace.

JOHN CLARE
1793–1864

Lord, Hear my Prayer
(*A paraphrase of Psalm 102*)

Lord, hear my prayer when trouble glooms,
Let sorrow find a way,
And when the day of trouble comes,
Turn not thy face away:
My bones like hearthstones burn away,
My life like vapoury smoke decays.

My heart is smitten like the grass,
That withered lies and dead,
And I, so lost to what I was,
Forget to eat my bread.
My voice is groaning all the day,
My bones prick through this skin of clay.

The wilderness's pelican,
The desert's lonely owl—
I am their like, a desert man
In ways as lone and foul.
As sparrows on the cottage top
I wait till I with fainting drop.

I hear my enemies reproach,
All silently I mourn;
They on my private peace encroach,
Against me they are sworn.
Ashes as bread my trouble shares,
And mix my food with weeping cares.

Yet not for them is sorrow's toil,
I fear no mortal's frowns—
But thou hast held me up awhile
And thou has cast me down.
My days like shadows waste from view,
I mourn like withered grass in dew.

But thou, Lord, shalt endure for ever,
All generations through;
Thou shalt to Zion be the giver
Of joy and mercy too.
Her very stones are in thy trust,
Thy servants reverence her dust.

Heathens shall hear and fear thy name,
All kings of earth thy glory know
When thou shalt build up Zion's fame
And live in glory there below.
He'll not despise their prayers, though mute,
But still regard the destitute.

THOMAS BINNEY

1798–1874

183   *Eternal Light*

'The King of Kings, and Lord of lords; Who
only hath immortality, dwelling in light
inapproachable; Whom no man hath seen, nor
can see.'

(*1 Tim. 5:15.16*)

Eternal Light! Eternal Light!
    How pure the soul must be
When, placed within Thy searching sight,
It shrinks not, but with calm delight
    Can live, and look on Thee!

The Spirits that surround Thy throne
    May bear the burning bliss;
But that is surely theirs alone,
Since they have never, never known
    A fallen world like this.

Oh how shall I, whose native sphere
    Is dark, whose mind is dim,
Before the Ineffable appear,
And on my naked spirit bear
    That uncreated beam?

THOMAS BINNEY

There is a way for man to rise
    To that sublime abode,—
An Offering and a Sacrifice
A HOLY SPIRIT's energies,
    An advocate with God:

These, these prepare us for the sight
    Of holiness above;
The sons of ignorance and night
May dwell in the Eternal Light,
    Through the Eternal Love.

JOHN HENRY NEWMAN
1801–1890

184   from *The Dream of Gerontius*

Praise to the holiest in the height,
    And in the depth be praise,
In all his words most wonderful,
    Most sure in all his ways.

Oh loving wisdom of our God!
    When all was sin and shame,
A second Adam to the fight
    And to the rescue came.

Oh wisest love! that flesh and blood,
    Which did in Adam fail,
Should strive afresh against the foe,
    Should strive and should prevail;

And that a higher gift than grace
    Should flesh and blood refine,
God's presence and his very self,
    And essence all-divine.

Oh generous love! that he who smote
    In man for man the foe,
The double agony in man
    For man should undergo;

And in the garden secretly,
  And on the cross on high,
Should teach his brethren, and inspire
  To suffer and to die.

Praise to the holiest in the height,
  And in the depth be praise,
In all his words most wonderful,
  Most sure in all his ways.

185   (*Guidance*)

Lead, kindly light, amid the encircling gloom,
        Lead thou me on;
The night is dark, and I am far from home;
        Lead thou me on.
Keep thou my feet; I do not ask to see
The distant scene: one step enough for me.

I was not ever thus, nor prayed that thou
        Shouldst lead me on;
I loved to choose and see my path; but now
        Lead thou me on.
I loved the garish day, and, spite of fears,
Pride ruled my will: remember not past years.

So long thy power hath blest me, sure it still
        Will lead me on
O'er moor and fen, o'er crag and torrent, till
        The night is gone,
And with the morn those angel faces smile
Which I have loved long since, and lost awhile.

JOHN GREENLEAF WHITTIER
1807–1892

The Over-Heart

'For of Him, and through Him, and to Him are
all things: to whom be glory forever!'
(Romans 11:36)

Above, below, in sky and sod,
　　In leaf and spar, in star and man,
　　Well might the wise Athenian scan
The geometric signs of God,
　　The measured order of His plan.

And India's mystics sang aright,
　　Of the One Life pervading all,—
　　One Being's tidal rise and fall
In soul and form, in sound and sight,—
　　Eternal outflow and recall.

God is: and man in guilt and fear
　　The central fact of Nature owns;
　　Kneels, trembling by his altar stones,
And darkly dreams the ghastly smear
　　Of blood appeases and atones.

Guilt shapes the Terror: deep within
　　The human heart the secret lies
　　Of all the hideous deities;
And, painted on a ground of sin,
　　The fabled gods of torment rise!

And what is He? The ripe grain nods,
　　The sweet dews fall, the sweet flowers blow;
　　But darker signs His presence show:
The earthquake and the storm are God's,
　　And good and evil interflow.

O hearts of love! O souls that turn
　　Like sunflowers to the pure and best!
　　To you the truth is manifest:
For they the mind of Christ discern
　　Who lean like John upon His breast!

In him of whom the sybil told,
　For whom the prophet's harp was toned,
　Whose need the sage and magian owned,
The loving heart of God behold,
　The hope for which the ages groaned!

Fade, pomp of dreadful imagery
　Wherewith mankind have deified
　Their hate, and selfishness, and pride!
Let the scared dreamer wake to see
　The Christ of Nazareth at his side!

What doth that holy Guide require?
　No rite of pain, nor gift of blood,
　But man a kindly brotherhood,
Looking, where duty is desire,
　To Him, the beautiful and good.

Gone be the faithlessness of fear,
　And let the pitying heaven's sweet rain
　Wash out the altar's bloody stain;
The law of Hatred disappear,
　The law of Love alone remain.

How fall the idols false and grim!
　And lo! their hideous wreck above
　The emblems of the Lamb and Dove!
Man turns from God, not God from him;
　And guilt, in suffering, whispers Love!

The world sits at the feet of Christ,
　Unknowing, blind, and unconsoled;
　It yet shall touch His garment's fold,
And feel the heavenly Alchemist
　Transform its very dust to gold.

The theme befitting angel tongues
　Beyond a mortal's scope has grown.
　O heart of mine! with reverence own
The fulness which to it belongs,
And trust the unknown for the known.

187 *The Call of the Christian*

Not always as the whirlwind's rush
　On Horeb's mount of fear,
Not always as the burning bush
　To Midian's shepherd seer,
Nor as the awful voice which came
　To Israel's prophet bards,
Nor as the tongues of cloven flame,
　Nor gift of fearful words,—

Not always thus, with outward sign
　Of fire or voice from Heaven,
The message of a truth divine,
　The call of God is given!
Awaking in the human heart
　Love for the true and right,—
Zeal for the Christian's better part,
　Strength for the Christian's fight.

Nor unto manhood's heart alone
　The holy influence steals:
Warm with a rapture not its own,
　The heart of woman feels!
As she who by Samaria's wall
　The Saviour's errand sought,—
As those who with the fervent Paul
　And meek Aquila wrought:

Or those meek ones whose martyrdom
　Rome's gathered grandeur saw:
Or those who in their Alpine home
　Braved the Crusader's war,
When the green Vaudois, trembling, heard,
　Through all its vales of death,
The martyr's song of triumph poured
　From woman's failing breath.

And gently, by a thousand things
　Which o'er our spirits pass,
Like breezes o'er the harp's fine strings,
　Or vapors o'er a glass,

Leaving their token strange and new
    Of music or of shade,
The summons to the right and true
    And merciful is made.

Oh, then, if gleams of truth and light
    Flash o'er thy waiting mind,
Unfolding to thy mental sight
    The wants of human-kind;
If, brooding over human grief,
    The earnest wish is known
To soothe and gladden with relief
    An anguish not thine own;

Though heralded with naught of fear,
    Or outward sign or show;
Though only to the inward ear
    It whispers soft and low;
Though dropping, as the manna fell,
    Unseen, yet from above,
Noiseless as dew-fall, heed it well,—
    Thy Father's call of love!

188   from *The Eternal Goodness*

I know not what the future hath
    Of marvel or surprise,
Assured alone that life and death
    His mercy underlies.

And if my heart and flesh are weak
    To bear an untried pain,
The bruisèd reed he will not break,
    But strengthen and sustain.

No offering of my own I have,
    Nor works my faith to prove;
I can but give the gifts he gave,
    And plead his love for love.

And so beside the silent sea
    I wait the muffled oar;
No harm from him can come to me
    On ocean or on shore.

I know not where his islands lift
　Their fronded palms in air;
I only know I cannot drift
　Beyond his love and care.

189　　　　　from *The Brewing of Soma*

Dear Lord and Father of mankind,
　Forgive our foolish ways!
Reclothe us in our rightful mind,
In purer lives thy service find,
　In deeper reverence, praise.

In simple trust like theirs who heard
　Beside the Syrian sea
The gracious calling of the Lord,
Let us, like them, without a word,
　Rise up and follow thee.

O Sabbath rest by Galilee!
　O calm of hills above,
Where Jesus knelt to share with thee
The silence of eternity
　Interpreted by love!

With that deep hush subduing all
　Our words and works that drown
The tender whisper of thy call,
As noiseless let thy blessing fall
　As fell thy manna down.

Drop thy still dews of quietness,
　Till all our strivings cease;
Take from our souls the strain and stress,
And let our ordered lives confess
　The beauty of thy peace.

Breathe through the heats of our desire
　Thy coolness and thy balm;
Let sense be dumb, let flesh retire;
Speak through the earthquake, wind, and fire,
　O still, small voice of calm!

190 *Worship*

'Pure religion and undefiled before God and the Father is this, To visit the fatherless and widows in their affliction, and to keep himself unspotted from the world.'

(*James 1:27*)

The Pagan's myths through marble lips are spoken,
    And ghosts of old Beliefs still flit and moan
Round fane and altar overthrown and broken,
    O'er tree-grown barrow and gray ring of stone.

Blind Faith had martyrs in those old high places,
    The Syrian hill grove and the Druid's wood,
With mothers offering, to the Fiend's embraces,
    Bone of their bone, and blood of their own blood.

Red altars, kindling through that night of error,
    Smoked with warm blood beneath the cruel eye
Of lawless Power and sanguinary Terror,
    Throned on the circle of a pitiless sky;

Beneath whose baleful shadow, over-casting
    All heaven above, and blighting earth below,
The scourge grew red, the lip grew pale with fasting,
    And man's oblation was his fear and woe!

Then through great temples swelled the dismal moaning
    Of dirge-like music and sepulchral prayer;
Pale wizard priests, o'er occult symbols droning,
    Swung their white censers in the burdened air:

As if the pomp of rituals, and the savor
    Of gums and spices could the Unseen One please;
As if His ear could bend, with childish favor,
    To the poor flattery of the organ keys!

Feet red from war-fields trod the church aisles holy,
    With trembling reverence: and the oppressor there,
Kneeling before his priest, abased and lowly,
    Crushed human hearts beneath his knee of prayer.

Not such the service the benignant Father
    Requireth at His earthly children's hands:

Not the poor offering of vain rites, but rather
   The simple duty man from man demands.

For Earth he asks it: the full joy of heaven
   Knoweth no change of waning or increase;
The great heart of the Infinite beats even,
   Untroubled flows the river of His peace.

He asks no taper lights, on high surrounding
   The priestly altar and the saintly grave,
No dolorous chant nor organ music sounding,
   Nor incense clouding up the twilight nave.

For he whom Jesus loved hath truly spoken:
   The holier worship which he deigns to bless
Restores the lost, and binds the spirit broken,
   And feeds the widow and the fatherless!

Types of our human weakness and our sorrow!
   Who lives unhaunted by his loved ones dead?
Who, with vain longing, seeketh not to borrow
   From stranger eyes the home lights which have fled?

O brother man! fold to thy heart thy brother;
   Where pity dwells, the peace of God is there;
To worship rightly is to love each other,
   Each smile a hymn, each kindly deed a prayer.

Follow with reverent steps the great example
   Of Him whose holy work was 'doing good';
So shall the wide earth seem our Father's temple,
   Each loving life a psalm of gratitude.

Then shall all shackles fall; the stormy clangor
   Of wild war music o'er the earth shall cease;
Love shall tread out the baleful fire of anger,
   And in its ashes plant the tree of peace!

ALFRED, LORD TENNYSON
1809–1892

from *In Memoriam*

XXVIII

The time draws near the birth of Christ:
    The moon is hid; the night is still;
    The Christmas bells from hill to hill
Answer each other in the mist.

Four voices of four hamlets round,
    From far and near, on mead and moor,
    Swell out and fail, as if a door
Were shut between me and the sound;

Each voice four changes on the wind,
    That now dilate and now decrease,
    Peace and goodwill, goodwill and peace,
Peace and goodwill, to all mankind.

This year I slept and woke with pain,
    I almost wished no more to wake,
    And that my hold on life would break
Before I heard those bells again;

But they my troubled spirit rule,
    For they controlled me when a boy;
    They bring me sorrow touched with joy,
The merry, merry bells of Yule.

XLIX

Be near me when my light is low,
    When the blood creeps, and the nerves prick
    And tingle; and the heart is sick,
And all the wheels of Being slow.

Be near me when the sensuous frame
    Is racked with pangs that conquer trust;
    And Time, a maniac scattering dust,
And Life, a Fury slinging flame.

Be near me when my faith is dry,
   And men the flies of latter spring,
   That lay their eggs, and sting and sing,
And weave their petty cells and die.

Be near me when I fade away,
   To point the term of human strife,
   And on the low dark verge of life
The twilight of eternal day.

XCV

You say, but with no touch of scorn,
   Sweet-hearted, you, whose light blue eyes
   Are tender over drowning flies,
You tell me, doubt is Devil-born.

I know not: one indeed I knew
   In many a subtle question versed,
   Who touched a jarring lyre at first,
But ever strove to make it true:

Perplexed in faith, but pure in deeds,
   At last he beat his music out.
   There lives more faith in honest doubt,
Believe me, than in half the creeds.

He fought his doubts and gathered strength,
   He would not make his judgement blind,
   He faced the spectres of the mind
And laid them: thus he came at length

To find a stronger faith his own;
   And Power was with him in the night,
   Which makes the darkness and the light,
And dwells not in the light alone,

But in the darkness and the cloud,
   As over Sinai's peaks of old,
   While Israel made their gods of gold,
Although the trumpet blew so loud.

CXXIII

That which we dare invoke to bless;
   Our dearest faith; our ghastliest doubt;
   He, They, One, All; within, without;
The Power in darkness whom we guess;

I found him not in world or sun,
   Or eagle's wing, or insect's eye;
   Nor through the questions men may try,
The petty cobwebs we have spun:

If e'er when faith had fallen asleep,
   I heard a voice 'believe no more'
   And heard an ever-breaking shore
That tumbled in the Godless deep;

A warmth within the breast would melt
   The freezing reason's colder part,
   And like a man in wrath the heart
Stood up and answered 'I have felt.'

No, like a child in doubt and fear:
   But that blind clamour made me wise;
   Then was I as a child that cries,
But, crying, knows his father near;

And what I am beheld again
   What is, and no man understands;
   And out of darkness came the hands
That reach through nature, moulding men.

CXXV

Love is and was my Lord and King,
   And in his presence I attend
   To hear the tidings of my friend,
Which every hour his couriers bring.

Love is and was my King and Lord,
   And will be, though as yet I keep
   Within his court on earth, and sleep
Encompassed by his faithful guard,

And hear at times a sentinel
   Who moves about from place to place,
   And whispers to the worlds of space,
In the deep night, that all is well.

JONES VERY
1813–1880

192   *The Created*

There is naught for thee by thy haste to gain;
'Tis not the swift with Me that win the race;
Through long endurance of delaying pain,
Thine opened eye shall see thy Father's face;
Nor here nor there, where now thy feet would turn,
Thou wilt find Him who ever seeks for thee;
But let obedience quench desires that burn,
And where thou art, thy Father, too, will be.
Behold! as day by day the spirit grows,
Thou see'st by inward light things hid before;
Till what God is, thyself, his image shows;
And thou dost wear the robe that first thou wore,
When bright with radiance from his forming hand,
He saw thee Lord of all his creatures stand.

JOHN MASON NEALE
1818–1866

193   *'Oh, give us back the days of old'*

Oh, give us back the days of old! oh! give me back an hour!
To make us feel that Holy Church o'er death hath might and power.
Take hence the heathen trappings, take hence the Pagan show,
The misery, the heartlessness, the unbelief of woe:
The nodding plumes, the painted staves, the mutes in black array,
That get their hard-won earnings by so much grief per day:

The steeds and scarves and crowds that gaze with half-suspended
  breath
As if, of all things terrible, most terrible was death:
And let us know to what we go, and wherefore we must weep,
Or o'er the Christian's hopeful rest, or everlasting sleep.
Lay in the dead man's hand the Cross—the Cross upon his breast
Because beneath the shadow of the Cross he went to rest:
And let the Cross go on before—the Crucified was first
To go before the people and their chains of death to burst;
And be the widow's heart made glad with charitable dole,
And pray with calm, yet earnest, faith for the departed soul.
And be the *De Profundis* said for one of Christ's own fold,
And—for a prisoner is set free—the bells be rung not tolled.
When face to face we stand with death, thus Holy Church records,
He is our slave, and we, through Her, his masters and his lords.
Deck the High Altar for the Mass! Let tapers guard the hearse!
For Christ, the Light that lighteneth all, to blessing turns our curse,
And be Nicea's Creed intoned and be the Gospel read,
In calm, low voice, for preaching can profit not the dead.
Then forth with banner, cross, and psalm, and chant, and hymn and
  prayer,
And look not on the coffin—for our brother is not there;
His soul, we trust assuredly, is safe in Abraham's breast,
And mid Christ's many faithful, his body shall have rest.
When earth its cares and turmoils, and many sorrows cease—
By all Thy woes, by all Thy joys, Lord Jesus grant them peace.

JULIA WARD HOWE

1819–1910

194   *Battle-Hymn of the Republic*

Mine eyes have seen the glory of the coming of the Lord:
He is trampling out the vintage where the grapes of wrath are stored;
He hath loosed the fateful lightning of his terrible swift sword:
    His truth is marching on.

I have seen Him in the watch-fires of a hundred circling camps;
They have builded Him an altar in the evening dews and damps;
I can read His righteous sentence by the dim and flaring lamps.
    His day is marching on.

I have read a fiery gospel, writ in burnished rows of steel:
'As ye deal with my contemners, so with you my grace shall deal;
Let the Hero, born of woman, crush the serpent with his heel,
       Since God is marching on.'

He has sounded forth the trumpet that shall never call retreat;
He is sifting out the hearts of men before his judgement-seat:
Oh! be swift, my soul, to answer Him! be jubilant, my feet!
       Our God is marching on.

In the beauty of the lilies Christ was born across the sea,
With a glory in his bosom that transfigures you and me:
As he died to make men holy, let us die to make men free,
       While God is marching on.

WILLIAM WHITING
1825–1878

195   *'Eternal Father, strong to save'*

Eternal Father, strong to save,
Whose arm doth bind the restless wave,
Who bidd'st the mighty ocean deep
Its own appointed limits keep;
    Oh, hear us when we cry to thee
    For those in peril on the sea.

O Saviour, whose almighty word
The winds and waves submissive heard,
Who walkedst on the foaming deep,
And calm amidst its rage didst sleep:
    Oh, hear us when we cry to thee
    For those in peril on the sea.

O sacred Spirit, who didst brood
Upon the chaos dark and rude,
Who bad'st its angry tumult cease,
And gavest light and life and peace:
    Oh, hear us when we cry to thee
    For those in peril on the sea.

O Trinity of love and power,
Our brethren shield in danger's hour;
From rock and tempest, fire and foe,
Protect them wheresoe'er they go:
  And ever let there rise to thee
  Glad hymns of praise from land and sea.

EMILY DICKINSON
1830–1886

196   *'Our journey had advanced'*

Our journey had advanced,
Our feet were almost come
To that odd fork in being's road,
Eternity by term.

Our pace took sudden awe,
Our feet reluctant led;
Before were cities, but between,
The forest of the dead.

Retreat was out of hope;
Behind, a sealed route,
Eternity's white flag before,
And God at every gate.

197   *'I shall know why'*

I shall know why, when time is over,
And I have ceased to wonder why;
Christ will explain each separate anguish
In the fair schoolroom of the sky.

He will tell me what Peter promised,
And I, for wonder at his woe,
I shall forget the drop of anguish
That scalds me now, that scalds me now.

239

198   *'Bring me the sunset in a cup'*

Bring me the sunset in a cup,
Reckon the morning's flagons up
And say how many dew,
Tell me how far the morning leaps,
Tell me what time the weaver sleeps
Who spun the breadths of blue.

Write me how many notes there be
In the new robin's exstasy
Among astonished boughs,
How many trips the tortoise makes,
How many cups the bee partakes,
The debauchee of dews.

Also, who laid the rainbow's piers,
Also, who leads the docile spheres
By withes of supple blue?
Whose fingers string the stalactite,
Who counts the wampum of the night
To see that none is due?

Who built this little alban house
And shut the windows down so close
My spirit cannot see?
Who'll let me out some gala day
With implements to fly away,
Passing pomposity?

199   *'We thirst at first'*

We thirst at first—'tis nature's act—
And later, when we die,
A little water supplicate
Of fingers going by.

It intimates the finer want
Whose adequate supply
Is that great water in the west
Termed Immortality.

200   *'Just lost when I was saved'*

Just lost when I was saved,
Just felt the world go by,
Just girt me for the onset with eternity,
When breath blew back,
And on the other side
I heard recede the disappointed tide.

Therefore as one returned I feel,
Odd secrets of the line to tell—
Some sailor skirting foreign shores,
Some pale reporter from the awful doors
Before the seal.

Next time, to stay.
Next time, the things to see
By ear unheard,
Unscrutinized by eye—

Next time, to tarry,
While the ages steal,
Slow tramp the centuries,
And the cycles wheel.

201   *'I stepped from plank to plank'*

I stepped from plank to plank,
A slow and cautious way;
The stars about my head I felt,
About my feet the sea.

I knew not but the next
Would be my final inch.
This gave me that precarious gait
Some call experience.

202   *'To learn the transport by the pain'*

To learn the transport by the pain
As blind men learn the sun,
To die of thirst suspecting
That brooks in meadows run,

To stay the homesick, homesick feet
Upon a foreign shore,
Haunted by native lands the while,
And blue, beloved air—

This is the sovreign anguish,
This the signal woe.
These are the patient laureates
Whose voices, trained below,

Ascend in ceaseless carol,
Inaudible indeed
To us, the duller scholars
Of the mysterious bard.

203   *''Tis so much joy!'*

'Tis so much joy! 'tis so much joy!
If I should fail, what poverty!
And yet, as poor as I
Have ventured all upon a throw,
Have gained—yes, hesitated so,
This side the victory.

Life is but life, and death but death.
Bliss is but bliss, and breath but breath.
And if indeed I fail,
At least to know the worst is sweet.
Defeat means nothing but defeat,
No drearier can befall.

And if I gain—Oh gun at sea,
Oh bells that in the steeples be,
At first repeat it slow!
For Heaven is a different thing,
Conjectured and waked sudden in,
And might extinguish me.

204   *'It is an honorable thought'*

It is an honorable thought
And makes one lift one's hat,
As one met sudden gentlefolk
Upon a daily street,

That we've immortal place
Though pyramids decay
And kingdoms like the orchard
Flit russetly away.

205   *'Heaven is what I cannot reach'*

Heaven is what I cannot reach.
The apple on the tree,
Provided it do hopeless hang,
That Heaven is to me.

The colour on the cruising cloud,
The interdicted land
Behind the hill, the house behind,
There paradise is found.

Her teazing purples, afternoons,
The credulous decoy,
Enamored of the conjuror
That spurned us yesterday.

206   *'Read, sweet, how others strove'*

Read, sweet, how others strove,
Till we are stouter;
What they renounced,
Till we are less afraid;
How many times they bore the faithful witness,
Till we are helped
As if a kingdom cared.

Read then of faith
That shone above the fagot,
Clear strains of hymn

The river could not drown,
Brave names of men
And celestial women
Passed out of record
Into renown.

207   *'I should have been too glad'*

I should have been too glad, I see,
Too lifted for the scant degree
Of life's penurious round;
My little circuit would have shamed
This new circumference, have blamed
The homelier time behind.

I should have been too saved, I see,
Too rescued; fear too dim to me
That I could spell the prayer
I knew so perfect yesterday,
That scalding one, 'Sabachthani',
Recited fluent here.

Earth would have been too much, I see,
And Heaven not enough for me.
I should have had the joy
Without the fear to justify,
The palm without the Calvary.
So, Savior, crucify.

Defeat whets victory, they say.
The reefs in old Gethsemane
Endear the shore beyond.
'Tis beggars banquets best define,
'Tis thirsting vitalizes wine.
Faith bleats to understand.

208   *'Great streets of silence led away'*

Great streets of silence led away
To neighborhoods of pause.
Here was no notice, no dissent,
No universe, no laws.

By clocks 'twas morning, and for night
The bells at distance called,
But epoch had no basis here
For period exhaled.

209   *'He fumbles at your soul'*

He fumbles at your soul
As players at the keys
Before they drop full music on.
He stuns you by degrees,
Prepares your brittle nature
For the ethereal blow
By fainter hammers further heard,
Then nearer, then so slow
Your breath has time to straighten,
Your brain to bubble cool,
Deals one imperial thunderbolt
That scalps your naked soul.

When winds take forests in their paws
The universe is still.

210   *'Immortal is an ample word'*

Immortal is an ample word
When what we need is by,
But when it leaves us for a time
'Tis a necessity.

Of Heaven above the firmest proof
We fundamental know,
Except for its marauding hand
It had been Heaven below.

211   *'Remorse is memory awake'*

Remorse is memory awake,
Her parties all astir,
A presence of departed acts
At window and at door.

It's past set down before the soul
And lighted with a match,
Perusal to facilitate
And help belief to stretch.

Remorse is cureless—the disease
Not even God can heal,
For 'tis his institution and
The adequate of Hell.

212   *'The only news I know'*

The only news I know
Is bulletins all day
From immortality;

The only shows I see
Tomorrow and today,
Perchance eternity.

The only one I meet
Is God, the only street
Existence; this traversed,

If other news there be
Or admirabler show,
I'll tell it you.

213   *'He preached upon "Breadth"'*

He preached upon 'Breadth' till it argued him narrow—
The broad are too broad to define;
And of 'Truth', until it proclaimed him a liar,
The truth never flaunted a sign.

Simplicity fled from his counterfeit presence
As gold the pyrites would shun.
What confusion would cover the innocent Jesus
To meet so enabled a man!

ANONYMOUS
19th century
The Bitter Withy

As it fell out upon a bright holiday,
Small hail from the sky did fall.
Our Saviour asked his mother mild,
'Can I go out and play at the ball?'

'At the ball, the ball, my own dear son
It's time that you was gone;
But it's don't let me hear of any mischief
At night when you come home.'

So it's up the hill and it's down the hill
Our sweet young Saviour ran,
Until he come to three rich lords' sons:
'Good morning, sirs, each one.'

'Good morn, good morn, and good morn,' says they;
'It's thrice good morn,' says he,
'And it's which of you three rich lords' sons
Is gonna play at the ball with me?'

'Why we, we're lords', we're ladies' sons
Born in a bower or hall.
But you, you're nothing but a poor maid's child,
You was born in an ox's stall.'

'Well, if I'm nothing but a poor maid's child
Born in an ox's stall,
I'll make you believe in your latter end
That I'm an angel above you all.'

And so he built him a bridge with the rays of the sun.
Over the river ran he.
Them three rich lords' sons, they followed him,
And it's drowned they were, all three.

And it's up the hill and it's down the hill
Three weeping mothers ran
Saying, 'Mary mild, take home your child,
For ours he's drowned, each one.'

And so it's Mary Mild, she took home her child,
She laid him across her knee,
And it's with a switch of the bitter withy
She's given him slashes three.

'Oh bitter withy, oh bitter withy,
You caused me to smart;
And now the willow shall be the very first tree
Gonna perish at the heart.'

CHRISTINA ROSSETTI
1830–1894

215   *Easter Monday*

Out in the rain a world is growing green,
  On half the trees quick buds are seen
    Where glued-up buds have been.
Out in the rain God's Acre stretches green,
  Its harvest quick tho' still unseen:
    For there the Life hath been.

If Christ hath died His brethren well may die,
  Sing in the gate of death, lay by
    This life without a sigh:
For Christ hath died and good it is to die;
  To sleep when so He lays us by,
    Then wake without a sigh.

Yea, Christ hath died, yea, Christ is risen again:
  Wherefore both life and death grow plain
    To us who wax and wane;
For Christ Who rose shall die no more again:
  Amen: till He makes all things plain
    Let us wax on and wane.

216   *St Peter*

St Peter once: 'Lord, dost Thou wash my feet?'—
   Much more I say: Lord, dost Thou stand and knock
   At my closed heart more rugged than a rock,
Bolted and barred, for Thy soft touch unmeet,
Nor garnished nor in any wise made sweet?
   Owls roost within and dancing satyrs mock.
   Lord, I have heard the crowing of the cock
And have not wept: ah, Lord, thou knowest it.
Yet still I hear Thee knocking, still I hear:
   'Open to Me, look on Me eye to eye,
That I may wring thy heart and make it whole;
And teach thee love because I hold thee dear
   And sup with thee in gladness soul with soul,
And sup with thee in glory by and by.'

GERARD MANLEY HOPKINS
1844–1889

217   *Heaven-Haven*
    A nun takes the veil

   I have desired to go
     Where springs not fail,
To fields where flies no sharp and sided hail
    And a few lilies blow.

   And I have asked to be
     Where no storms come,
Where the green swell is in the havens dumb,
    And out of the swing of the sea.

218   '*As kingfishers catch fire*'

As kingfishers catch fire, dragonflies draw flame;
   As tumbled over rim in roundy wells
   Stones ring; like each tucked string tells, each hung bell's
Bow swung finds tongue to fling out broad its name;
Each mortal thing does one thing and the same:
   Deals out that being indoors each one dwells;
   Selves—goes itself; *myself* it speaks and spells,
Crying *What I do is me: for that I came.*

I say more: the just man justices;
   Keeps gráce: thát keeps all his goings graces;
Acts in God's eye what in God's eye he is—
   Chríst. For Christ plays in ten thousand places,
Lovely in limbs, and lovely in eyes not his
   To the Father through the features of men's faces.

219   *'I wake and feel the fell of dark'*

I wake and feel the fell of dark, not day.
What hours, O what black hoürs we have spent
This night! what sights you, heart, saw; ways you went!
And more must, in yet longer light's delay.

With witness I speak this. But where I say
Hours I mean years, mean life. And my lament
Is cries countless, cries like dead letters sent
To dearest him that lives alas! away.

I am gall, I am heartburn. God's most deep decree
Bitter would have me taste: my taste was me;
Bones built in me, flesh filled, blood brimmed the curse.

Selfyeast of spirit a dull dough sours. I see
The lost are like this, and their scourge to be
As I am mine, their sweating selves; but worse.

220   *In the Valley of the Elwy*

I remember a house where all were good
   To me, God knows, deserving no such thing:
   Comforting smell breathed at very entering,
Fetched fresh, as I suppose, off some sweet wood.

That cordial air made those kind people a hood
   All over, as a bevy of eggs the mothering wing
   Will, or mild nights the new morsels of Spring:
Why, it seemed of course; seemed of right it should.

Lovely the woods, waters, meadows, combes, vales,
All the air things wear that build this world of Wales;
   Only the inmate does not correspond:

God, lover of souls, swaying considerate scales,
Complete thy creature dear O where it fails,
   Being mighty a master, being a father and fond.

ALICE MEYNELL
1847–1922

221   *A General Communion*

I saw the throng, so deeply separate,
    Fed at one only board—
The devout people, moved, intent, elate,
    And the devoted Lord.

Oh struck apart! not side from human side,
    But soul from human soul,
As each asunder absorbed the multiplied,
    The ever unparted whole.

I saw this people as a field of flowers,
    Each grown at such a price
The sum of unimaginable powers
    Did no more than suffice.

A thousand single central daisies they,
    A thousand of the one;
For each, the entire monopoly of day;
    For each, the whole of the devoted sun.

222   *The Fugitive*
       '*Nous avons chassé ce Jésus-Christ*'
            —French publicist.

Yes, from the ingrate heart, the street
Of garrulous tongue, the warm retreat
    Within the village and the town;
    Not from the lands where ripen brown
A thousand thousand hills of wheat;

Not from the long Burgundian line,
The Southward, sunward range of vine.
　　Hunted, He never will escape
　　The flesh, the blood, the sheaf, the grape,
That feed His man—the bread, the wine.

223　　　　　*In Portugal, 1912*

And will they cast the altars down,
　　Scatter the chalice, crush the bread?
In field, in village, and in town
　　He hides an unregarded head;

Waits in the corn-lands far and near,
　　Bright in His sun, dark in His frost,
Sweet in the vine, ripe in the ear—
　　Lonely unconsecrated Host.

In ambush at the merry board
　　The Victim lurks unsacrificed;
The mill conceals the harvest's Lord,
　　The wine-press holds the unbidden Christ.

ROBERT BRIDGES
1844–1930

224　　　　*Noel: Christmas Eve, 1913*
　　　　　Pax hominibus bonae voluntatis

A frosty Christmas Eve
　　when the stars were shining
Fared I forth alone
　　where westward falls the hill,
And from many a village
　　in the water'd valley
Distant music reach'd me
　　peals of bells aringing:
The constellated sounds
　　ran sprinkling on earth's floor
As the dark vault above

with stars was spangled o'er.
  Then sped my thought to keep
  that first Christmas of all
When the shepherds watching
  by their folds ere the dawn
Heard music in the fields
  and marvelling could not tell
Whether it were angels
  or the bright stars singing.
Now blessed be the tow'rs
  that crown England so fair
That stand up strong in prayer
  unto God for our souls:
Blessed be their founders
  (said I) an' our country folk
Who are ringing for Christ
  in the belfries tonight
With arms lifted to clutch
  the rattling ropes that race
Into the dark above
  and the mad romping din.
But to me heard afar
  it was starry music
Angels' song, comforting
  as the comfort of Christ
When he spake tenderly
  to his sorrowful flock:
The old words came to me
  by the riches of time
Mellow'd and transfigured
  as I stood on the hill
Heark'ning in the aspect
  of th'eternal silence.

225   *Low Barometer*

The southwind strengthens to a gale,
Across the moon the clouds fly fast,
The house is smitten as with a flail,
The chimney shudders to the blast.

On such a night, when air has loosed
Its guardian grasp on blood and brain,
Old terrors then of god or ghost
Creep from their caves to life again;

And Reason kens he herits in
A haunted house. Tenants unknown
Assert their squalid lease of sin
With earlier title than his own.

Unbodied presences, the pack'd
Pollution and Remorse of Time,
Slipped from oblivion, reenact
The horrors of unhouseled crime.

Some men would quell the thing with prayer
Whose sightless footsteps pad the floor,
Whose fearful trespass mounts the stair
Or bursts the lock'd forbidden door.

Some have seen corpses long interr'd
Escape from hallowing control,
Pale charnel forms—nay ev'n have heard
The shrilling of a troubled soul,

That wanders till the dawn hath cross'd
The dolorous dark, or Earth hath wound
Closer her storm-spredd cloke, and thrust
The baleful phantoms underground.

JOHN MEADE FALKNER
1858–1922

226 *Christmas Day. The Family Sitting*

In the days of Caesar Augustus
    There went forth this decree:
Si quis rectus et justus
    Liveth in Galilee,
Let him go up to Jerusalem
    And pay his scot to me.

JOHN MEADE FALKNER

There are passed one after the other
    Christmases fifty-three,
Since I sat here with my mother
    And heard the great decree:
How they went up to Jerusalem
    Out of Galilee.

They have passed one after the other;
    Father and mother died,
Brother and sister and brother
    Taken and sanctified.
I am left alone in the sitting,
    With none to sit beside.

On the fly-leaves of these old prayer-books
    The childish writings fade,
Which show that once they were their books
    In the days when prayer was made
For other kings and princesses,
    William and Adelaide.

The pillars are twisted with holly,
    And the font is wreathed with yew.
Christ forgive me for folly,
    Youth's lapses—not a few,
For the hardness of my middle life,
    For age's fretful view.

Cotton-wool letters on scarlet,
    All the ancient lore,
Tell how the chieftains starlit
    To Bethlehem came to adore;
To hail Him King in the manger,
    Wonderful, Counsellor.

The bells ring out in the steeple
    The gladness of erstwhile,
And the children of other people
Are walking up the aisle;
They brush my elbow in passing,
    Some turn to give me a smile.

Is the almond-blossom bitter?
　Is the grasshopper heavy to bear?
Christ make me happier, fitter
　To go to my own over there:
Jerusalem the Golden,
　What bliss beyond compare!

My Lord, where I have offended
　Do Thou forgive it me.
That so when, all being ended,
　I hear Thy last decree,
I may go up to Jerusalem
　Out of Galilee.

FRANCIS THOMPSON
1859–1907

227　　*The Kingdom of God*
　　　　'*In no strange land*'

O world invisible, we view thee,
O world intangible, we touch thee,
O world unknowable, we know thee,
Inapprehensible, we clutch thee!

Does the fish soar to find the ocean,
The eagle plunge to find the air—
That we ask of the stars in motion
If they have rumour of thee there?

Not where the wheeling systems darken,
And our benumbed conceiving soars!—
The drift of pinions, would we hearken,
Beats at our own clay-shuttered doors.

The angels keep their ancient places;—
Turn but a stone and start a wing!
'Tis ye, 'tis your estrangèd faces,
That miss the many-splendoured thing.

But (when so sad thou canst not sadder)
Cry,—and upon thy so sore loss
Shall shine the traffic of Jacob's ladder
Pitched betwixt Heaven and Charing Cross.

Yea, in the night, my Soul, my daughter,
Cry—clinging Heaven by the hems;
And lo, Christ walking on the water
Not of Gennesareth, but Thames!

CHARLES WILLIAMS
1886–1945

228   *At the 'Ye that do truly'*

Now are our prayers divided, now
Must you go lonelily, and I;
For penitence shall disallow
Communion and propinquity.

Together we commandments heard,
Paid tithes together and professed:
Now mourns a solitary word
Where solitary deeds transgressed.

Averted be that head of grace,
And turned those melancholy eyes
To weep, within a narrow place
And shadow of iniquities.

Farewell! we may no more be kind,
Nor either ease the other's breath:
Death shall our marriage vows unbind,
Death, and this sharp foretaste of death.

Farewell! before this hour is done
We shall have met or missed, my dear,
In a remoter union,
But now the solitudes are here.

CLIFFORD BAX
1886–1962

229   *'Turn back, O man'*

Turn back, O man, forswear thy foolish ways;
Old now is earth, and none may count her days,
Yet thou, her child, whose head is crowned with flame,
Still wilt not hear thine inner God proclaim:
Turn back, O man, forswear thy foolish ways.

Earth might be fair and all men glad and wise.
Age after age their tragic empires rise,
Built while they dream, and in that dreaming weep;
Would man but wake from out his haunted sleep,
Earth might be fair and all men glad and wise.

Earth shall be fair, and all her people one:
Not till that hour shall God's whole will be done;
Now, even now, once more from earth to sky
Peals forth in joy man's old undaunted cry:
Earth shall be fair, and all her folk be one.

H. D. (HILDA DOOLITTLE)
1886–1961

230   from *Sagesse*
              (Summer–Winter 1957)

I

You look at me, a hut or cage contains
your fantasy, your frantic stare;

'a white-faced Scops owl from Sierra Leone,
West Africa,' I read, under a picture in *The Listener*,

and this is Whitsun, June the ninth, and I must find
the Angel or the Power that rules this hour;

I find the name *Aneb*, with the attribute,
Dieu clément for the hour, and for the day,

H. D. (HILDA DOOLITTLE)

Dieu propice with the name *Siré*;
Viroaso is the angel for the day, and for the hour,

we may invoke the angel, *Thopitus*;
do these rebuke me? what can I do, my friend?

I can only say, 'O white-faced Scops,
stare out, glare out, live on . . .'

2

May those who file before you feel
something of what you are—that God is kept within

the narrow confines of a cage, a pen;
they will laugh and linger and some child may shudder,

touched by the majesty, the lifted wings,
the white mask and the eyes that seem to see,

like God, everything and like God, see nothing;
our small impertinence, our little worth

is invisible in the day; when darkness comes,
you will be no more a fool, a clown,

a white-faced Scops, a captive and in prison,
but noble and priest and soldier, scribe and king

will hail you, sacrosanct, while frail women
bend and sway between the temple pillars,

till the torches flicker and fail,
and there is only faint light from the braziers

and the ghostly trail of incense, and cries of recognition
and of gladness in the fragrant air.

3

'O, look, he's comical, his baggy trousers
and his spindly legs—you've still got half a bun',

H. D. (HILDA DOOLITTLE)

'he won't eat buns,' the father says,
'but mice and such, look at his claws,

a vampire—yes, he's comical, look at his nose
and whiskers—proper make-up for a Guy',

the child remembers something, draws away,
she thinks, 'I never saw a farthing,

it's half a ha'pence, but she said, teacher or somebody,
or Mr Spence, that there were two, not owls,

some other birds, sold for a farthing—and what else?'
He said, *without your Father, no bird falls,*

I don't know where or what it's all about;
I wish I could go home, get out of here;

he must be angry if he liked the birds;
I wish they wouldn't laugh, it isn't funny,

and this one's bigger than—than a hundred others,
sparrows, I think it was.

T. S. ELIOT
1888–1965

231   *Journey of the Magi*

'A cold coming we had of it,
Just the worst time of the year
For a journey, and such a long journey:
The ways deep and the weather sharp,
The very dead of winter.'
And the camels galled, sore-footed, refractory,
Lying down in the melting snow.
There were times we regretted
The summer palaces on slopes, the terraces,
And the silken girls bringing sherbet.
Then the camel men cursing and grumbling
And running away, and wanting their liquor and women,

And the night-fires going out, and the lack of shelters,
And the cities hostile and the towns unfriendly
And the villages dirty and charging high prices:
A hard time we had of it.
At the end we preferred to travel all night,
Sleeping in snatches,
With the voices singing in our ears, saying
That this was all folly.

Then at dawn we came down to a temperate valley,
Wet, below the snow line, smelling of vegetation;
With a running stream and a water-mill beating the darkness,
And three trees on the low sky,
And an old white horse galloped away in the meadow.
Then we came to a tavern with vine-leaves over the lintel,
Six hands at an open door dicing for pieces of silver,
And feet kicking the empty wine-skins.
But there was no information, and so we continued
And arrived at evening, not a moment too soon
Finding the place; it was (you may say) satisfactory.

All this was a long time ago, I remember,
And I would do it again, but set down
This set down
This: were we led all that way for
Birth or Death? There was a Birth, certainly,
We had evidence and no doubt. I had seen birth and death,
But had thought they were different; this Birth was
Hard and bitter agony for us, like Death, our death.
We returned to our places, these Kingdoms,
But no longer at ease here, in the old dispensation,
With an alien people clutching their gods.
I should be glad of another death.

232 *A Song for Simeon*

Lord, the Roman hyacinths are blooming in bowls and
The winter sun creeps by the snow hills;
The stubborn season has made stand.
My life is light, waiting for the death wind,
Like a feather on the back of my hand.
Dust in sunlight and memory in corners
Wait for the wind that chills towards the dead land.

Grant us thy peace.
I have walked many years in this city,
Kept faith and fast, provided for the poor,
Have given and taken honour and ease.
There went never any rejected from my door.
Who shall remember my house, where shall live my children's
  children
When the time of sorrow is come?
They will take to the goat's path, and the fox's home,
Fleeing from the foreign faces and the foreign swords.

Before the time of cords and scourges and lamentation
Grant us thy peace.
Before the stations of the mountain of desolation,
Before the certain hour of maternal sorrow,
Now at this birth season of decease,
Let the Infant, the still unspeaking and unspoken Word,
Grant Israel's consolation
To one who has eighty years and no tomorrow.

According to thy word.
They shall praise Thee and suffer in every generation
With glory and derision,
Light upon light, mounting the saints' stair.
Not for me the martyrdom, the ecstasy of thought and prayer,
Not for me the ultimate vision.
Grant me thy peace.
(And a sword shall pierce thy heart,
Thine also.)
I am tired with my own life and the lives of those after me,
I am dying in my own death and the deaths of those after me.
Let thy servant depart,
Having seen thy salvation.

233 *Marina*

Quis hic locus, quae regio, quae mundi plaga?

What seas what shores what grey rocks and what islands
What water lapping the bow
And scent of pine and the woodthrush singing through the fog
What images return
O my daughter.

Those who sharpen the tooth of the dog, meaning
Death
Those who glitter with the glory of the humming-bird, meaning
Death
Those who sit in the sty of contentment, meaning
Death
Those who suffer the ecstasy of the animals, meaning
Death

Are become unsubstantial, reduced by a wind,
A breath of pine, and the woodsong fog
By this grace dissolved in place

What is this face, less clear and clearer
The pulse in the arm, less strong and stronger—
Given or lent? more distant than stars and nearer than the eye

Whispers and small laughter between leaves and hurrying feet
Under sleep, where all the waters meet.

Bowsprit cracked with ice and paint cracked with heat.
I made this, I have forgotten
And remember.
The rigging weak and the canvas rotten
Between one June and another September.
Made this unknowing, half conscious, unknown, my own.
The garboard strake leaks, the seams need caulking.
This form, this face, this life
Living to live in a world of time beyond me; let me
Resign my life for this life, my speech for that unspoken,
The awakened, lips parted, the hope, the new ships.

What seas what shores what granite islands towards my timbers
And woodthrush calling through the fog
My daughter.

234   *Usk*

        Do not suddenly break the branch, or
        Hope to find
        The white hart behind the white well.
        Glance aside, not for lance, do not spell
        Old enchantments. Let them sleep.

'Gently dip, but not too deep',
Lift your eyes
Where the roads dip and where the roads rise
Seek only there
Where the grey light meets the green air
The hermit's chapel, the pilgrim's prayer.

EDWIN MUIR

1887–1958

235   *The Annunciation*

The angel and the girl are met.
Earth was the only meeting place.
For the embodied never yet
Travelled beyond the shore of space.
The eternal spirits in freedom go.

See, they have come together, see,
While the destroying minutes flow,
Each reflects the other's face
Till heaven in hers and earth in his
Shine steady there. He's come to her
From far beyond the farthest star,
Feathered through time. Immediacy
Of strangest strangeness is the bliss
That from their limbs all movement takes.
Yet the increasing rapture brings
So great a wonder that it makes
Each feather tremble on his wings.

Outside the window footsteps fall
Into the ordinary day
And with the sun along the wall
Pursue their unreturning way.
Sound's perpetual roundabout
Rolls its numbered octaves out
And hoarsely grinds its battered tune.

But through the endless afternoon
These neither speak nor movement make,

But stare into their deepening trance
As if their grace would never break.

ELIZABETH DARYUSH

1887–1977

236   '*How on solemn fields of space*'

How on solemn fields of space
Black with amplitude sublime
Form the starry flowers of time;

How the centuries replace
Lifeless worlds with worlds of green,
Scenes of rock with forest scene;

How the city, proud yet mean,
For whose sake a wildwood burned
In its turn at last despairs,

Falls before the horde of years,
All this is but thought returned,
This that we have fixed we find ...

Till on proof by proof destroyed,
On the waste-mounds of the mind,
Soul's vague lily scents the void.

DAVID JONES

1895–1974

237   *A, a, a, Domine Deus*

I said, Ah! what shall I write?
I inquired up and down.
        (He's tricked me before
with his manifold lurking-places.)
I looked for His symbol at the door.
I have looked for a long while
        at the textures and contours.

I have run a hand over the trivial intersections.
I have journeyed among the dead forms
    causation projects from pillar to pylon.
I have tired the eyes of the mind
    regarding the colours and lights.
I have felt for His Wounds
    in nozzles and containers.
I have wondered for the automatic devices.
I have tested the inane patterns
    without prejudice.
I have been on my guard
    not to condemn the unfamiliar.
For it is easy to miss Him
    at the turn of a civilization.
I have watched the wheels go round in case I might see the living
creatures like the appearance of lamps, in case I might see the Living
God projected from the Machine. I have said to the perfected steel,
be my sister and for the glassy towers I thought I felt some beginnings
of His creature, but *A, a, a, Domine Deus*, my hands found the glazed
work unrefined and the terrible crystal a stage-paste ... *Eia Domine
Deus.*

JOHN BROOKS WHEELWRIGHT
1897–1940

238   from *Forty Days*
              (*The Second Ascension of Christ*)

The doubting Apostle speaks:
  —Forty days
and forty nights, which were as days
starlight, moonlight, lamplight, sunlight
fell on his form, compact of light,
as, on dark form shade falls.
To feel him with us was enough
enough to have a look in flashing moments
how his neck behind his ear
sloped to the beam-like shoulder of the Carpenter.
He was made visible
by no shadow, shade, nor any modeling;

only the bright body of his body's light
made dark all light I knew.
O! whirring feathers, darting Dove,
that dripping twig
those drops of chrism, and—
the Christ!

—The fortieth day was spent.
He took a wild black iris between his toes
plucked it, and let it fall.
(I thought even him reluctant to give up
friendships he had found sweetly
bedded in life's bitterness.)
—'I go!
Going, I precede you.
I come
and coming, judge you by those things
in which I precede you.
Nor shall I come again till two be one:
till top be bottom; left be right;
all that which is without, within;
male with the female, each both male and female:
future and forward, past and left behind.'
And speaking, grew less tangible
than to the three on the transfigured mount.
'I have shown you my glory.
As a bee leaves the flower
I go,
but cleave a seed—I am there;
split the rock, you shall find me,
and where the lonely ones
gather together, there I am.'

I saw him stretch his arms,
I thought him tired and yawning,
but, with a shock of shame, I knew
the benediction in the attitude.
(I had not seen him die.)
We saw his wounds glow red,
the body fulminate
and Him of Fire,
mounting on subservient Seraphim
whirl, twist away.

The arms had stretched as if for flight—
the five Scars glowed—
his chest lifted as for breath,
and his heels, as if for dancing;
between, beneath his toes
the red clay clung and kissed them.—
The legs hung from the hips
a bell below the torse,
swung like a bell below the hips;
he lifted his chin in song.
The smoking robe consumed in flame:
White flames, Petals of Lilies
Lilies of Flame, Dimmed by the effulgence of the Flesh.
There, a triumphal statue with no pedestal, he stood;
then mounted higher on the air.
The footprints ringed wider
like footprints on still water
ringed, broke into stars, wings, legionary eyes.
In rushing flight about him
in spheres and disks, the Seraphim
Span, Whirled, Twisted
Flickered, Gleamed away.
Away, toward the opened Firmament
through the triangular Name above it.
Above It,
away.

—We gaped and shook our heads and gazed
after what had passed before our eyes.
He.
Not a cynic, no blasphemer
no Rabbi; not a daemon
not a devil, and no Prophet.
He.
The One, the True God, going to his Father in Heaven
as to his Mother on Earth, he came, the One, the True,
the Lord.
We stared not only in wonder, not with loneliness,
feeling him with us, permanent . . .

'Gluttonous bees! Come forth!'
—Two Strangers sudden beside us
standing in the midst of praise.

'Forth, gluttonous bees!
Swarm!
Come from the blossomed eye
the germ of act, the seed to split the rock
forth; come forth; swarm.'

We turned and fled; not as we had fled
from that disturbed suburban orchard
not so now, we were fleeing
toward the City, not away from it.
Our heads were buffeted by Clubs, by Stones
Swords, Glaives, Knives, Saws, Spears, bit our feet.
Our blood spattered our paths.
Forward, Sideward, Backward, Forward
four pitched prone;
lay, like fallen crucifixions
a moment, then on again.

I, and the other Son of Thunder
plunged down hill
with backs bowed, with eager brows
like angelic Centaurs we saw riding
Above, Behind, Below, Before, About us
whom, Within us and Without us,
we heard shouting:
—'Rome!
to Rome,
Rome!
Go to Rome!
Go tell the Roman Synagogue.
Tell Rome!'

JANET LEWIS

1899–

239   *A Lullaby*

Lullee, lullay,
I could not love thee more
If thou wast Christ the King.
Now tell me, how did Mary know
That in her womb should sleep and grow
The Lord of everything?

JANET LEWIS

Lullee, lullay,
An angel stood with her
Who said, 'That which doth stir
Like summer in thy side
Shall save the world from sin.
Then stable, hall and inn
Shall cherish Christmas-tide.'

Lullee, lullay,
And so it was that Day.
And did she love Him more
Because an angel came
To prophesy His name?
Ah no, not so,
She could not love Him more,
But loved Him just the same.
Lullee, lullee, lullay.

STEVIE SMITH

1902–1971

240   *The Airy Christ*
(*After reading Dr Rieu's translation of St Mark's Gospel*)

Who is this that comes in splendour, coming from the blazing East?
This is he we had not thought of, this is he the airy Christ.

Airy, in an airy manner in an airy parkland walking,
Others take him by the hand, lead him, do the talking.

But the Form, the airy One, frowns an airy frown,
What they say he knows must be, but he looks aloofly down,

Looks aloofly at his feet, looks aloofly at his hands,
Knows they must, as prophets say, nailèd be to wooden bands.

As he knows the words he sings, that he sings so happily
Must be changed to working laws, yet sings he ceaselessly.

Those who truly hear the voice, the words, the happy song,
Never shall need working laws to keep from doing wrong.

Deaf men will pretend sometimes they hear the song, the words,
And make excuse to sin extremely; this will be absurd.

Heed it not. Whatever foolish men may do the song is cried
For those who hear, and the sweet singer does not care that he
   was crucified.

For he does not wish that men should love him more than anything
Because he died; he only wishes they would hear him sing.

PADRAIC FALLON

1905–1974

241   *Mater Dei*

In March the seed
Fell, when the month leaned over, looking
Down into her valley.
And none but the woman knew it where she sat
In the tree of her veins and tended him
The red and ripening Adam of the year.

Her autumn was late and human.
Trees were nude, the lights were on the pole
All night when he came,
Her own man;
In the cry of a child she sat, not knowing
That this was a stranger.

Milk ran wild
Across the heavens. Imperiously He
Sipped at the delicate beakers she proffered him.
How was she to know
How huge a body she was, how she corrected
The very tilt of the earth on its new course?

ROBERT PENN WARREN

1905–

242   *Original Sin: A Short Story*

Nodding, its great head rattling like a gourd,
And locks like seaweed strung on the stinking stone,
The nightmare stumbles past, and you have heard
It fumble your door before it whimpers and is gone:
It acts like the old hound that used to snuffle your door and moan.

You thought you had lost it when you left Omaha,
For it seemed connected then with your grandpa, who
Had a wen on his forehead and sat on the veranda
To finger the precious protuberance, as was his habit to do,
Which glinted in sun like rough garnet or the rich old brain bulging
    through.

But you met it in Harvard Yard as the historic steeple
Was confirming the midnight with its hideous racket,
And you wondered how it had come, for it stood so imbecile,
With empty hands, humble, and surely nothing in pocket:
Riding the rods, perhaps—or grandpa's will paid the ticket.

You were almost kindly then, in your first homesickness,
As it tortured its stiff face to speak, but scarcely mewed.
Since then you have outlived all your homesickness,
But have met it in many another distempered latitude:
Oh, nothing is lost, ever lost! at last you understood.

It never came in the quantum glare of sun
To shame you before your friends, and had nothing to do
With your public experience or private reformation:
But it thought no bed too narrow—it stood with lips askew
And shook its great head sadly like the abstract Jew.

Never met you in the lyric arsenical meadow
When children call and your heart goes stone in the bosom,
At the orchard anguish never, nor ovoid horror,
Which is furred like a peach or avid like the delicious plum.
It takes no part in your classic prudence or fondled axiom.

Not there when you exclaimed: 'Hope is betrayed by
Disastrous glory of sea-capes, sun-torment of whitecaps
—There must be a new innocence for us to be stayed by.'
But there it stood, after all the timetables, all the maps,
In the crepuscular clutter of *always*, *always*, or *perhaps*.

You have moved often and rarely left an address,
And hear of the deaths of friends with a sly pleasure,
A sense of cleansing and hope which blooms from distress;
But it has not died, it comes, its hand childish, unsure,
Clutching the bribe of chocolate or a toy you used to treasure.

It tries the lock. You hear, but simply drowse:
There is nothing remarkable in that sound at the door.
Later you may hear it wander the dark house
Like a mother who rises at night to seek a childhood picture;
Or it goes to the backyard and stands like an old horse cold in the
  pasture.

SIR JOHN BETJEMAN
1906–1984

243 *Sunday Afternoon Service in
St Enodoc Church, Cornwall*

Come on! come on! This hillock hides the spire,
Now that one and now none. As winds about
The burnished path through lady's finger, thyme
And bright varieties of saxifrage,
So grows the tinny tenor faint or loud
And all things draw towards St Enodoc.

Come on! come on! and it is five to three.

Paths, unfamiliar to golfers' brogues,
Cross the eleventh fairway broadside on
And leave the fourteenth tee for thirteenth green,
Ignoring Royal and Ancient, bound for God.
   Come on! come on! no longer bare of foot,
The sole grows hot in London shoes again.

Jack Lamburne in his Sunday navy-blue
Wears tie and collar, all from Selfridge's.
There's Enid with a silly parasol,
And Graham in grey flannel with a crease
Across the middle of his coat which lay
Pressed 'neath the box of his Meccano set,
Sunday to Sunday.
           Still, Come on! come on!
The tinny tenor. Hover-flies remain
More than a moment on a ragwort bunch,
And people's passing shadows don't disturb
Red Admirals basking with their wings apart.
    A mile of sunny, empty sand away,
A mile of shallow pools and lugworm casts,
Safe, faint and surfy, laps the lowest tide.
    Even the villas have a Sunday look.
The Ransom mower's locked into the shed.
'I have a splitting headache from the sun,'
And bedroom windows flutter cheerful chintz
Where, double-aspirined, a mother sleeps;
While father in the loggia reads a book,
Large, desultory, birthday-present size,
Published with coloured plates by *Country Life*,
A Bernard Darwin on *The English Links*
Or Braid and Taylor on *The Mashie Shot*.
Come on! come on! he thinks of Monday's round—
Come on! come on! that interlocking grip!
Come on! come on! he drops into a doze—
Come on! come on! more far and far away
The children climb a final stile to church;
Electoral Roll still flapping in the porch—
Then the cool silence of St Enodoc.

My eyes, recovering in the sudden shade,
Discern the long-known little things within—
A map of France in damp above my pew,
Grey-blue of granite in the small arcade
(Late Perp: and not a Parker specimen
But roughly hewn on windy Bodmin Moor),
The modest windows palely glazed with green,
The smooth slate floor, the rounded wooden roof,
The Norman arch, the cable-moulded font—
All have a humble and West Country look.

Oh 'drastic restoration' of the guide!
Oh three-light window by a Plymouth firm!
Absurd, truncated screen! oh sticky pews!
Embroidered altar-cloth! untended lamps!
So soaked in worship you are loved too well
For that dispassionate and critic stare
That I would use beyond the parish bounds
Biking in high-banked lanes from tower to tower
On sunny, antiquarian afternoons.
   Come on! come on! a final pull. Tom Blake
Stalks over from the bell-rope to his pew
Just as he slopes about the windy cliffs
Looking for wreckage in a likely tide,
Nor gives the Holy Table glance or nod.
A rattle as red baize is drawn aside,
Miss Rhoda Poulden pulls the tremolo,
The oboe, flute and vox humana stops;
A Village Voluntary fills the air
And ceases suddenly as it began,
Save for one oboe faintly humming on,
As slow the weary clergyman subsides
Tired with his bike-ride from the parish church.
He runs his hands once, twice, across his face
'Dearly beloved . . .' and a bumble-bee
Zooms itself free into the churchyard sun
And so my thoughts this happy Sabbathtide.
   Where deep cliffs loom enormous, where cascade
Mesembryanthemum and stone-crop down,
Where the gull looks no larger than a lark
Hung midway twixt the cliff-top and the sand,
Sun-shadowed valleys roll along the sea.
Forced by the backwash, see the nearest wave
Rise to a wall of huge, translucent green
And crumble into spray along the top
Blown seaward by the land-breeze. Now she breaks
And in an arch of thunder plunges down
To burst and tumble, foam on top of foam,
Criss-crossing, baffled, sucked and shot again,
A waterfall of whiteness, down a rock,
Without a source but roller's furthest reach:
And tufts of sea-pink, high and dry for years,
Are flooded out of ledges, boulders seem
No bigger than a pebble washed about

In this tremendous tide. Oh kindly slate!
To give me shelter in this crevice dry.
These shivering stalks of bent-grass, lucky plant,
Have better chance than I to last the storm.
Oh kindly slate of these unaltered cliffs,
Firm, barren substrate of our windy fields!
Oh lichened slate in walls, they knew your worth
Who raised you up to make this House of God.
What faith was his, that dim, that Cornish saint,
Small rushlight of a long-forgotten church,
Who lived with God on this unfriendly shore,
Who knew He made the Atlantic and the stones
And destined seamen here to end their lives
Dashed on a rock, rolled over in the surf,
And not one hair forgotten. Now they lie
In centuries of sand beside the church.
Less pitiable are they than the corpse
Of a large golfer, only four weeks dead,
This sunlit and sea-distant afternoon.
'Praise ye the Lord!' and in another key
The Lord's name by harmonium be praised.
'The Second Evening and the Fourteenth Psalm.'

W. H. AUDEN

1907–1974

244   *The Shield of Achilles*

She looked over his shoulder
    For vines and olive trees,
Marble well-governed cities
    And ships upon untamed seas,
But there on the shining metal
    His hands had put instead
An artificial wilderness
    And a sky like lead.

A plain without a feature, bare and brown,
    No blade of grass, no sign of neighbourhood,
Nothing to eat and nowhere to sit down,
    Yet, congregated on its blankness, stood

An unintelligible multitude.
A million eyes, a million boots in line,
Without expression, waiting for a sign.

Out of the air a voice without a face
    Proved by statistics that some cause was just
In tones as dry and level as the place:
    No one was cheered and nothing was discussed;
    Column by column in a cloud of dust
They marched away enduring a belief
Whose logic brought them, somewhere else, to grief.

        She looked over his shoulder
           For ritual pieties,
      White flower-garlanded heifers,
           Libation and sacrifice,
      But there on the shining metal
           Where the altar should have been,
      She saw by his flickering forge-light
           Quite another scene.

Barbed wire enclosed an arbitrary spot
    Where bored officials lounged (one cracked a joke)
And sentries sweated, for the day was hot:
    A crowd of ordinary decent folk
    Watched from without and neither moved nor spoke
As three pale figures were led forth and bound
To three posts driven upright in the ground.

The mass and majesty of this world, all
    That carries weight and always weighs the same
Lay in the hands of others; they were small
    And could not hope for help and no help came:
    What their foes liked to do was done, their shame
Was all the worst could wish; they lost their pride
And died as men before their bodies died.

        She looked over his shoulder
           For athletes at their games,
      Men and women in a dance
           Moving their sweet limbs
      Quick, quick, to music,
           But there on the shining shield

His hands had set no dancing-floor
But a weed-choked field.

A ragged urchin, aimless and alone,
    Loitered about that vacancy; a bird
Flew up to safety from his well-aimed stone:
    That girls are raped, that two boys knife a third,
    Were axioms to him, who'd never heard
Of any world where promises were kept,
Or one could weep because another wept.

        The thin-lipped armourer,
            Hephaestos, hobbled away;
        Thetis of the shining breasts
            Cried out in dismay
        At what the god had wrought
            To please her son, the strong
        Iron-hearted man-slaying Achilles
            Who would not live long.

245   *Anthem*

Let us praise our Maker, with true passion extol Him.
Let the whole creation give out another sweetness,
Nicer in our nostrils, a novel fragrance
From cleansed occasions in accord together
As one feeling fabric, all flushed and intact,
Phenomena and numbers announcing in one
Multitudinous œcumenical song
Their grand givenness of gratitude and joy,
Peaceable and plural, their positive truth
An authoritative This, an unthreatened Now
When, in love and in laughter, each lives itself,
For, united by His Word, cognition and power,
System and Order, are a single glory,
And the pattern is complex, their places safe.

246 *Amor Loci*

I could draw its map by heart,
showing its contours,
strata and vegetation,
name every height,
small burn and lonely shieling,
but nameless to me,
faceless as heather or grouse,
are those who live there,

its dead too vague for judgement,
tangible only
what they wrought, their giant works
of delve and drainage
in days preterite: long since
their hammering stopped
as the lodes all petered out
in the Jew Limestone.

Here and there a tough chimney
still towers over
dejected masonry, moss,
decomposed machines,
with no one about, no chance
of buttering bread,
a land postured in my time
for marginal farms.

Any musical future
is most unlikely.
Industry wants Cheap Power,
romantic muscle
a perilous wilderness,
Mr Pleasure pays
for surf–riding, claret, sex:
it offers them none.

To me, though, much: a vision,
not (as perhaps at
twelve I thought it) of Eden,
still less of a New

Jerusalem but, for one,
convinced he will die,
more comely, more credible
than either daydream.

How, but with some real focus
of desolation
could I, by analogy,
imagine a love
that, however often smeared,
shrugged at, abandoned
by a frivolous worldling,
does not abandon?

F. T. PRINCE

1912 –

247   *Soldiers Bathing*

The sea at evening moves across the sand.
Under a reddening sky I watch the freedom of a band
Of soldiers who belong to me. Stripped bare
For bathing in the sea, they shout and run in the warm air;
Their flesh worn by the trade of war, revives
And my mind towards the meaning of it strives.

All's pathos now. The body that was gross,
Rank, ravenous, disgusting in the act or in repose,
All fever, filth and sweat, its bestial strength
And bestial decay, by pain and labour grows at length
Fragile and luminous. 'Poor bare forked animal,'
Conscious of his desires and needs and flesh that rise and fall,
Stands in the soft air, tasting after toil
The sweetness of his nakedness: letting the sea-waves coil
Their frothy tongues about his feet, forgets
His hatred of the war, its terrible pressure that begets
A machinery of death and slavery,
Each being a slave and making slaves of others: finds that he
Remembers his old freedom in a game
Mocking himself, and comically mimics fear and shame.

He plays with death and animality;
And reading in the shadows of his pallid flesh, I see
The idea of Michelangelo's cartoon
Of soldiers bathing, breaking off before they were half done
At some sortie of the enemy, an episode
Of the Pisan wars with Florence. I remember how he showed
Their muscular limbs that clamber from the water,
And heads that turn across the shoulder, eager for the slaughter,
Forgetful of their bodies that are bare,
And hot to buckle on and use the weapons lying there.
—And I think too of the theme another found
When, shadowing men's bodies on a sinister red ground,
Another Florentine, Pollaiuolo,
Painted a naked battle: warriors, straddled, hacked the foe,
Dug their bare toes into the ground and slew
The brother-naked man who lay between their feet and drew
His lips back from his teeth in a grimace.

They were Italians who knew war's sorrow and disgrace
And showed the thing suspended, stripped: a theme
Born out of the experience of war's horrible extreme
Beneath a sky where even the air flows
With *lacrimae Christi*. For that rage, that bitterness, those blows,
That hatred of the slain, what could they be
But indirectly or directly a commentary
On the Crucifixion? And the picture burns
With indignation and pity and despair by turns,
Because it is the obverse of the scene
Where Christ hangs murdered, stripped, upon the Cross. I mean,
That is the explanation of its rage.

And we too have our bitterness and pity that engage
Blood, spirit, in this war. But night begins,
Night of the mind: who nowadays is conscious of our sins?
Though every human deed concerns our blood,
And even we must know, what nobody has understood,
That some great love is over all we do,
And that is what has driven us to this fury, for so few
Can suffer all the terror of that love:
The terror of that love has set us spinning in this groove
Greased with our blood.

These dry themselves and dress,
Combing their hair, forget the fear and shame of nakedness.
Because to love is frightening we prefer
The freedom of our crimes. Yet, as I drink the dusky air,
I feel a strange delight that fills me full.
Strange gratitude, as if evil itself were beautiful,
And kiss the wound in thought, while in the west
I watch a streak of red that might have issued from Christ's breast.

R. S. THOMAS
1913–

248   *The Hand*

It was a hand. God looked at it
and looked away. There was a coldness
about his heart, as though the hand
clasped it. As at the end
of a dark tunnel, he saw cities
the hand would build, engines
that it would raze them with. His sight
dimmed. Tempted to undo the joints
of the fingers, he picked it up.
But the hand wrestled with him. 'Tell
me your name,' it cried, 'and I will write it
in bright gold. Are there not deeds
to be done, children to make, poems
to be written? The world
is without meaning, awaiting
my coming.' But God, feeling the nails
in his side, the unnerving warmth
of the contact, fought on in
silence. This was the long war with himself
always foreseen, the question not
to be answered. What is the hand
for? The immaculate conception
preceding the delivery
of the first tool? 'I let you go,'
he said, 'but without blessing.
Messenger to the mixed things
of your making, tell them I am.'

249   *The Porch*

Do you want to know his name?
It is forgotten. Would you learn
what he was like? He was like
anyone else, a man with ears
and eyes. Be it sufficient
that in a church porch on an evening
in winter, the moon rising, the frost
sharp, he was driven
to his knees and for no reason
he knew. The cold came at him;
his breath was carved angularly
as the tombstones; an owl screamed.

He had no power to pray.
His back turned on the interior
he looked out on a universe
that was without knowledge
of him and kept his place
there for an hour on that lean
threshold, neither outside nor in.

C. H. SISSON
1914–

250   *Knole*

The white hill-side is prickled with antlers
And the deer wade to me through the snow.
From John Donne's church the muffled and galoshed
Patiently to their holy dinners go.

And never do those antlered heads reflect
On the gentle flanks where in autumn they put their seed
Nor Christians on the word which, that very hour,
Their upturned faces or their hearts received.

But spring will bring the heavy doe to bed;
The fawn will wobble and soon after leap.
Those others will die at this or the next year's turn
And find the resurrection encased in sleep.

251   *A Letter to John Donne*

Note: On 27 July 1617, Donne preached at the parish church at
Sevenoaks, of which he was rector, and was entertained at Knole, then
the country residence of Richard Sackville, third Earl of Dorset.

I understand you well enough, John Donne
First, that you were a man of ability
Eaten by lust and by the love of God
Then, that you crossed the Sevenoaks High Street
As rector of Saint Nicholas:
I am of that parish.

To be a man of ability is not much
You may see them on the Sevenoaks platform any day
Eager men with despatch cases
Whom ambition drives as they drive the machine
Whom the certainty of meticulous operation
Pleasures as a morbid sex a heart of stone.

That you could have spent your time in the corruption of courts
As these in that of cities, gives you no place among us:
Ability is not even the game of a fool
But the click of a computer operating in a waste
Your cleverness is dismissed from this suit
Bring out your genitals and your theology.

What makes you familiar is this dual obsession;
Lust is not what the rutting stag knows
It is to take Eve's apple and to lose
The stag's paradisal look:
The love of God comes readily
To those who have most need.

You brought body and soul to this church
Walking there through the park alive with deer
But now what animal has climbed into your pulpit?
One whose pretension is that the fear
Of God has heated him into a spirit
An evaporated man no physical ill can hurt.

Well might you hesitate at the Latin gate
Seeing such apes denying the church of God:
I am grateful particularly that you were not a saint
But extravagant whether in bed or in your shroud.
You would understand that in the presence of folly
I am not sanctified but angry.

Come down and speak to the men of ability
On the Sevenoaks platform and tell them
That at your Saint Nicholas the faith
Is not exclusive in the fools it chooses
That the vain, the ambitious and the highly sexed
Are the natural prey of the incarnate Christ.

252   *The Usk*

Christ is a language in which we speak to God
And also God, so that we speak in truth;
He in us, we in him, speaking
To one another, to him, the City of God.

I

Such a fool as I am you had better ignore
Tongue twist, malevolent, fat mouthed
I have no language but that other one
His the Devil's, no mouse I, creeping out of the cheese
With a peaked cap scanning the distance
Looking for truth.
Words when I have them, come out, the Devil
Encouraging, grinning from the other side of the street
And my tears
Streaming, a blubbered face, when I am not laughing
Where in all this
Is calm, measure,
Exactness
The Lord's peace?

2

Nothing is in my own voice because I have not
Any. Nothing in my own name
Here inscribed on water, nothing but flow
A ripple, outwards. Standing beside the Usk
You flow like truth, river, I will get in
Over me, through me perhaps, river let me be crystalline
As I shall not be, shivering upon the bank.
A swan passed. So it is, the surface, sometimes
Benign like a mirror, but not I passing, the bird.

3

Under the bridge, meet reward, the water
Falling in cascades or worse, you devil, for truthfulness
Is no part of the illusion, the clear sky
Is not yours, the water
Falling not yours
Only the sheep
Munching at the river brim
Perhaps

4

What I had hoped for, the clear line
Tremulous like water but
Clear also to the stones underneath
Has not come that way, for my truth
Was not public enough, nor perhaps true.
Holy Father, Almighty God
Stop me before I speak

                        —*per Christum*.

5

Lies on my tongue. Get up and bolt the door
For I am coming not to be believed
The messenger of anything I say.
So I am come, stand in the cold tonight
The servant of the grain upon my tongue,
Beware, I am the man, and let me in.

6

So speech is treasured, for the things it gives
Which I can not have, for I speak too plain
Yet not so plain as to be understood

It is confusion and a madman's tongue.
Where drops the reason, there is no one by.
Torture my mind: and so swim through the night
As envy cannot touch you, or myself
Sleep comes, and let her, warm at my side, like death.
The Holy Spirit and the Holy One
Of Israel be my guide. So among tombs
Truth may be sought, and found, if we rejoice
With Ham and Shem and Japhet in the dark.
The ark rolls onward over a wide sea.
Come sleep, come lightning, comes the dove at last.

253 *Cato*

How can I climb the Mount of Purgatory?
Cato, are you there?
—Looking so virtuous while your dream associates,
Dante and Virgil, cough behind their hands.

I who have never seen the last evening
—No more had Dante then—slip in behind
It is not for me to intrude upon the company
No supreme lady called me; if I go upwards
It will be stumbling, by myself, unobserved.
I should avoid all company on the way
And fall flat on my face if I saw Paradise,
Over the loose screes till I hit the earth
Head-first. There is so little content in this idea
Of a progression towards beatitude.
Beatitude is here or not at all
'The kingdom of heaven is at hand', or under the counter
For special purchasers who have enough money,
Coin of Caesarea. I wanted three things,
Lechery, success, never at any time virtue
But a faint approbation that makes life tolerable
As long as one lives in the city of weak smiles.
I have run counter to every device
That could bring happiness as I suppose it
Which is quite contrary to the way I have it.
O my dear absent one, oh my dear absence
When shall I be absent from myself?
Absence is mourning; absence is also love;

That presence may be love is all I pray.
I wait here and hope it may be morning.

JOHN BERRYMAN
1914–1972

254   (*Alcoholic*)

O all the problems other people face
we have intensified & could not face
until at last we feel completely alone
thick in a quart of company a day.

I knew I had a problem with that stuff
& problems with my wife & child & work;
But all what help I found left me intact
safe with a quart of feral help a day.

DT's, convulsions. Hospitals galore.
Projectile vomiting hours, intravenous,
back in the nearest bar the seventh day.
God made a suggestion. I went home

and I am in the 4th week of the third treatment
& I am *hurting*, daily, & when I jerk
a few scales seem to fall away from my eyes
until with perfect clarity enough

seems to be visible to keep me sane
& sober toward the bed where I will die.
I pray that You may grant me a yielding will.

I pray that my will may be attuned to
Your will for & with me.

JACK CLEMO

1916–

255   *'Neither Shadow of Turning'*

I could not name a single blessing
　　That came to me in disguise;
The gifts I asked arrived unmasked
　　Under broad day's honest skies.

God does not play a senile game
　　That wraps His mercies round
With a leprous sheet, a scabbed deceit:
　　His good, from the start, is sound.

There is no heaven disguised as hell,
　　No jail by which we're freed;
A twist that mocks is no paradox—
　　It's the devil's twist indeed.

'Deliver us from evil'—why,
　　If the evil has good inside?
God's war is grim—we are bruised with Him:
　　HIS gifts never mystified.

256   *Mould of Castile*
            (*to St Teresa*)

A streak of Sappho, it is said,
Inflamed you, the painted and imperious
Charmer in velvet robes at Avila;
But soon your withered young bones rattled
On convent stones: gaunt postulant,
You had fled, still dead to God, from a goblin-flare.

No mist or dream had softened
The bold Castilian flint: there was sun-glare
On bull-fights and flashing lizards
And the hot black stems of olives, pungent cistus,
Awaiting the shift and shock, an El Greco storm.

Did you waste thirty years
In fighting the sun, flashing out
With a gay jest between swoons and fears
Of those winged visions? Did election dare
Molest your Spanish pride
To that length, fan a fury of love
That soared, bled in the trap,
Lapped a wilful ease, lastly, in brisk reform?

You were ageing, an enigma still,
When your mules arrived at San José,
And a thunder that thrills my flint
In Cornwall now, spread from the wooden waggons,
Filled with your nuns, lurching over calcined plains,
Up primitive mountain tracks, drifting aground
On river ferries. You and they were bound
For new cells in Elisha's shadow:
Traditional rock like that which my poet-soul,
As wasted and adamant,
Split and gay as yours, descried
Beyond sly bramble, misted kiln
And the dried voluptuary veins.

257   *Growing in Grace*

My native clay
Symbols grow unreal.
Blunt clanging tools
Corroded rock
Kiln-scorching . . .
O Shepherd
Of green pastures!

Purgation's landscape
Fails to purge,
Makes us afraid.
Slap of hose-jets
Blinding
Deafening blast
Rattle on bleared dunes
Scoops and sirens'
Howl over stagnant mud.

Waters of Meribah.
I proved thee at the...
I proved thee.
Baptised into the death...
O Shepherd
Of green pastures!

258 *On the Death of Karl Barth*

He ascended from a lonely crag in winter,
His thunder fading in the Alpine dusk;
And a blizzard was back on the Church,
A convenient cloak, sprinkling harlot and husk—
Back again, after all his labour
To clear the passes, give us access
Once more to the old prophetic tongues,
Peak-heats in which man, time, progress
Are lost in reconciliation
With outcast and angered Deity.

He has not gone silenced in defeat:
The suffocating swirl of heresy
Confirms the law he taught us; we keep the glow,
Knowing the season, the rhythm, the consummation.

Truth predicts the eclipse of truth,
And in that eclipse it condemns man,
Whose self-love with its useful schools of thought,
Its pious camouflage of a God within,
Is always the cause of the shadow, the fall, the burial,
The smug rub of hands
Amid a reek of research.

The cyclic, well-meant smothering
Of the accursed footprints inside man's frontier;
The militant revival,
Within time and as an unchanged creed,
Of the eternal form and substance of the Word:
This has marked Western history,
Its life's chief need and counter-need,
From the hour God's feet shook Jordan.

JACK CLEMO

We touched His crag of paradox
Through our tempestuous leader, now dead,
Who ploughed from Safenwil to show us greatness
In a God lonely, exiled, homeless in our sphere,
Since his footfall breeds guilt, stirs dread
Of a love fire-tongued, cleaving our sin,
Retrieving the soul from racial evolution,
Giving it grace to mortify,
In deeps or shallows, all projections of the divine.

ANONYMOUS
c. 1935

259   *The Heavenly Aeroplane*

One of these nights about twelve o'clock
The old world's going to reel and rock,
The sinner's going to tremble and cry for pain
And the Lord will come in his aeroplane.

> Oh ye thirsty of every tribe
> Get your ticket for an aeroplane ride,
> Jesus our Savior is a-coming to reign
> And take you up to glory in His aeroplane.

Talk about your joy-rides in automobiles,
Talk about your fast time on motor wheels,
We'll break all records as we upward fly
For an aeroplane joy-ride through the sky.

There will be no punctures or muddy roads,
No broken axles from overloads,
No shocks to give trouble or cause delay
As we soon will rapture up the narrow way.

You will have to get ready if you take this ride,
Quit all your sins and humble your pride,
You must furnish a lamp both bright and clean
And a vessel of oil to run the machine.

When our journey is over and we'll all sit down
At the marriage supper with a robe and a crown
We'll blend our voices with the heavenly throng
And praise our Savior as the years roll on.

JAMES McAULEY
1917–1976

To Vincent Buckley

Since all our keys are lost or broken,
Shall it be thought absurd
If for an art of words I turn
Discreetly to the Word?

Drawn inward by his love, we trace
Art to its secret springs:
What, are we masters in Israel
And do not know these things?

Lord Christ from out his treasury
Brings forth things new and old:
We have those treasures in earthen vessels,
In parables he told,

And in the single images
Of seed, and fish, and stone,
Or, shaped in deed and miracle,
To living poems grown.

Scorn then to darken and contract
The landscape of the heart
By individual, arbitrary
And self-expressive art.

Let your speech be ordered wholly
By an intellectual love;
Elucidate the carnal maze
With clear light from above.

Give every image space and air
To grow, or as bird to fly;
So shall one grain of mustard-seed
Quite overspread the sky.

Let your literal figures shine
With pure transparency:
Not in opaque but limpid wells
Lie truth and mystery.

And universal meanings spring
From what the proud pass by:
Only the simplest forms can hold
A vast complexity.

We know, where Christ has set his hand
Only the real remains:
I am impatient for that loss
By which the spirit gains.

261   *New Guinea*

In memory of Archbishop Alain de Boismenu, M.S.C.

Bird-shaped island, with secretive bird-voices,
Land of apocalypse, where the earth dances,
The mountains speak, the doors of the spirit open,
And men are shaken by obscure trances.

The forest-odours, insects, clouds and fountains
Are like the figures of my inmost dream,
Vibrant with untellable recognition;
A wordless revelation is their theme.

The stranger is engulfed in those high valleys,
Where mists of morning linger like the breath
Of Wisdom moving on our specular darkness.
Regions of prayer, of solitude, and of death!

Life holds its shape in the modes of dance and music,
The hands of craftsmen trace its patternings;
But stains of blood, and evil spirits, lurk
Like cockroaches in the interstices of things.

We in that land begin our rule in courage,
The seal of peace gives warrant to intrusion;
But then our grin of emptiness breaks the skin,
Formless dishonour spreads its proud confusion.

JAMES McAULEY

Whence that deep longing for an exorcizer,
For Christ descending as a thaumaturge
Into his saints, as formerly in the desert,
Warring with demons on the outer verge.

Only by this can life become authentic,
Configured henceforth in eternal mode:
Splendour, simplicity, joy—such as were seen
In one who now rests by his mountain road.

CLIFF ASHBY

1918–

262   *Latter Day Psalms*

1

Somewhere there is Grace, Lord,
Was I not told it as a child
When the sound of the sparrow
Filled my heart with delight
And the rain fell like friendship on my head.
 Now the call of the cuckoo
Cannot calm my aching heart
And my soul is tormented with fear.
 Have mercy, Lord, for I have travelled far
Yet all my knowledge is as nothing.
My days are numbered. Time titters
As I stumble down the street.

Forgiveness, O forgive me, Lord,
Close my critical eye
Take me to your breast
For how else may I die.

2

The tree waves in the wind
But does not break unless
The bough is over-burdened.
When spring disrupts the dead days
Buds, leaves, and birds praise God
In song and silent sound.

CLIFF ASHBY

The dead dock, stiff
With last year's pride,
Leans unwillingly in the gale.

My heart, Lord, is unyielding.
My joints are stiff
The knuckles of my knees
Refuse to bend.
The knife is at my neck,
My back breaks.

I will say my matutinal prayers
From a crippled position,
Perhaps the Lord will hear?

3

I lived among lewd men
Beneath the Crouch End clock
Waiting for God to speak.
But my ears were dull
And what my brain received
My mind misunderstood.
So I took my mean heart to the hills,
Beside the Palace of Alexandra
Gazed on Barbican and grieved.
　　Lord speak to me in the morning
　　Or the night will be everlasting.
Now all the dogs of Dewsbury
Bay about my heels
And the foul water of the Calder
Weeps into the sea.

4

On the estate, Lord, the people
Take counsel one with another
And in the public house
There is lamentation.
The cost of living soars
Like wild duck rising
After morning feed.
Man has neither means nor meaning.
The cry of the young in the street
Rouses a protest in the market place.
　　What shall I do, Lord?

CLIFF ASHBY

Though I bring my sad soul
And place it at Your feet,
My mouth is bitter, for fear
Infects my hand and heart.
The pit of hell yawns wide
Before my floundering feet,
I slip, I slide, I fall,
I try to grasp a skylark
But it flies south for summer.
    My mind is melancholic,
    I cannot praise my maker.

263   *A Stranger in this Land*

Lord, I am lonely
And the sun is shining,
Listless, while the wind
Shakes the ageing leaves.
The harvest has been gathered
All is bagged and barned,
Silos burst with grain.
    Why, Lord, must I still stand
Dropping blind seeds
On to a barren soil?

Come, sweet Jesus, cut me down
With the sickle of Your mercy,
For I am lonely
And a stranger in this land.

ELIZABETH JENNINGS
1926–

264   *In a Garden*

When the gardener has gone this garden
Looks wistful and seems waiting an event.
It is so spruce, a metaphor of Eden
And even more so since the gardener went,

Quietly godlike, but, of course, he had
Not made me promise anything, and I
Had no one tempting me to make the bad
Choice. Yet I still felt lost and wonder why.

Even the beech tree from next door which shares
Its shadow with me, seemed a kind of threat.
Everything was too neat and someone cares

In the wrong way. I need not have stood long
Mocked by the smell of a mown lawn, and yet
I did. Sickness for Eden was so strong.

THOMAS KINSELLA
1928–

265   *The Dispossessed*

The lake is deserted now
but the water is still clean and transparent,
the headlands covered with laurels,
the little estuaries full of shells,
with enchanting parterres where the waves
ebb and flow over masses of turf and flowers.

It was like a miracle, a long pastoral, long ago.
The intoxication of a life gliding away
in the face of heaven: Spring, a plain of flowers;
Autumn, with grape-clusters and chestnuts
formed in its depths; our warm nights
passing under starlight.   We had established peace,
having learnt to practise virtue without
expectation of recompense—that we must be virtuous
without hope. (The Law is just; observe it,
maintain it, and it will bring contentment.)

Then, by the waterside, among the tortoises
with their mild and lively eyes, with crested larks
fluttering around Him, so light
they rested on a blade of grass

without bending it, He came among us
and lifted His unmangled hand:

                       These beauties,
these earth-flowers growing and blowing, what are they?
The spectacle of your humiliation!
If a man choose to enter the kingdom of peace
he shall not cease from struggle until he fail,
and having failed he will be astonished,
and having been astonished will rule,
and having ruled will rest.

                       Our dream curdled.
We awoke, and began to thirst
for the restoration of our house.
One morning, in a slow paroxysm of rage,
we found His corpse stretched on the threshold.

GEOFFREY HILL
1932–

266   *Christmas Trees*

Bonhoeffer in his skylit cell
bleached by the flares' candescent fall,
pacing out his own citadel,

restores the broken themes of praise,
encourages our borrowed days,
by logic of his sacrifice.

Against wild reasons of the state
his words are quiet but not too quiet.
We hear too late or not too late.

267   *Lachrimae Amantis*

What is there in my heart that you should sue
so fiercely for its love? What kind of care
brings you as though a stranger to my door
through the long night and in the icy dew

seeking the heart that will not harbour you,
that keeps itself religiously secure?
At this dark solstice filled with frost and fire
your passion's ancient wounds must bleed anew.

So many nights the angel of my house
has fed such urgent comfort through a dream,
whispered 'your lord is coming, he is close'

that I have drowsed half-faithful for a time
bathed in pure tones of promise and remorse:
'tomorrow I shall wake to welcome him.'

WENDELL BERRY

1934–

268

The Slip

The river takes the land, and leaves nothing.
Where the great slip gave way in the bank
and an acre disappeared, all human plans
dissolve. An aweful clarification occurs
where a place was. Its memory breaks
from what is known now, and begins to drift.
Where cattle grazed and trees stood, emptiness
widens the air for birdflight, wind, and rain.
As before the beginning, nothing is there.
Human wrong is in the cause, human
ruin in the effect—but no matter;
all will be lost, no matter the reason.
Nothing, having arrived, will stay.
The earth, even, is like a flower, so soon
passeth it away. And yet this nothing
is the seed of all—heaven's clear
eye, where all the worlds appear.
Where the imperfect has departed, the perfect
begins its struggle to return. The good gift
begins again its descent. The maker moves
in the unmade, stirring the water until
it clouds, dark beneath the surface,
stirring and darkening the soul until pain

perceives new possibility. There is nothing
to do but learn and wait, return to work
on what remains. Seed will sprout in the scar.
Though death is in the healing, it will heal.

PETER DALE
1938–

from *The Fragments*

Few ever came to help you speak or sell
your tracts and gospels in the village square
to neighbours queued for buses to a town
of cinemas and more than one hotel.
I saw your gesture tear
archaic period and noun
across the dusk, but walked with friends to the. pub,
pretending not to see your stand or the. stare
of neighbours as they noticed one more snub.
And he could do no miracle there.

' "Being in the form of God,
he thought it not robbery
to be equal with God
but made himself of no reputation
and took upon himself the form of a servant
and was brought to the likeness of man . . ." '
Your odd, tobyjug figure shook:
' "and fashioned as a man
he humbled himself
and became obedient unto death,
even the death of the cross.
Wherefore God hath given him a name . . ." '
And then you gasped for breath.

Strawlight stuffing poked from the bare light.
Crumpets of foam topped each icicled glass.
You entered the bar to sell your magazines
around the mellow. When they claimed their right
to hymns from bible-class,
recalling childhood scenes,

I watched your hands fumble out some harmony.
You offered me your box. Coins would chink
in silence and you whisper: ' "He that hath no money
come ye to the waters and drink." '

And now I watch my hands fumble the keys,
my type no better than your tunes—those weak,
incurving little-fingers, the family trait,
never to make the furthest stretch with ease.
All you have left: a unique
inheritance I hate.
Downstairs the strumming guts of guitars
and gramophones replace your wheezing tunes.
I watch acquaintances head for various bars.
The docile bus-queue moons.

ACKNOWLEDGEMENTS

The editor and publishers gratefully acknowledge permission to reproduce the following copyright material:

Michael Alexander: From *The Earliest English Poems*, trans. Michael Alexander (Penguin Classics, 1966). © Michael Alexander 1966. Reprinted by permission of Penguin Books Ltd.

Anon: 'The Heavenly Aeroplane' reprinted from *Ozark Folksongs*, collected and edited by Vance Randolph, by permission of the University of Missouri Press. Copyright 1980 by the Curators of the University of Missouri.

Cliff Ashby: From *The Dogs of Dewsbury* (1976). Reprinted by permission of Carcanet Press Ltd.

Donald Attwater: From Donald Attwater's translation of the B text of *The Book Concerning Piers the Plowman* by William Langland.

W. H. Auden: 'The Shield of Achilles' copyright 1952 by W. H. Auden; 'Amor Loci' copyright © 1966 by W. H. Auden; and 'Anthem', all from *W. H. Auden: Collected Poems*, edited by Edward Mendelson, copyright © 1976 by Edward Mendelson, William Meredith and Monroe K. Spears, Executors of the Estate of W. H. Auden. Reprinted by permission of Random House Inc. These poems are also from *Collected Poems* by W. H. Auden by permission of Faber and Faber Ltd.

Clifford Bax: Reprinted by permission of A. D. Peters & Co. Ltd.

Wendell Berry: From *A Part* (North Point Press, 1980). © 1980 Wendell Berry.

John Berryman: From *Henry's Fate* (1977). Copyright © 1969 by John Berryman, copyright © 1975, 1976, 1977 by Kate Berryman. Reprinted by permission of Faber & Faber Ltd., and Farrar Straus & Giroux Inc.

John Betjeman: From *Collected Poems* (1970). Reprinted by permission of John Murray (Publishers) Ltd. and Houghton Mifflin Co.

Jack Clemo: 'Mould of Castile (to St Teresa)' from *The Echoing Tip* (1971). Reprinted by permission of Methuen & Co. Ltd. 'On the Death of Karl Barth', 'Neither Shadow of Turning' and 'Growing in Grace' from *I Proved Thee At the Waters—the Testimony of a Blind Writer's Mother* (Eveline Clemo, 1976). Reprinted by permission of Moorley's Bible and Bookshop Ltd., Ilkeston, Derbyshire.

Peter Dale: Extract from 'The Fragments' from *Mortal Fire* (1976). Reprinted by permission of Agenda Editions, London.

Elizabeth Daryush: From *Collected Poems* (1976). Reprinted by permission of Carcanet Press Ltd.

Donald Davie: These translations are appearing for the first time in this anthology. Copyright © 1981 Donald Davie. By permission of the author.

Emily Dickinson: 'I stepped from plank to plank'; ' 'Tis so much joy!'; 'It is an honorable thought'; 'Heaven is what I cannot reach'; 'I should have

ACKNOWLEDGEMENTS

been too glad'; 'He fumbles at your soul'; 'Remorse is memory awake'. Reprinted by permission of the publishers and the Trustees of Amherst College from *The Poems of Emily Dickinson*, edited by Thomas H. Johnson, Cambridge, Mass.: The Belknap Press of Harvard University Press, Copyright 1951, © 1955, 1979 by The President and Fellows of Harvard College. 'The only news I know' from *The Complete Poems of Emily Dickinson* edited by T. H. Johnson. Copyright 1929 by Martha Dickinson Bianchi, Copyright © 1957 by Mary L. Hampson. By permission of Little, Brown & Company.

Hilda Doolittle: From *Hermetic Definition*. Copyright 1958 by Norman Holmes Pearson. Reprinted by permission of New Directions.

T. S. Eliot: From *Collected Poems 1909–1962* (1963). Copyright 1936 by Harcourt Brace Jovanovich, Inc; copyright © 1963, 1964 by T. S. Eliot. Reprinted by permission of Faber & Faber Ltd. and Harcourt, Brace Jovanovich, Inc.

Padraic Fallon: From *Poems* (Dolmen Press, 1974).

Geoffrey Hill: From *Tenebrae* (1978). Copyright © 1978 by Geoffrey Hill. Reprinted by permission of Andre Deutsch Ltd. and in the United States by permission of Houghton Mifflin Company.

Elizabeth Jennings: From *Growing Points* (Carcanet, 1975). By permission of David Higham Associates Ltd.

David Jones: From *The Sleeping Lord*. Reprinted by permission of Faber & Faber Ltd.

Thomas Kinsella: From *New Poems 1973* (Dolmen Press/OUP, 1973).

Janet Lewis: From *Poems 1924–1944* (Alan Swallow, 1950). Reprinted with the permission of The Ohio University Press, Athens.

Edwin Muir: From *The Collected Poems of Edwin Muir* (1964). Copyright © 1960 by Willa Muir. Reprinted by permission of Faber & Faber Ltd. and Oxford University Press, Inc.

F. T. Prince: From *Collected Poems* (Anvil Press Poetry/The Menard Press, 1979). Copyright © 1979 F. T. Prince. Reprinted by permission of Anvil Press Poetry.

C. H. Sisson: 'Cato' from *Anchises* (1976); 'Knole', 'A Letter to John Donne' and 'The Usk', all from *In the Trojan Ditch* (1974). Reprinted by permission of Carcanet Press Ltd.

Stevie Smith: From *The Collected Poems of Stevie Smith* (Allen Lane, 1975) and also in *Selected Poems* (New Directions, 1964). Copyright © 1964 by Stevie Smith. Reprinted by permission of James MacGibbon Executor and New Directions, New York.

Brian Stone: 'Now fade the rose and lily-flower' from *Medieval Verse*, trans. Brian Stone (Penguin Classics, 1964). © Brian Stone, 1964. Extract from 'Cleanness' from *The Owl and the Nightingale/Cleanness/St Erkenwald*, trans. Brian Stone (Penguin Classics, 1971). © Brian Stone, 1971. Reprinted by permission of Penguin Books Ltd.

R. S. Thomas: 'The Hand' from *Laboratories of the Spirit* (1975), and 'The Porch' from *Frequencies* (1978). Reprinted by permission of Macmillan, London and Basingstoke.

ACKNOWLEDGEMENTS

R. P. Warren: From *Selected Poems, 1923–1975* (1976). Copyright 1942 by Robert Penn Warren. Reprinted by permission of Alfred A. Knopf, Inc. and William Morris Agency, Inc. on behalf of the author.

John Brooks Wheelwright: From *Collected Poems of John Wheelwright* (ed. by Alvin H. Rosenfeld, 1972). Copyright © 1971 by Louise Wheelwright Damon. All rights reserved. Reprinted by permission of New Directions.

Charles Williams: From *Divorce* (1920). Reprinted by permission of Oxford University Press.

While every effort has been made to secure permission, we may have failed in a few cases to trace or contact the copyright holder. We apologize for any apparent negligence.

NOTES AND REFERENCES

A note on modernization. I do not pretend to have been consistent about this. Occasionally I have used modernized versions that were ready to hand (as the Notes that follow indicate). When in doubt, I have been conservative, preferring the risk of baffling or irritating some readers to the risk of destroying the character, especially the *musical* character, of some old and beautiful poems. I have however re-punctuated rather extensively, even in the case of poems of the last three-hundred years. Some spellings that seemed exceptionally idiosyncratic or misleading have also been silently changed, even in relatively modern poems. But with these exceptions I have supposed that no modernizing was called for in respect of texts originating since about 1680.

D.D.

1. Dame Helen Gardner in her version of the poem in *The Faber Book of Religious Verse*, 1972, translates '*Hwaet!*' as 'Listen!'
   The poem survives only in one MS., the Vercelli Book, dating from the tenth century, but quotations from it are found in runes on the Ruthwell Cross, Dumfriesshire, between two and three centuries earlier.

5. From *Medieval English Verse*, translated with an Introduction by Brian Stone (Penguin Books, 1964). The original is in *The Harley Lyrics* (ed. G. L. Brook; Manchester University Press, 1956).

6. Brian Stone, who translated this in his *Medieval English Verse*, remarks: 'The reneguing and reaffirmation of faith in the last stanza but one give the poem a strong personal touch: this makes a welcome contrast to the naive orthodoxy which tends to dominate medieval poetry.' The original is in Carleton Brown's *Religious Lyrics of the Fourteenth Century* (Oxford University Press, 1952).

9. *Troilus and Criseyde*, Bk. V, lns. 1835–69.

11. Modernized as by Helen Gardner in *The Faber Book of Religious Verse*. The refrain means: 'For I am sick with love.' There is another poem with the same refrain and in the same stanza, dating from about the same period, in which the speaker is not Christ but the Virgin.

13. From Chambers and Sidgwick, *Early English Lyrics* (Sidgwick & Jackson, 1949).

17. From *The Canticles or Ballads of Solomon*, 1549.

22. This famous anonymous Elizabethan poem exists in many versions, one of them running to fifty-five stanzas. This version is the shortest known to me. A longer version, itself excerpted from a still longer one, is printed in *The Faber Book of Religious Verse*, by Helen Gardner, who points out that it marries a famous Latin hymn by Peter Damien with the native ballad tradition.

23. I follow the text in R. D. S. Jack, *A Choice of Scottish Verse 1560–1660*, where the poem is printed from MS.

NOTES AND REFERENCES

26. This curious poem should be compared with 'The Bitter Withy' (no. 214), the same traditional poem surfacing out of folk-memory, and further debased, three-hundred years later.

31. Alexander Hume was a Presbyterian courtier of the circle round James VI of Scotland. His diction is very elaborate and courtly, despite the strong element of Scots vernacular. The poem, first printed in 1599, is printed here from the text in R. D. S. Jack, *A Choice of Scottish Verse 1560–1660*, though I have repunctuated extensively.

36–39. For the first ever full and scholarly edition of *The Sidney Psalter*, vastly influential when it circulated in MS. in its own day, we are indebted to Dr J. C. A. Rathmell. It reveals, in the Countess of Pembroke, apparently a Calvinist like her brother Philip Sidney, the first woman-poet of genius in the history of English poetry. Of the very few who have appreciated these poems at something like their true worth, the most distinguished and the most perceptive was John Ruskin, in *Rock Honeycomb*.

27–29. Texts of the Sonnets from *Caelica* are from the very scarce *Poems and Dramas of Fulke Greville, first Lord Brooke*, in two volumes edited by Geoffrey Bullough (Edinburgh, 1938). Because a crabbed quaintness (in no disparaging sense) is so central to the flavour of this poet, I have modernized him somewhat less than other poets.

42. From J. Danyel's *Songs for the Lute*, 1606.

43. From the Francis Turpyn Book, *c.* 1615.

44. From John Attey's *First Book of Ayres*, 1622. It appears in W. H. Auden and Chester Kallman (eds.), *An Anthology of Elizabethan Lute Songs, Madrigals, and Rounds*, 1970.

53. From *Christ's Victory and Triumph*, 1610.

56. This appears to be a reproach addressed to the Puritan clergy who chose to be deprived or suspended rather than obey the Canons of 1604, requiring that surplices and copes be worn, and that the sign of the cross be made in baptizing.

65. The most relevant text from Chapter 13 of St Matthew's Gospel may be this: 'For verily I say unto you, That many prophets and righteous men have desired to see those things which ye see, and have not seen them; and to hear those things which ye hear, and have not heard them.'

73. This, like the preceding poem, is from *The Poems of Thomas Washbourne, D. D.*, edited by A. B. Grosart in 1868. The poem has, as epigraph, *Ecclesiastes*, xii:7: 'Then shall the dust return to the earth as it was and the spirit shall return to God that gave it.' William Harvey, who discovered the circulation of the blood, died in 1657.

78–79. *Paradise Lost*, Book V, lns. 507–543; Book XII, lns. 607–649.

80. *Samson Agonistes*, lns. 1268–1296 (Chorus).

86. Verses 6–10 are omitted.

100. Vaughan, or else his printer, transposed the numerals. The apposite text is St John's Gospel, 3:1–2: 'There was a man of the Pharisees, named Nicodemus, a ruler of the Jews: The same came to Jesus by night, and said unto him, Rabbi, we know that thou art a teacher come from God:...'

102. Urian Oakes's Elegy, in 52 stanzas, was published in Cambridge,

Massachusetts in 1677. It is excerpted here, spelling and punctuation modernized, from *Colonial American Poetry*, edited with introductions by Kenneth Silverman, 1968.

103. Dryden's *State of Innocence*, which he called an 'opera', is his dramatized version of Milton's *Paradise Lost*, which he admired.

104. *Religio Laici*, lns. 62–71; 99–110.

105. Dryden's expanded version of a section from Chaucer's *Prologue* to the *Canterbury Tales* (see no. 10) could not be published in his lifetime, because it reveals with dangerous clarity his Jacobite opposition to the so-called 'revolutionary settlement', the dynastic double-dealing that had ensured a protestant succession for the Crown.

109. The original, written for the scholars of Winchester College, has twelve stanzas, of which however few editors have ever printed more than six, and none in the last century more than seven.

110–112. Texts are modernized from Donald E. Stanford's edition of a previously unknown poet, *The Poems of Edward Taylor* (New Haven, 1960).

114. The text is from H. B. Wright and M. K. Spears (eds.), *The Literary Works of Matthew Prior* (2nd ed., Oxford, 1971). *Exodus*, iii:14 reads: 'And God said unto Moses, I AM THAT I AM: and he said. Thus shalt thou say unto the children of Israel, I AM hath sent me unto you.' Though the poem was first published in 1693, the text given is the rather different one of 1718.

Though Prior is now remembered by anthologists chiefly for certain pieces of elegant amorous badinage, he was known for a century after his death as a serious religious poet, on the score of this poem and his *Solomon*, 1708.

At ln. 58, 'new HYPOTHESIS' may refer to Isaac Newton's *Principia*, published 1687.

116. *Galatians*, vi:14 reads: 'But God forbid that I should glory, save in the cross of our Lord Jesus Christ, by whom the world is crucified unto me, and I unto the world.'

117. *Job*, i:21 reads: 'And said, Naked came I out of my mother's womb, and naked shall I return thither: the Lord gave, and the Lord hath taken away; blessed be the name of the Lord.'

119. Capitalization as in the first printings.

120. There is a tradition that this famous hymn was inspired by the view across Southampton Water to the Isle of Wight.

121. The first two words were originally 'Our God'. John Wesley's emendation to 'O God' is here adopted, since this is the form most familiar to generations of Christians in all denominations.

127. These verses, allegedly written by Hann after reading the life of Mrs Catherine Stubbs, in Isaac Ambrose's 'War with the Devils', hang framed in the ancient Loughwood Baptist Meeting House where Hann once ministered, a seventeenth-century thatched building now preserved by the National Trust near Axminster, Devon.

130. The text is from *Hymns Founded on Various Texts in the Holy Scriptures, by the late Reverend Philip Doddridge, D. D. Published from the Author's*

Manuscript by Job Orton (Shrewsbury, 1755).

St John's Gospel, xix:41 reads: 'Now in the place where he was crucified there was a garden: and in the garden a new sepulchre, wherein was never man yet laid.'

132. From *Hymns and Sacred Poems*, 1739.

133. From *Hymns on the Lord's Supper*, 1745.

134. From *Nativity Hymns*, 1745. Capitalization and italics as in Wesley's original.

135. From *Hymns on God's Everlasting Love* (1741), this is a good example of Charles Wesley's gift for pungent polemic and lampoon. Calvin himself had confessed that the doctrine of predestination was 'horrible', but he did not see in logic how it could be avoided. Wesley does not address himself to the logical crux, but appeals to common sense and common sensibility.

136. This piece, which was composed 1748–1749, was first printed from MS. by Frank Baker in *Representative Verse of Charles Wesley* (1962).

137. From *Family Hymns*, 1767, where it is entitled, 'On the Birth-day of a Friend'.

138. First published in *Funeral Hymns*, 1759, under the title, '*On the Death of a Child*.' Wesley's first-born son died at just over a year old in 1753. Text is from Baker's *Representative Verse of Charles Wesley*, op. cit. Note that 'officious' has the approving meaning it has in Dr Johnson's verses on Robert Levett.

139. Written probably in 1782, and first printed in full in Baker's *Representative Verse of Charles Wesley*, op. cit. Both the Wesley brothers were fervent Tory loyalists.

141. Printed in the first two editions of John Wesley's *The Character of a Methodist*, 1742, in *Hymns and Sacred Poems*, 1749, and also in an undated broadside.

156. From *Truth*: lns. 1–20; 44–78; 283–300; 345–356; 381–428; 463–514.

163. *Jeremiah* xxiii: 6 reads: 'In his days Judah shall be saved, and Israel shall dwell safely; and this is his name whereby he shall be called, THE LORD OF RIGHTEOUSNESS.'

172. Wordsworth's great poem of 1802 is seldom or never considered 'Christian'. My conviction that it is so rests on the frequently overlooked stanza 14, where the old man who inspires in the poet an unforeseen and unprecedented resolution (his 'Ode to Duty' was yet to be written) seems plainly identified as a Scottish presbyterian.

177. The five quatrains of this famous hymn are quarried out of no less than sixteen in *The Christian Year*.

193. Written in 1839, this seems to record the poet's change from Evangelicism to sacramental High Churchmanship. It was first printed from MS. by Geoffrey Rowell, in *Hell and the Victorians* (Oxford, 1974).

214. Compare *ante*, no. 26. It is printed from the jacket-sleeve of a gramophone disc by 'the Wattersons' (Topic Records, London, 1977). The Wattersons record chapbook copies of the poem circulating in the 1840s in Birmingham.

224. The Latin epigraph means: 'Peace to men of good will.'

228. In the *Book of Common Prayer*, the priest is directed to say to those who come to receive the holy Communion: 'Ye that do truly and earnestly repent you of your sins, and are in love and charity with your neighbours, and intend to lead a new life, following the commandments of God, and walking from henceforth in his holy ways; Draw near with faith, and take this holy Sacrament to your comfort; . . .'

233. The Latin epigraph means: 'What is this place, what country, what region of the world?'

257. From *I Proved Thee at the Waters, The Testimony of a Blind Writer's Mother*, by Eveline Clemo. See Psalm 81, verse 7: 'Thou calledst in trouble, and I delivered thee; I answered thee in the secret place of thunder: I proved thee at the waters of Meribah.'

258. Karl Barth (1886–1968), after studying theology in his native Switzerland and in Germany, and being ordained in the Reformed (i.e. Calvinist) church, was from 1911 to 1921 pastor in the village of Safenwil, between Basle and Zurich. Barth was later Professor of Theology at several German universities, but refused to take the oath of loyalty to Hitler, whereupon he was deprived of his professorship and in 1935 was expelled from Germany.

259. From Volume IV of *Ozark Folksongs*, collected and edited by Vance Randolph, and published by the State Historical Society of Missouri in 1950. It was sung at many 'Holy Roller' meetings in the late 1930s, both in Missouri and Arkansas.

260–261. The late James McAuley (1917–1976) was an Australian.

266. Dietrich Bonhoeffer was a German protestant pastor imprisoned and finally killed by the Nazis for his opposition to World War Two.

INDEX OF FIRST LINES

The numbers are page numbers

INDEX OF FIRST LINES

INDEX OF FIRST LINES

INDEX OF FIRST LINES

INDEX OF AUTHORS

The numbers are those of the poems

INDEX OF AUTHORS